Lee ☆ The Last Years

☆ BY CHARLES BRACELEN FLOOD ☆

Love Is a Bridge

A Distant Drum

Tell Me, Stranger

Monmouth

More Lives Than One

The War of the Innocents

Trouble at the Top

Rise, and Fight Again

Lee — The Last Years

☆ Lee ☆

The Last Years

Charles Bracelen Flood

Houghton Mifflin Company   Boston

For information about permission to reproduce selections
from this book, write to Permissions, Houghton Mifflin
Company, 2 Park Street. Boston, Massachusetts 02108.

Library of Congress Cataloging in Publication Data

Flood, Charles Bracelen.
Lee—The Last Years.
Bibliography: p.
Includes index.
1. Lee, Robert E. (Robert Edward), 1807–1870.
2. Generals—Confederate States of America—Biography.
3. Confederate States of America. Army—Biography.
I. Title.
E467.1.L4F56   973.8′1 ′0924 [B]   81-4231
ISBN 0-395-31292-2
ISBN 0-395-34637-1 (pbk.)   AACR2

Printed in the United States of America

V 18 17 16 15 14 13 12 11

In dedicating this book, I think first of my mother, the late Ellen Bracelen Flood, who shared with her children her love for the English language. I wish also to express my admiration for L. Randolph Mason, a Virginian whose conversations led this Northerner to realize that this was a story that belonged not only to the South but to our nation as a whole.

Acknowledgments

I WISH TO THANK General Lee's granddaughter, Mrs. Hunter deButts of Upperville, Virginia, for permission to consult and quote from the deButts-Ely Collection of Robert E. Lee Family Papers in the Library of Congress, and for allowing me to use her photographs of the Lee children in this book. I am similarly indebted to Mrs. Charles K. Lennig, Jr., of Philadelphia, for permission to quote from her collection of twenty letters from General Lee to her grandmother Annette Carter, none of which have been previously published.

Of the many people who assisted me in my research, I am particularly grateful to Betty Ruth Kondayan, Reference and Public Services Librarian at Washington and Lee University, who at this writing has just been appointed Librarian of the Julia Rogers Library at Goucher College. For more than three years, Mrs. Kondayan was of invaluable help, both during my trips to Lexington, Virginia, to consult the Lee Papers at Washington and Lee University, and in her swift, friendly, and efficient responses to what must have seemed endless further questions by mail and telephone. Her efforts were ably complemented by those of Susan Coblentz Lane. I am also very much indebted to Professor Holt Merchant of the Department of History at Washington and Lee, who gave the manuscript of this book two readings at different stages and made many exceedingly valuable suggestions. Whatever its remaining faults, the book profited greatly by his efforts.

Professor Gérard Maurice Doyon, Chairman of the Art Department and Director of the duPont Gallery at Washington and Lee, shared with me his information and translations concerning the Swiss painter

Frank Buchser, whose trip to Lexington to paint the last portrait from life of General Lee was apparently unknown to previous biographers. Mrs. Mary P. Coulling of Lexington, who is writing a book about the Lee daughters, gave my manuscript a most helpful reading, and is in my judgment the first person to clarify the confusion surrounding the chaotic weather conditions at the time of General Lee's death. Also at Washington and Lee University, I received the assistance of Maurice D. Leach, Jr., Librarian of the University Library; Robert S. Keefe, Director of the News Office; Romulus T. Weatherman, Director of Publications, and Captain Robert C. Peniston, USN (Ret.), Director of the Lee Chapel. Patrick Brennan of the Class of 1978 acted as a most enthusiastic, knowledgeable, and helpful guide while I was in Lexington. I also made use of the Preston Library at the Virginia Military Institute in Lexington.

At the Library of Congress, Ms. Marianne Roos was extremely helpful during my days spent consulting the deButts-Ely Collection. Other institutions that have assisted me are: the National Archives; Virginia Historical Society; the duPont Library at Stratford Hall Plantation; the New-York Historical Society, and the State Historical Society of Missouri. Inquiries were helpfully answered by the Duke University Library and by Gettysburg College. Among the individuals who wrote prompt and useful answers to questions are Charles E. Thomas of Greenville, South Carolina, and Dr. Arthur Ben Chitty of the Association of Episcopal Colleges. Frederick C. Maisell III, Historian of the McDonogh School in McDonogh, Maryland, made available to the author the last letter written by General Lee. Dr. Robert S. Conte, Greenbrier Historian, answered questions concerning the White Sulphur Springs resort in West Virginia now known as the Greenbrier, where General Lee and his family spent time during his last summers.

On my research trip to Appomattox Court House National Historical Park, I received excellent cooperation from Ronald G. Wilson, Park Historian, who later answered further inquiries. In Richmond, Virginia, Mr. and Mrs. Lawrence M. Barnes, Jr., were indefatigable in finding the answers to a variety of questions concerning General Lee's days there after the surrender at Appomattox. In Charlotte, North Carolina, Miss Elizabeth Lawrence made numerous exceedingly helpful suggestions after reading the manuscript, as did Mrs. Benjamin

Withers. The Honorable Francis O. Clarkson of Charlotte answered legal questions concerning the status of Arlington, and directed my attention to information about the grave of General Lee's daughter Anne Carter Lee. James B. Craighill of Charlotte was generous in making available the unpublished reminiscences of his grandfather James B. Craighill. Jules Larsen, formerly of Louisville, Kentucky, and now of Charlotte, was the first to direct my attention to this period of American history in a conversation in 1976. Warren W. Way of Charlotte verified certain North Carolina references.

A special sort of gratitude is due to my agent, Sterling Lord, whose excellent representation has enabled me to pursue my writing on a full-time basis. I am also deeply appreciative of the sensitive and effective contribution made at different stages in the writing of this book by my editor, Austin Olney, Editor-in-Chief of the Trade Division of Houghton Mifflin. He has brought to the task a dedication and a willingness to spend time on a manuscript that can no longer be taken for granted in contemporary publishing.

I am indebted to my sister, Mary Ellen Reese, herself an author, for an insightful reading of my manuscript at an early stage in its development, and to another author, Thomas Parrish, for constructive comments at a later stage. Among the libraries located near my home in Richmond, Kentucky, I made great use of books possessed by the John Grant Crabbe Library at Eastern Kentucky University, and am indebted to its staff and to Dean Ernest E. Weyhrauch, its Director. I am similarly grateful to the Hutchins Library of Berea College, in Berea, Kentucky. Use was also made of the collections in the library system of the University of Kentucky.

In my research on the founding of the Kappa Alpha Order at Washington College while General Lee was the school's president, I was assisted by Professor Idris Rhea Traylor, Jr., of the History Department at Texas Tech University, a Councilor of that national fraternity, and by William E. Forester, its Executive Director. I am grateful to my friend Edward S. Chenault for first bringing to my attention the early history of Kappa Alpha.

Among my friends and neighbors in Richmond, Kentucky, three have volunteered special and most useful assistance. James T. Coy III, M.D., gave me valuable research materials in his possession. William H. Mitchell, M.D., read my manuscript and compared it with earlier descriptions and analyses of General Lee's physical condition during the last years of his life, reviewing all of it in terms of present medical knowledge. Jane H. Clouse supervised the preparation of the manuscript.

Last and most important has been the immeasurable contribution made to this book by my wife, Katherine Burnam Flood. She has improved the manuscript by her comments about it; she has sustained the author with steadfast devotion. This book would not be here without her, and I thank her with all my heart.

Lee ☆ The Last Years

Chapter 1

GENERAL ROBERT E. LEE stood on a hilltop, studying the fog-covered woods ahead. Listening to the artillery fire and musketry, he tried to judge the progress of the crucial attack that his men were making. It was shortly after eight o'clock in the morning on Palm Sunday, April 9, 1865, and the shattered remnants of Lee's Army of Northern Virginia were in a column strung along four miles of road near the village of Appomattox Court House.

A few minutes earlier, Lee had ordered Lieutenant Colonel Charles Venable of his staff to ride forward through these woods and find Major General John B. Gordon, the able and aggressive Georgian whose corps was making this assault. When Venable returned through the mist, the report he brought would determine whether this army was to fight on or surrender.

After four years of war, the northern front of the Confederate States of America had collapsed. A week before, unable to hold their overextended lines against the massive Union forces being thrown at them by General Ulysses S. Grant, Lee's battered, worn-out army had evacuated both Petersburg and the Confederate capital, Richmond. Since then they had slogged westward across Virginia through a hundred miles of spring mud, marching and fighting in an effort to break away from pursuing Federal columns. Lee's plan was to move west parallel to the railroad lines, and pick up food that was to await his army at supply depots. Then they would turn south to join the Confederate army under Joseph E. Johnston that was opposing Sherman's march north through the Carolinas from Savannah.

That turn to the south had never come. The march west became a nightmare retreat under incessant attacks that produced terrible losses — three days before this Palm Sunday, in the rout at Sayler's Creek, eight thousand of Lee's men were captured at one stroke. The food had not materialized. Starving horses collapsed and died in the mud. Reeling from hunger, soldiers who had won amazing victories in the past threw away their muskets and lay down in the fields, waiting to be picked up as prisoners. At its peak, this once-fearsome army had numbered seventy thousand men. A week before, thirty thousand began this withdrawal to the west, with sixty to seventy thousand Union Army soldiers on their heels. On this misty morning, the Army of Northern Virginia was reduced to eleven thousand gaunt, tenacious veterans. During the night, Federal troops had thrown themselves in strength across the Confederate line of march, and Lee's army was at last surrounded. At five this morning Lee had launched this final drive to break out to the west and continue the retreat.

Waiting for Lieutenant Colonel Venable to return with the message that would tell him whether further fighting would be useless, Lee stood silent amidst a few of his staff officers. He was a strikingly hand-some man of fifty-eight, nearly six feet tall, with grey hair and a trim silver beard. Years of campaigning had burnt his clear ruddy skin to a deep red-brown; there were crow's-feet at the corners of his luminous brown eyes. He had a broad forehead, prominent nose, short thick neck, big shoulders and deep chest, and stood erect as the West Point cadet he once had been. Because he thought he might end this day as General Grant's prisoner, Lee was not wearing his usual grey sack coat. To represent his thousands of mud-caked scarecrows who were still ready to fight on, this morning Lee was resplendent in a double-breasted grey dress coat with gilt buttons. Around his waist was a deep red silk sash, and over that was a sword belt of gold braid. At his side hung a dress sword in a leather and gilt scabbard; on the blade was an inscription in French, *Aide toi et Dieu t'aidera* — Help yourself and God will help you.

Standing on this hillside, Lee knew the consequences of the choice he must soon make. In the past forty-eight hours Ulysses S. Grant had opened a correspondence with him, sending messages under flags of truce, urging him to surrender this army. If he surrendered these men now, the other armies of the Confederacy might stagger on briefly, but his action would mean the end of the war.

For Lee, there was a special problem faced by no other Confederate officer. He was not only the field commander of this army, but he was the general in command of all Confederate forces. If the rider coming back through the woods brought him reason to think he could get his men through to Johnston's army in North Carolina and assume direct command of both armies, it might be his duty to continue the bloodshed. He had produced near-miracles before; if he could fashion one more sharp blow, it might ease the terms of the inevitable surrender.

Everything was converging. Two days before, he had sent a message to his son Major General W. H. Fitzhugh Lee, a young cavalry commander who had served in the United States Army before the war: "Keep your command together and in good spirits, General; don't let it think of surrender. I will get you out of this." Earlier in the war he had written this same son, whose nickname was Rooney, "If victorious, we have every thing to live for in the future. If defeated, nothing will be left for us to live for."

All the hopes were crashing now, in a way that affected his flesh and blood. Rooney was up there in the fighting in those misty trees; so was another Major General Fitzhugh Lee, his nephew. His oldest son, Major General Custis Lee, a West Pointer like himself, had been missing since Sayler's Creek; there were rumors that he was dead. His youngest son, Captain Robert E. Lee, Jr., had been missing in action for a week.

Those were the bonds of family, but this entire army was filled with love for Lee. They were proud of his appearance, proud of his brilliant leadership, but their hearts went out to him because he shared their risks and hardships, constantly showing them how much he admired them and appreciated their sacrifices. Thousands of them referred to him as "Uncle Robert." His soldiers saw their cause embodied in him; one of his generals told him, "You are the country to these men." In the horrendous confusion of the defeat at Sayler's Creek, Lee had cantered into the midst of his scattered troops. Facing the enemy, he grabbed up a red Confederate battle flag and held it high in the dusk, the banner waving against the flames of destroyed supplies. A staff officer told what happened next.

> . . . The sight of him aroused a tumult. Fierce cries resounded on all sides and, with hands clinched violently and raised aloft, the men called on him to lead them against the enemy. "It's General Lee!"

"Uncle Robert!" "Where's the man who won't follow Uncle Robert?" I heard on all sides — the swarthy faces full of dirt and courage, lit up every instant by the glare of the burning wagons.

☆   ☆   ☆

Lieutenant Colonel Venable emerged from the misty woods and rode up the slope to Lee. He had an oral message from Major General Gordon on the front line: "I have fought my corps to a frazzle, and I fear I can do nothing unless I am heavily supported by Longstreet's corps."

Longstreet's corps. Lee knew that Gordon could not have the reinforcements he said he needed to break through; they were committed and fighting as the army's rear guard, holding off twice their numbers. There were no reserves left, and no hope of breaking out.

Lee said in his deep voice, addressing no one, "Then there is nothing left me but to go and see General Grant, and I would rather die a thousand deaths."

His words broke the respectful silence and dignified bearing of the officers near him. Years of dedication, of comrades killed, had come to naught in an instant. "Convulsed with passionate grief," an artilleryman said, "many were the wild words we spoke as we stood around him."

As the fog began to lift and Lee finally could see his last battlefield, he spoke again, this time in what an officer beside him called a voice "filled with hopeless sadness."

"How easily I could be rid of this," Lee said, again addressing no one, "and be at rest! I have only to ride along the line and all will be over!" He meant that it would be easy to commit suicide by riding in front of his lines, drawing enemy fire. Lee crossed his arms over his chest, his hands gripping his biceps; an inward battle was being fought to a decision. Finally he said with a deep sigh: "But it is our duty to live. What will become of the women and children of the South if we are not here to protect them?"

Amidst arrangements for a temporary cease-fire while he went to confer with Grant, Lee was presented with a dramatic last-ditch suggestion. It came from Brigadier General E. Porter Alexander, the young chief of Longstreet's artillery. Lee had returned from his hilltop vantage point to the simple headquarters of a few tents and wagons where he had spent the night. Alexander came walking through the headquarters area, unaware that Lee had decided to meet with Grant.

As he had done so often with so many officers, Lee reviewed the battlefield situation with Alexander and then said, giving no hint of his decision, "What have we got to do today?" Lee's motives in doing this throughout the war were twofold: he wanted to make sure that no alternate plan escaped him, and it was also a form of Socratic teaching, making younger leaders learn by asking them what they would do if they were in his place.

Instead of surrendering, Alexander replied, let these loyal thousands of excellent soldiers slip away through the woods, singly or in small groups. Most of them could sneak through the Union lines today or tonight. Then they could make their way to their home states — the Army of Northern Virginia had units from places as distant as Florida and Texas — and continue the war as guerrillas.

Lee crushed this idea in a few words. "If I took your advice, the men would be without rations and under no control of officers. They would be compelled to rob and steal in order to live. They would become mere bands of marauders, and the enemy's cavalry would pursue them and overrun many sections they may never have occasion to visit. We would bring on a state of affairs it would take the country years to recover from." Although Lee meant "the South" when he said "the country," he was doing something for which the North as well as the South had reason to thank him, even before he went to see Grant.

The shooting stopped all around the defensive positions into which Lee's men had moved and along the Union lines encircling them. Some of the Confederates knew what was happening, others guessed, and thousands expected to go on fighting later in the day. They had seen flags of truce before.

From the Union lines, the hopeless position of Lee's army was apparent to every Federal soldier. Like the men opposing them, they kept their weapons at their sides. It was too soon to celebrate, but they had no doubt that the end was at hand. A soldier from New Hampshire sat on a slope with his comrades, looking over at the surrounded and greatly outnumbered Confederates, and later remembered how they "pitied and sympathized with these courageous Southern men who had fought for four long and dreary years, all so stubbornly, so bravely and so well, and now, whipped, beaten, completely used up, were fully at our mercy — it was pitiful, sad, hard, and seemed to us altogether too bad."

Among the mounted messengers cantering around the wooded countryside carrying white flags, one came to Lee's headquarters with an entirely personal message. His son Major General Custis Lee was safe and unharmed, a prisoner in Union hands.

The Federal officer who sent this news through the lines was Brigadier General Lawrence Williams; his mother and Lee's wife were first cousins. His name summoned memories of the way this war had ripped the fabric of relationships. Lawrence's father and Lee had been fellow officers of the Engineers during the Mexican War, and he had been killed at Monterrey. A West Pointer, Lawrence had at the outset of this war chosen to fight for the North; his brother Orton, also an officer, had resigned from the United States Army to fight for the Confederacy. Orton was in love with Lee's daughter Agnes, his childhood playmate; at Christmas of 1862 he proposed marriage and was tearfully rejected by her, although she loved him, because twenty months of war had turned him into a drinker and an unpredictably violent man. Later Orton was apprehended within Union lines, dressed as a Federal officer, and was hanged as a spy.

II

By one o'clock in the afternoon of this Palm Sunday, Lee was sitting in the corner of a parlor in the village of Appomattox Court House, inside enemy lines. Grant was riding to this meeting place from a point sixteen miles away, and there was nothing to do but wait.

The silence in the room was painful. Lieutenant Colonel Charles Marshall of Lee's staff sat next to Brevet Brigadier General Orville E. Babcock of Grant's staff, who had escorted them here under a white flag of truce. Both officers occasionally ventured a few pleasant words, but each time fell silent, wishing they could get this behind them.

Lee sat motionless in the corner, his broad-brimmed military hat and riding gauntlets on the small table beside him. It was a moment of supreme irony. When the war began, Robert Edward Lee, who had served in the United States Army as cadet and officer for a total of thirty-five years, was offered command of the army to which he must now surrender. Although he was opposed to secession, he had replied that "I could take no part in an invasion of the Southern States," had resigned his commission, and had gone on to fight superbly in defense of his native Virginia.

It was irony enough that Lee could on this day have been the victor instead of the vanquished, but the contrast between his own impeccable prewar career and Grant's added another dimension. In 1854, when Lee was superintendent of the United States Military Academy at West Point, Captain Ulysses S. Grant resigned from the army — a decision reputedly forced on him by his superiors because of habitual drunkenness. By 1860, when Colonel Robert E. Lee was commander of all United States Army forces in the Department of Texas, Grant had in six civilian years failed as a farmer and as a real estate salesman, and was a clerk in his father's harness and leather-goods shop in Galena, Illinois. Scraping for a living, he wept on a street in Galena when no one bought a load of firewood he was peddling.

The war had given Grant the opportunity to re-enter his profession and to demonstrate a courage and resolve that strengthened with every crisis. Like Lee, he never lost sight of his objectives; unlike Lee, he had the resources to attain them. Now Grant was at the head of the most powerful army the world had seen. Two nights before, his endless columns had come pouring through Farmville, exhausted but moving fast, sensing that victory was near. When the men in the leading ranks saw Grant quietly watching them from the darkened porch of a hotel beside the road, a forced march by night turned into something else.

> Bonfires were lighted on both sides of the street, the men seized straw and pine knots, and improvised torches. Cheers arose from throats already hoarse with shouts of victory, bands played, banners waved, arms were tossed high and caught again. The night march had become a grand review, with Grant as the reviewing officer.

Here at Appomattox these two careers were to intersect. Eleven months before this meeting, after his first day fighting Lee, Grant had thrown himself on the cot in his tent in a near-hysterical condition that

8

an aide described by saying, "I never saw a man so agitated in my life." The next day Grant went right on fighting.

As Lee waited in this room in a little Virginia village, the question hanging over his army involved the terms of surrender. If Grant wished, every one of Lee's surrounded men, and the thousands of stragglers wandering the countryside, could be marched off to confinement as prisoners of war.

There was a rattle of many hooves coming down the road, turning into the yard. The horses stopped. Feet swung to earth; boots came up the steps. General Ulysses S. Grant hurried into the room. Three inches shorter than Lee, with dark brown hair and a rough close beard, he was wearing a private's tunic fitted with general's shoulder straps. One of his buttons was buttoned in the wrong buttonhole, and mud was spattered on his boots and dark blue uniform. He shook hands with Lee in the most friendly manner; neither triumph nor sympathy appeared on Grant's square face. The one thing he exuded was a profound relief that it was over. Less than two hours before, when a courier had finally found Grant and delivered Lee's written request for surrender, Grant had told one of his generals to read it aloud to the rest of the staff. When the officer did so, someone proposed three cheers; the group managed one or two feeble efforts, and burst into tears instead. Grant had been suffering "the most excruciating pain" from a "sick-headache; but the instant I saw the contents of the note I was cured."

As Lee settled back at the table in the corner, and Grant sat down at a table in the center of the room, a dozen Federal officers entered. One of them noted that they took their places along the wall as quietly as possible, "very much as people enter a sick chamber where they expect to find the patient dangerously ill."

Grant began the conversation with a reference to their one previous meeting, during the Mexican War, and followed this with a number of incidents from those campaigns, in which several of the Union officers present had fought. Lee barely entered into what was almost a monologue by Grant, but he did ask quietly if it would be possible to see and thank Brigadier General Lawrence Williams, who had sent him word that his son Custis was safe.

Grant immediately dispatched someone to find Williams, and went on talking about Mexico. Later, Grant was to say that he felt "much embarrassed" during this conversation, despite his seeming spontaneity. Perhaps he went on reminiscing because he felt it would be easier for the loser to raise the subject at hand, rather than for the victor to thrust it upon him.

Soon enough, Lee said the hardest words he had ever had to utter. "I suppose, General Grant, that the object of our present meeting is fully understood. I asked to see you to ascertain upon what terms you would receive the surrender of my army."

Grant answered as if it were an everyday thing to be ending the worst war in American history. Referring to their earlier exchange of notes, he repeated the terms he had offered in one of them — generous terms that Lee feared might no longer be offered, now that his army was surrounded by six times its numbers.

"The terms I propose," Grant said, "are those stated substantially in my letter of yesterday — that is, the officers and men surrendered to be paroled and disqualified from taking up arms again until properly exchanged, and all arms, ammunition and supplies to be delivered up as captured property."

Lee nodded and gave an inward sigh of relief. His men would not be marched off to prison camps. On the strength of their promise to behave peaceably, they could leave here as disarmed individuals, paroled prisoners who need not spend a day in captivity but were free to make their way home as best they could.

In a few minutes, the terms were being written out by Grant, who lit a cigar and puffed on it as he thought between sentences. When Grant rose and brought the draft over to him, Lee got out his reading glasses, wiped them off, perched them on his nose, and studied the document. In addition to the mechanics of the surrender, Grant was allowing the officers to keep their swords and pistols, as well as their private horses and baggage. Legend has Lee offering his sword and Grant refusing it; in fact, Grant was making such an offer unnecessary by stipulating that his opponents were to keep their swords.

Lee's eyes went to the last sentence, which was to have great importance in his life some weeks hence, although neither he nor Grant now recognized its full implications. Once the details of surrender and parole were accomplished, Grant had written, "each officer and man will be allowed to return to their homes not to be disturbed by United States authority so long as they observe their paroles and the laws in force where they may reside."

Lee was to refer to Grant's surrender terms as being extremely generous, but after reading this document, and before a final copy was made for him to sign, he mentioned an omission that troubled him. He explained to Grant, who did not know it, that the Confederate cavalrymen and some of the artillerymen owned their own horses. Lee did not beg, but by pointing this out he was hoping that Grant would see what it would mean in a war-ravaged land, right now, at the time of spring planting, to have not only the officers' horses, but all the horses, come home with their owners and be set to plowing.

Grant had learned a lot on that street in Galena. In an instant he was following Lee's thought, musing aloud that "I take it that most of the men in the ranks are small farmers, and as the country has been so raided by the two armies, it is doubtful whether they will be able to put in a crop to carry themselves through the next winter without the aid of the horses they are now riding, and I will arrange it this way: I will not change the terms as now written, but I will instruct the officers I shall appoint to receive the paroles to let all the men who claim to own a horse or mule take the animals home with them to work their little farms."

Grant's words were a beacon in Lee's dark hour; this could make the difference between full stomachs and near-starvation for the children of some of the soldiers for whom Lee was negotiating. Acts like these could turn despair into hope. Moved, Lee said thankfully, "This will have the best possible effect upon the men." Thinking of the defeated and embittered civilian population of the South, he added, "It will be very gratifying and will do much toward conciliating our people."

As the surrender terms were being copied in a final draft, with Lieutenant Colonel Marshall of Lee's staff simultaneously writing an acceptance, Grant introduced his officers who had been standing along the walls during these historic moments. It was in some ways a West Point reunion, although Lee remained grave, politely shaking hands with those who extended theirs, and bowing silently to the others. Brigadier General Lawrence Williams had been found and was brought in; Lee thanked him for sending the message that Custis was safe. There was another Brigadier General Williams present, Seth Williams, who as a captain had been adjutant at West Point when Lee was superintendent. Lee talked with him for a few moments, but when Williams offered an amusing anecdote from their close association of those days, Lee had no heart for it. He just nodded that he had heard.

The last man presented by Grant to Lee was Lieutenant Colonel Ely S. Parker, Grant's military secretary, who had just finished making the final draft of the surrender document. Parker was a Seneca Indian, chief of his tribe.

With the introductions complete, Lee brought up a keenly felt responsibility. During the retreat, his army had taken between a thousand and fifteen hundred of Grant's men as prisoners, herding them along because they could do nothing else with them. Like his own men, these prisoners were surviving on a few handfuls of parched corn, if that, and he wanted to hand them over to Grant. It was immediately agreed that this would be done.

This raised the dreadful condition of Lee's army, and again Grant forestalled the need to plead for anything.

"I will take steps at once to have your army supplied with rations," Grant volunteered. When Lee said that he had no clear idea as to how many men were still in ranks, and how many were wandering around as stragglers, Grant said casually, "Suppose I send over twenty-five thousand rations, do you think that will be a sufficient supply?"

There was an army! They could feed themselves, and spare twenty-five thousand extra meals! "Plenty," Lee said, "plenty." He spoke as if overcome by this evidence of the resources of the enemy that had hammered him down. "An abundance." In a moment he added, "And it will be a great relief, I can assure you."

A few minutes later, Lee signed the letter in which he accepted Grant's terms for the surrender of the Army of Northern Virginia. Lieutenant Colonel Marshall took it from Lee and handed it to Lieutenant Colonel Parker, who gave Marshall Grant's signed letter setting forth the surrender terms. Thus it was that the two men who exchanged the documents that ended the fighting were a grandson of Chief Justice John Marshall, who in civilian life had been a lawyer in Baltimore, and an Indian chief who had studied to be a lawyer and was refused admission to the bar because of his race.

It was done. Lee stood and shook hands with Grant. He had come to this room fearing that his men might face humiliation and prison camps; from this moment to the end of his life he never allowed an unkind word about Grant to be spoken in his presence.

Lee bowed to the other Federal officers. Carrying his hat in his right hand and his gauntlets in his left, he walked from the room, followed by Marshall. There was a hallway, and Lee paused just inside the open door to the porch, pulling himself together. He thought that no one but Marshall could see him, but George Forsyth, a Union general who had not been in the parlor, was watching from a room across the hall. Forsyth saw that Lee was turning red, "a deep crimson flush, that rising from his neck overspread his face and even tinged his broad forehead . . . Booted and spurred, still vigorous and erect, he stood bareheaded, looking out of the open doorway, sad-faced and weary."

Lee put on his hat and stepped out. Several tired Union officers who were resting on the porch, having no idea that the meeting was over, jumped to their feet and saluted. Lee returned the salute "mechanically but courteously." At the top of the steps he pulled on his gauntlets and gazed to the northeast, where his men remained in defensive positions a mile away, many of them with no idea that he had just surrendered them all. With the exception of deaths in his family, this session in the parlor had been the worst ordeal of his life, despite Grant's efforts to ease it. Now he had to face the splendidly loyal troops who had given him a thousand proofs of their courage and determination.

Some Union officers in the yard below had come to attention, but Lee was still standing at the top of the steps, staring toward his army, noticing nothing around him. Now he looked to his right and left, wondering where his horse was. "Orderly!" he called in a choked voice, "orderly!" Sergeant G. W. Tucker, the one other Confederate who had come to this meeting, appeared instantly, leading Lee's horse Traveller.

Lee went down the steps, Marshall behind him, and paused on the lowest step while Tucker replaced Traveller's bridle. Again he looked sadly in the direction of his army, and "thrice smote the palm of his left hand slowly with his right fist in an absent sort of way." Then, as Tucker buckled the throat latch, Lee finally looked at this grey horse he loved. He lifted Traveller's black forelock from under the brow band, parted and smoothed it, and patted his forehead.

Sergeant Tucker stepped back. Lee "swung himself slowly and wearily, but nevertheless firmly, into the saddle . . . as he did so there broke unguardedly from his lips a long, low, deep sigh, almost a groan in its intensity, while the flush on his neck seemed, if possible, to take on a still deeper hue."

As Lee turned Traveller's head away from the house, General Grant came down the steps and started across the yard toward his horse. Grant, too, was in an abstracted state. When he realized that this was Lee leaving, he stopped and took off his hat. So did every other Union soldier in the yard. Lee raised his hat silently, and turned through the gate into the road.

Grant stood watching him ride away. The Union officers wanted to mount their horses and get back to their commands, but as long as Grant stood there they had to remain standing as they were. One of Grant's staff said to him, "This will live in history."

Grant did not reply, and watched Lee until he was out of sight.

Chapter 2

LEE'S MEN watched him riding back to them from the Federal lines, a grey-clad man on his muscular grey horse with its black mane and tail. As Lee crossed the narrow Appomattox River, the woods behind him were in the first vivid green of spring.

Weapons at their sides, expecting to go on fighting, these soldiers in rags had written an astonishing page of military history. For four years they had held the Confederacy's main northern battlefront against forces that were frequently two and three times as large. Their situation had mirrored the disparity between the North, an industrial society with a population in excess of twenty million, and the South, an agricultural society with a white population of eight million and four million black slaves. Even the most ardent Confederates had never believed that they could take the war far into Northern territory; the South's war aim was to win battlefield victories so decisive that they would force the North to abandon its military effort and recognize the Confederate States of America as a separate Southern nation. There was also the hope that European nations, impressed by Confederate successes, might enter formal alliances to achieve this end. In their doomed but tenacious efforts, these often hungry Southern soldiers had fought with an absolute minimum of supplies. At the war's outset, the South had possessed only one ironworks capable of making cannon and railroad rails; all the textile mills were then in the North, and there was no way to manufacture wool blankets. Although the South had some domestic manufacture of various supplies, and some equipment bought in Europe got through the ever-tightening Northern naval blockade, the Confederate forces had relied heavily on fitting themselves out with captured Federal equipment. A British observer had noted that Lee's modest headquarters consisted of Union Army wagons, camp chairs, blankets — even Lee's sleeping tent bore the markings of a New Jersey regiment.

Consistently outnumbered but aggressively led by Lee, the Army of Northern Virginia inflicted terrible losses on an enemy able to replace every casualty. Lee's men won remarkable victories against great odds; even in their defeats they bled the North. In the process, these soldiers from all over the South achieved a tremendous belief in themselves and in their commander, and evolved a style that combined squalor and dash. When the Texas Brigade marched past at a review, a foreign officer commented that their shirts and trousers had innumerable rips in them. Lee looked at him and said, "The enemy never sees the backs of my Texans." The infantrymen of "Stonewall" Jackson's corps marched great distances so quickly that they became known as Jackson's "foot cavalry." As for the horsemen themselves, a boy in Maryland, used to seeing only Federal troops, gave this description of his first glimpse of Lee's cavalry:

> . . . the dirtiest men I ever saw, a most ragged, lean and hungry set of wolves. Yet there was a dash about them that the Northern men lacked. They rode like circus riders.

This army had captured the world's imagination; a Northern war correspondent who had seen Lee's advancing ranks at uncomfortably close quarters wrote admiringly of "that array of tattered uniforms and bright muskets."

These soldiers watching Lee come toward them were simple men. Slavery had been the principal issue that led to this war, but nine out of ten of these foot soldiers and artillerymen had never owned a slave. They were fighting because the Union Army had invaded the South. Here from Louisiana, Alabama, Arkansas, Mississippi, Tennessee, Georgia, the Carolinas, fighting beside Virginians on the Confederacy's northern front, they all believed that they had a right to take their states out of the Union and create their own Confederacy, a separate Southern nation.

Some of these soldiers, now twenty years old, had been in the ranks since they were sixteen. Most of them had not been paid for a year or more. After four years of fighting in what they believed to be a sacred cause, all of them knew what it was to lose a battle, but many of them could not conceive of final defeat.

They were able to see Lee's face now as he approached their lines. Their eyes softened. They loved him as a commander has seldom been loved. His effect on his men was almost hypnotic. Before one battle Lee silently rode bareheaded along the lines of a regiment that was about to attack, paying tribute to the sacrifice they were going to make. It was a gesture so eloquent that one young soldier thought Lee had in fact made a speech, and charged the enemy sobbing and shouting, "Any man who will not fight after what Marse Robert said, is a damned coward!" On another occasion he rode out of camp to greet a column of his troops who were returning to his command after long duty elsewhere; simply the way he sat on his horse and looked at them sent them into wild cheering, and one of them said, "The effect was as of a military benediction." The men watching him now believed that he was invincible, that he would get them through this horrible retreat and into some position from which they could again smash the Yankees.

Lee rode into the lines. Men raised their soft, wide-brimmed hats, ready to cheer him as always, but Lee kept riding straight through them, staring ahead with an expression they had never seen. A terrible thought came to hundreds of them. They ran from their positions and crowded about him as he tried to ride on.

"General," they said, "General? General, are we surrendered?"

Lee took off his hat and looked down into the hungry sleepless faces that surrounded him as he sat astride Traveller. Again he tried to ride forward, but a sea of his soldiers enclosed him.

"Men, we have fought the war together, and I have done the best I could for you. You will all be paroled and go to your homes . . ." Tears flooded his eyes. He tried to continue, but all he could manage was "Good-bye."

They parted for him now, their mouths open. As if there were some misunderstanding, they began to assure him, "General, we'll fight 'em yet."

It was all they had to offer, this unshaven phalanx, and they came along quickly beside Traveller. "General, say the word and we'll go in and fight 'em yet."

"We'll go after 'em again."

Lee rode toward an apple orchard that was serving as a temporary command post. Weeping, cheering him, cursing the news, men moved alongside Lee to reach up and touch him, to comfort him and be comforted by him. Some grasped his hand and walked along for a few steps like a child beside a father, sobbing; others patted Traveller, and the proud horse mistook this for yet another victory ovation for his master after a battle, and pranced amidst the tears.

Lee passed through the cordon of sentries at the apple orchard, and the crowd dispersed to spread the news.

Inside the Union lines the word of victory produced frenzied cheering. The euphoria was seen this way by a Federal officer: "The air was filled with hats, canteens, haversacks and everything that could be displayed as an expression of great rejoicing. The grim warriors embraced each other and rolled on the turf with tears of joy coursing down their bronzed faces."

Amid the cheering, musicians of the regimental bands raced to assemble and strike up "Hail, Columbia" and "The Star Spangled Banner." A young soldier wrote a letter that began, "My Dear Mother, I am almost too much excited to write. You will know the reason why long before you receive this. Lee has surrendered with his whole army, and from this day the war is virtually over. Thank God we have been permitted to see this glorious day."

☆ ☆ ☆

An hour later, with the sun setting, Lee rode out of the apple orchard, heading the mile up this sloping road to his headquarters tents. Now everyone in the Confederate encampment knew. They crowded along both sides of the road — all eleven thousand men who had marched to the end with Lee. A major of Engineers described it.

> As soon as he entered this avenue of these old soldiers, the flower of the army, the men who had stuck to their duty through thick and thin in so many battles, wild, heartfelt cheers arose which so touched General Lee that tears filled his eyes and trickled down his cheeks as he rode on his splendid charger, hat in hand, bowing his acknowledgments . . .
>
> Each group began in the same way, with cheers, and ended in the same way, with sobs, all along the route to his quarters. Grim, bearded men threw themselves on the ground, covered their faces with their hands and wept like children. Officers of all ranks made no attempt to conceal their feelings, but sat on their horses and cried aloud . . .

A dirt-crusted soldier embodied the broken heart of the Confederacy when he reached out his arms and shouted, "I love you just as well as ever, General Lee!"

By nightfall, the Union Army began bringing in wagons loaded with food for the starving Confederates. Even before this first official distribution of Federal rations, hundreds of the recent enemies had been visiting back and forth, despite orders that each army was to stay within its own lines. Union soldiers, sometimes with little food in their own packs, were so struck by the plight of the hunger-dizzy Southerners that they did what a Pennsylvania volunteer recorded: "shared our food until every haversack was empty. The sweet aroma of real coffee staggered the Confederates, condensed milk and sugar appalled them. And they stood aghast at just a little butter."

The food was gratefully received, but some other Union overtures were not. A Federal colonel gave a little speech to a group of Confederates, in effect telling them that all was forgiven. He closed by saying, "We are all a band of brothers now," and waited for applause.

One of his ragged audience looked at him and said, "If I had you out in the woods by yourself I'd brother you."

A less physical but more passionate response came when a Union general spoke to Confederate Brigadier General Henry A. Wise, who was a former governor of Virginia and the man who had signed the order that John Brown be hanged after his raid on Harpers Ferry. When the Federal officer expressed the hope that there would be good relations between North and South, Wise answered, "There is a rancor in our hearts which you little dream of. We hate you, sir."

II

They were surrendered, but they were still an army, sleeping in rows that marked their decimated units. Their muskets were still stacked in orderly lines, as they had been at hundreds of bivouacs. They had their cartridges, musketballs, and bayonets, all to be handed over as directed.

Around the campfires, some men huddled late. Few talked. They stared into the flames and remembered the things that soldiers remember. The Army of Northern Virginia was about to pass into the hands of partisan historians, mythmakers, sentimentalists. These men knew facts. Some could remember the overture to Second Manassas at Groveton, Virginia, on August 28, 1862. Stonewall Jackson gave the order to attack by mildly telling a group of mounted officers, "Bring up your men, gentlemen." A participant depicted what happened next — not a Southern lady's image of her ancestors at war.

> Every officer turned around and scurried back to the woods at full gallop. The men had been watching their officers with much interest and when they wheeled and dashed toward them they knew what it meant, and from the woods arose a hoarse roar like that from cages of wild animals at the scent of blood.

As for the Stonewall Brigade, one of the finest infantry units the world has seen, it had some bad days that were to be conveniently forgotten. At Cedar Mountain the commander of a North Carolina brigade, ordered into the fighting to plug a gap, recounted with some satisfaction, "I had not gone 100 yards into the woods before we met the celebrated Stonewall Brigade, utterly routed and fleeing as fast as they could run." The North Carolinians opened their ranks, let the Stonewall Brigade's Twenty-seventh Virginia Infantry run through them to the rear, and pushed on to the front, where they drove back the Federals.

Not only were units to march into history with unblemished records; soon it was to be an article of faith in the South that amateur hard-riding gentlemen had overnight become a corps of superbly professional officers. On both sides, a few men with no previous military experience had shown an intuitive feel for high command, but they were great exceptions. One colonel at Appomattox remembered Lee at Spotsylvania in May of 1864, after three years of war, quietly overruling Major General A. P. Hill, who wanted to place Brigadier General Ambrose R. Wright of Georgia before a board of inquiry because of his costly tactical errors.

"These men are not an army," Lee explained to Hill, a West Pointer who had spent thirteen years in the Regular Army; "they are citizens defending their country. General Wright is not a soldier; he's a lawyer. I cannot do many things that I could do with a trained army. The soldiers know their duties better than the general officers do, and they have fought magnificently . . . You'll have to do what I do: when a man makes a mistake, I call him to my tent, and use the authority of my position to make him do the right thing the next time."

During this night, by Lee's statement eleven days later in one of his letters to Confederate President Jefferson Davis, "when the surrender became known, more than ten thousand men came in, as reported to me by the Commissary of the Army . . ."

This matter-of-fact recitation was the nearest that Lee ever came to criticizing his beloved enlisted men. The implication was that ten thousand stragglers were suddenly able to come walking in from the surrounding countryside when the shooting stopped, and perhaps should not have dropped out during the terrible final retreat.

The Federal troops already knew that Lee's men were creatures of flesh and blood like themselves. Both sides had a full measure of the American soldier's sense of humor. Two days before this, a desperately hungry North Carolina soldier, trailing at the very end of the retreating army, had been poking the bushes along a rail fence trying to flush out a chicken. Suddenly an entire squad of Union soldiers surrounded him shouting, "Surrender, surrender, we've got you!"

"Yes," the starving North Carolinian said, dropping his musket and raising his hands, "you've got me, and the hell of a git you got!"

As for the qualities of that "git," no one had a greater respect for Confederate fighting ability than did Grant, who was sitting up at his headquarters on the night of this Palm Sunday, telling tales of the Mexican War and apparently unable to discuss the events of the day. When he did write about the soldiers of the South, he spoke of "that enemy, whose manhood, however mistaken the cause, drew forth such herculean deeds of valor."

Chapter 3

AT TEN O'CLOCK the next morning, Lee rode to a small knoll between the two armies where Grant, mounted on his horse Cincinnati, was waiting to see him. The framework for the surrender of Lee's army had been agreed upon the day before, but now Grant wanted to see if Lee would assist him in bringing about the surrender of the Confederate forces to the south that were not under Lee's direct field command and were still fighting.

The two generals raised their hats as they met. It was another misty morning, with occasional drizzling rain, and over his grey uniform Lee was wearing an old blue overcoat that he had worn in the United States Army. Grant's staff stepped off to one side, leaving them alone in a way that had been impossible during yesterday's signing of the surrender terms.

"We had there between the lines," Grant wrote, "sitting on horseback, a very pleasant conversation of over half an hour." Since Grant had also characterized yesterday's conversation as "pleasant," while others who saw Lee at Appomattox found him in a state of manly grief bordering on shock, Grant's description of mood may have been inaccurate, but he gave a detailed description of what they discussed:

> ... Lee said to me that the South was a big country, and that we might have to march over it three or four times before the war entirely ended, but that now we would be able to do it, as they could no longer resist us. He expressed it as his earnest hope, however, that we would not be called upon to cause more loss and sacrifice of life; but he could not foretell the result.

This gave Grant the opportunity he sought.

I then suggested to General Lee that there was not a man in the Confederacy whose influence with the soldiery and the whole people was as great as his, and that if he would now advise the surrender of all the armies I had no doubt his advice would be followed with alacrity.

Like the nation from which it had seceded, the Confederacy had adopted the concept that the military authority must be subordinate to a civilian commander-in-chief. Although Lee was the general commanding all Confederate forces, he felt that an overall surrender involved a political rather than a purely military decision, and must be made by President Jefferson Davis.

Lee explained to Grant that he would have to consult with Davis before issuing orders for a general surrender. Since both Lee and Grant knew that Davis and the remnants of his administration were in the situation of refugees who were avoiding Federal columns while they sought a solid base from which to continue the war, Grant realized that it was going to be impossible for Lee and Davis to have any rapid and effective communication. Hope vanished that Lee would sit here on Traveller and authorize a quick general surrender.

"I knew there was no use to urge him to do anything against his ideas of what was right," Grant said of this moment, and dropped the matter. Their talk switched to the implementation of the surrender agreement governing Lee's forces in the immediate area. It was agreed that a printing press that accompanied Grant's forces should start turning out parole forms that would give legal protection to Lee's men when they traveled home.

In a few minutes, Lee and Grant reached across to each other from their horses and shook hands. When they met again, Grant would be President of the United States, and Lee, in the great forgotten chapter of his life, would be doing more than any other American to heal the wounds of war.

As Lee turned Traveller, three Federal officers came forward on their horses and asked if they could come with him to enter the Confederate lines. They wanted to look up some friends, now Confederate officers, with whom they had served in "the old army," as both sides called the prewar regular force.

Nearing Lee's headquarters, the mounted group encountered one of the most prominent Federal officers, Major General George Gordon

Meade, commander of the Army of the Potomac, and a friend of Lee's from earlier days. The Army of Northern Virginia had given Meade's men many a horrible day, but it was Meade who had thrown back Lee at Gettysburg.

Lee greeted Meade kindly and then said, "But what are you doing with all that grey in your beard?"

Meade cheerfully shot back, "You have to answer for most of it!"

As Lee and Meade talked, one of Meade's aides formed this impression of how the stress and exhaustion of these days was telling on Lee. He found Lee "in manner exceedingly grave and dignified — this, I believe, he always was; but there was evidently added an extreme depression, which gave him the air of a man who has kept up his pride to the last, but was entirely overwhelmed. From his speech I judge he was inclined to wander in his thoughts."

Lee shunned oratory, but he wished to make a final statement — really a declaration of love — to the men who had marched with him to the end. Throughout the war, he had been awed by his soldiers' dedication. "There were never such men in an army before," he had said to General John Bell Hood of Texas. The way for these thousands of soldiers to be told a last time of his admiration for them and appreciation of their services was to publish a General Order to be read to the respective units by their officers. It was also to be posted in places where the men could read and reread it for themselves.

With all else that he had to do, and possibly because of the exhaustion noted by the Union officer, Lee gave the task of writing this farewell order to Lieutenant Colonel Charles Marshall. When Marshall was slow in getting it done, due to the number of officers, both Confederate and Union, who were milling about on official and unofficial business, Lee told Marshall to get into the captured Federal ambulance that he used as an office in the field, and not to come out of it until he was finished. Lee posted a guard outside the ambulance to make certain the colonel could work in peace.

Marshall eventually emerged with a document that expressed the feelings of a man with whom he had been closely associated for three years, and whose thoughts and words he had transmitted to others on a daily basis. Lee deleted a bitter paragraph that seemed likely to keep alive the wounds of war, and changed a few words. This is what was read to his soldiers — General Order Number Nine, his last official communication to his army, and a tribute so eloquent that generations of Southern schoolchildren would recite it as their counterpart to Lincoln's Gettysburg Address.

> After four years of arduous service marked by unsurpassed courage and fortitude, the Army of Northern Virginia has been compelled to yield to overwhelming numbers and resources.
>
> I need not tell the brave survivors of so many hard fought battles, who have remained steadfast to the last, that I have consented to this result from no distrust of them; but feeling that valor and devotion could accomplish nothing that could compensate for the loss that must have attended the continuance of the contest, I determined to avoid the useless sacrifice of those whose past services have endeared them to their countrymen.
>
> By the terms of the agreement, officers and men can return to their homes until exchanged. You will take with you the satisfaction that proceeds from the consciousness of duty faithfully performed; and I earnestly pray that a Merciful God will extend to you His blessing and protection.
>
> With an unceasing admiration of your constancy and devotion to your Country, and a grateful remembrance of your kind and generous consideration for myself, I bid you all an affectionate farewell.
>
> R. E. Lee
> Genl.

Chapter 4

O N THE CHILL and overcast morning of April 12, three days after
the signing of the surrender terms, the Army of Northern Virginia was to perform its last act as a unit. It was to march up the sloping road to Appomattox Court House. There, on the outskirts of the
village, where the road flattened out, each successive division was to
halt, face the blue-clad Federal formations, and lay down its arms.
Grant had already left this area, and Lee was closing down his headquarters; neither would be present at this ceremony, although Lee
would still be with his troops when they returned to camp without
their muskets.

By chance, the Union general appointed to receive the surrender,
and the Confederate general who was to lead up the first of the Southern divisions, were living symbols of the distances that men had traveled to kill each other in this war. They were also representative of the
diverse sources from which both North and South drew officers who
had never previously served in the military.

Joshua Chamberlain of Maine, newly promoted to major general,
had been a professor of religion and Romance languages at Bowdoin
College. Given a leave of absence to study in Europe during the years
1862 and 1863, he had instead entered the army and risen to be colonel
of the famous Twentieth Maine, winning the Congressional Medal of
Honor for his defense of Little Round Top at the Battle of Gettysburg.
He had received the last of his several wounds when he was hit twice at
Hatcher's Run, just two weeks before.

Chamberlain was as fine a Union soldier as could be found; his
Southern opposite number in this last necessary business was Major

General John B. Gordon of Georgia, whose Second Corps had made the final doomed attack on Palm Sunday morning. This war's start had found him, aged thirty, in the business of developing coal mines. Some of his miners formed an infantry company and elected him captain; from this totally inexperienced beginning, he had risen to be a general of exceptional ability, and was Lee's hardest-fighting corps commander during the last year of the war. The most obvious of his many wounds was a deep gash in his thin face.

Shortly after breakfast, six thousand men of a Federal division lined up to receive the surrender. There were troops from Maine, Massachusetts, Michigan, New York, and Pennsylvania. Soon they saw the long, dispirited column of Confederates trudging up the road from the river, muskets on their shoulders for the last time. Gordon was at their head on horseback, the expression on his scarred face as crushed as those of his men. The first unit behind him was an understrength regiment of two hundred and ten men, the survivors of the Stonewall Brigade, which had started the war with forty-five hundred eager recruits. Behind them came many famous regiments, so few left in each that the red Confederate battle flags at their heads followed each other by short intervals. At a distance it looked like a parade of massed banners — to Chamberlain, watching them come, "The whole column seemed crowned with red."

The Confederates were nearly abreast of the Union ranks. As far as they knew, the blue-clad division of their late enemies was simply there to see to it that they laid down their arms. Suddenly the Southerners heard bugles and drums. The soldiers of the United States Army were lifting their muskets to the position of Carry Arms in a salute to the Confederate States Army.

The effect was electric. Chamberlain, who had given the order to salute, watched the Confederate general react:

> Gordon at the head of the column, riding with heavy spirit and downcast face, catches the sound . . . looks up . . . wheels superbly, making with himself and his horse one uplifted figure, with profound salutation as he drops the point of his sword to the boot toe; then, facing to his own command, gives word for his successive brigades to pass us with the same position of the manual, — honor answering honor. On our part not a sound of trumpet more, nor roll of drum . . . but an awed stillness rather, and breath-holding, as if it were the passing of the dead!

The Confederates halted and turned, lines of men in grey rags looking from twelve feet away into the eyes of men they had been shooting at seventy-two hours before. Chamberlain thought, "It is by miracles we have lived to see this day, — any of us standing here."

It was the soldiers who were showing the nation how a war should be ended. No Southern poet could say more than this, from General Chamberlain:

> Before us in proud humiliation stood the embodiment of manhood, men whom neither toils and sufferings, nor the fact of death, nor disaster, nor hopelessness could bend from their resolve; standing before us now, thin, worn, and famished, but erect, and with eyes looking level into ours, waking memories that bound us together as no other bond . . .

Veterans that they were, Lee's soldiers stacked their muskets with precision and few shows of emotion, but when each regiment in succession had to give up the flag it had followed into battle, placing it on a stack of surrendered muskets, the tears and curses and cries of pain began again. Men ran out from the ranks to kiss their flags good-bye. Some tore them from their staffs and hid them among themselves as they marched off — a practice quickly stopped after consultation between Union and Confederate officers. A few regiments marched up without a banner; the flag was tucked inside someone's tunic, or torn into a score of small secreted pieces that would become framed heirlooms in Southern houses.

The surrendering went on for six hours. When the last of the casualty-shrunken grey units marched up, a Confederate described what happened: ". . . someone in the blue line broke the silence and called for three cheers for the last brigade to surrender. It was taken up all about him by those who knew what it meant. But for us this soldierly generosity was more than we could bear. Many grizzled veterans wept like women, and my own eyes were as blind as my voice was dumb."

II

As the first of Lee's surrendered contingents marched back into their camp, feeling naked without their muskets, bayonets, and cartridge boxes, Lee and his staff were disbanding the headquarters of the Army of Northern Virginia. Later this morning Lee would give the order "Strike the tent!" So often this command to take down the tent and pack it in a wagon had been called out by Lee's deep voice on a morning that saw great movements, and thousands dead by sunset. Now it would mean that the last reports had been received, the last orders given, and this army would cease to exist.

It was left to a Union cavalry sergeant from Massachusetts to record Lee's departure from his army. Assigned to the detachment of horsemen who were to escort Lee and some of his staff along the road to his rented house in Richmond, this trooper found a headquarters that was, as it had been all through the war, a place of spartan simplicity. In this grove of white oaks, chestnut oaks, and Virginia pines, there were the captured tents with "U.S." on them, and the captured ambulance that Lee used as an office. A few wagons, some horses — the only hint that some of the officers under these trees had lived on handsome plantations was the presence of several black servants who cooked, washed clothes, and chopped wood. Some had been freed by their masters before this war; others had been slaves until today.

The Union cavalry sergeant wrote that his detachment was:

> . . . courteously received and asked to wait until General Lee and his staff had breakfasted and completed arrangements for their departure. We dismounted a short distance away. General Lee seated himself at a table made from a hard tack box and ate his last breakfast (consisting of hard tack, fried pork and coffee without milk), with the Army of Northern Virginia. He was dressed in a neat, gray uniform and was a splendid looking soldier.
>
> Commanding officers of corps and divisions of the Confederate army and other officers then came to take leave of him. He was a short distance from me and his conversation was evidently words of encouragement and advice. Almost every one of the officers went away

in tears. Then we mounted, and General Lee's party started through the lines of the remnant of the Army of Northern Virginia for his home in Richmond.

Then commenced an ovation that seemed to me a wonderful manifestation of confidence and affection for this great military chieftain. From the time we left his camp till we passed the last of his regiments the men seemed to come from everywhere and the "Rebel Yell" was continuous.

The lieutenant in charge of the sixteen Union cavalrymen of the escort had been told to render whatever service Lee wished — ride with him the hundred miles to Richmond, or let him proceed by himself whenever he wished to do that. The lieutenant later noted in his diary that he "escorted them about 12 miles on the road to Richmond, which was strewn with dead mules and wreckage." At that point Lee overtook a few soldiers of the Stonewall Brigade who, having been the first to lay down their arms in the morning, were already along the road to their homes, two hundred and fifty miles away at the far end of the Valley of Virginia. Lee took out a map he had used for less peaceful purposes and went over it with his veterans, pointing out their quickest route home. When he said good-bye to them, he told them to think of the future and not the past, and to be as loyal citizens as they had been soldiers.

Then Lee said to the Union cavalry lieutenant, "You see I am in my own country and among friends and do not need an escort. I am giving you unnecessary trouble, and now request you to withdraw your men and rejoin your command."

That was Lee speaking as a professional officer; the lieutenant told the last of their parting: ". . . he shook my hand and wished me a safe return to my home, with tears in his eyes."

Back at Appomattox, General Chamberlain watched the rest of the Confederate camp dissolve:

Now on the morrow, over all the hillsides in the peaceful sunshine, are clouds of men on foot or horse, singly or in groups, making their earnest way as if by the instinct of the ant, each with his own little burden, each for his own little home.

Chapter 5

ONCE HE HAD MARCHED at the head of seventy thousand men. Now, following him as he rode Traveller, came an old wagon, an unmilitary quilt rigged over its top and sides to replace rotted-away canvas. Behind that was the captured Federal ambulance that had served as his office, and then another Federal ambulance, this one loaned by the victors to carry home a wounded officer of his staff.

Two years before, Lee had stood on a hillock and taken the salute as eight thousand of his horsemen jingled past on parade. Now there were twenty "bony, weary old horses" with him, some pulling the vehicles, others carrying the few riders who accompanied him east toward Richmond. The group included Lieutenant Colonel Charles Marshall and Lieutenant Colonel Walter H. Taylor, a slight young man who had mixed his indispensable office work with free-lance participation in every battle he could ride into when not otherwise occupied. A man along the road saw Marshall and Taylor "gaunt and pallid in ragged uniforms." Major Giles B. Cooke, the wounded staff officer who was lying in the borrowed Union ambulance, was far worse off than the haggard men on horseback. The others, mounted or in the wagons, were a handful of enlisted men, and the few black servants, some riding beside men who had owned them. This exhausted, tattered procession crossed the green, war-slashed country, none of them knowing his future.

For Lee, the future might be short. The attitude of Grant and his men at Appomattox was no indication of Northern public feeling. Three hundred and sixty thousand Union soldiers were dead; their parents, their widows, their children, thought of Confederate soldiers as armed rebels guilty of treason. In this view, there could be no worse traitors than those officers of the United States Army, educated at West Point, who had fought against the government they had sworn to serve. There was a high probability that Robert E. Lee would be indicted for treason, a crime punishable by hanging or a long prison term.

Whatever the action taken against him, Lee's body might collapse before an arresting officer could appear in Richmond. Two years before, in camp at Fredericksburg, Virginia, he had experienced a heart attack. Neither he nor his doctors had understood what the seizure was. His exceptional strength and determination had kept him going, despite later complications. On this ride from Appomattox to Richmond, he looked more robust than his younger officers and considered himself to be physically sound, though he suffered from pain that the doctors said was rheumatism. In fact, it was angina pectoris, and his deteriorating circulatory system made him vulnerable to another heart attack or to a stroke.

Even if he escaped immediate medical crises and Federal punishment, Lee's future was clouded. His thirty-nine years as a soldier were at an enforced end. He had no job. Apart from the rented house in Richmond, there was no place where he and his family could live. Arlington, his wife's estate on the Potomac, opposite Washington, and the place where they had lived with their children many of the years before the war, had been occupied by Federal troops at the beginning of this conflict. Part of its eleven hundred acres had been pressed into service as a cemetery for the Union dead; there were thousands of graves there. Lee had hopes of recovering Arlington for his family, but had no idea of what he might encounter in the attempt. Another family farm in Virginia, known as the White House, had been put to the torch by Union soldiers, its principal house leveled. The third farm, Romancoke, near the White House, was in an area so ravaged by war that there was not a fence post left standing within eight miles.

Lee was not bankrupt — a few of his small investments had survived the war — but waiting for him in Richmond was a wife who was an invalid, and their three unmarried daughters. His sons Custis and Rooney had come through the final battles unscathed; even if he were so fortunate as to find that his son Robert, now missing, was alive and well, it would mean that he had three sons who were emerging from the Confederate Army with neither jobs nor money.

Along this road to Richmond were constant reminders that Lee had been a central figure in a stupendous failure. On the road itself was the wreckage of his army — dead horses, shattered wagons in ditches, bloody bandages in the April mud. When he turned his head, he saw weed-choked fields and burnt houses. Blasted trestles and torn-up railroad tracks were silent witness that there was no public transport, no shipment of goods. There was nothing on the shelves of country stores. In towns, the banks were closed. Confederate money was worthless. Amputees in grey poked along red-clay roads on crutches while blue-clad columns marched to occupy strategic points in the South.

☆　☆　☆

Like his army, Lee was riding into history. In what was left of his life, many millions of Americans would know just where he was and what he was doing, but after his death the national memory would simplify Lee. He would come striding out of some plantation at the beginning of the Civil War, swing up on Traveller, put up a fabulous fight, surrender to Grant at Appomattox, and then — he and Traveller were instantly transformed into a stone statue, with his name revered in the South and his campaigns studied in the world's military academies.

Future Southern generations would think of Lee as a well-to-do, landed aristocrat, quintessentially a man of the South. It was true that his family had been prominent in Virginia for two hundred years, and that his father was at one time governor of Virginia; but by the time Lee was born of his improvident father's second marriage he was a poor relation, raised just a cut above genteel poverty by a mother who was in effect abandoned, and later widowed. He had sought the appointment to the United States Military Academy partly because the only way he could get a college education was to be educated at public expense. Thousands of acres had come into his life when, as a young army officer, he married Mary Anna Randolph Custis, the great-granddaughter of Martha Washington, a spoiled only child who was the sole heiress to Arlington and the two other large farms. Even this relationship with the land was deceptive; his military life kept him from taking an active role in farming until the years just before the war. Then, when his charming but inefficient father-in-law died, leaving the mismanaged Custis farms in chaos, Lee took a long leave of absence in a desperate effort to put them back on a paying basis. The war had wiped out the gains he made; as he rode east to rejoin his family in Richmond, the only money that any of the Lees possessed was from the investments that Lee had made from his pay as an officer in the United States Army. It was a long way from the days when his father-in-law had felt that a poor young lieutenant of Engineers, no matter how handsome and pleasant, was not much of a match for his rich daughter.

Others would romanticize Lee. He was a realist who learned from experience, and few Southerners understood how much of that experience, invaluable to the Confederate cause, was acquired outside the South. There was Lee in his cadet days on the cliffs above the Hudson River, getting to know young men from every state, studying under instructors from many parts of the nation, and passing in review under the watchful eye of Colonel Sylvanus Thayer of Massachusetts, the superintendent known as "the Father of the Military Academy." There was Lee's early assignment, in 1835, as a topographical engineer surveying the disputed boundary between Ohio and Michigan. Bearing the title of Assistant Astronomer, he paddled a canoe through a wild frontier area of the Great Lakes, reporting in a letter to his young wife an encounter with "a handsome Bark Canoe, guided by one squaw sitting in the stern, and *towed* by two others on the Beach . . . In the canoe were three small children, the whole party was very neatly dressed the women in short petticoats coming no lower than the knee, with a kind of short gown or jacket above them, their hair in one long plait at their backs and a large silver plate suspended at the breast."

Two years later Lee was at St. Louis, in charge of cutting a channel for the Mississippi there as part of the first effort by the Corps of Engineers to control the great river's course. Mary and his little children joined him in his second year of this work; he wrote a friend that the children delighted in imitating the paddle-wheel river boats. "They convert themselves into steamboats, ring their bells, raise their steam (high pressure), and put off. They fire up so frequently, and keep on so heavy a pressure of steam that I am constantly fearing that they will burst their boilers."

New York City was Lee's next assignment; with some interruptions, he spent five years there, repairing and improving four forts that guarded the nation's busiest harbor. He left New York for the Mexican War, during which he impressed General Winfield Scott as being "the very best soldier I ever saw in the field." Other duty outside the South included his three years as superintendent at West Point, and a number of inspection trips that took him as far north as Rhode Island. Although Texas was to become a Confederate state, for Lee it was the West in its wildest form; as commander of the United States Second Cavalry, he chased Comanche Indians and tracked down Mexican bandits. Later, as commander of the Department of Texas, he witnessed the experimental cross-country marches being conducted with seventy-five camels imported from North Africa. The man who had ordered the test to determine whether camels would be suitable army pack animals in the Southwest was the nation's secretary of war — Jefferson Davis.

So it was that the man riding away from Appomattox was a product of more than the South. There was never a more loyal Virginian, but if Lee had been only what most Southerners thought he was, he could never have done what he did in their defense, nor raise himself to certain heights that lay between him and the grave. He was not a typical anything — Southerner, soldier, citizen, man of prayer — and even on this heartbreaking ride through April mists his active mind was probing the future. He knew the feeling for revenge that was in many Southern hearts, and the danger that new fighting might explode anywhere, at any time. The wrong word from Lee — even a word that could be misconstrued — and his veterans would come pouring out of the hills with anything they could get their hands on — pistols, squirrel guns, scythes, axes. "You have only to blow the bugle," one of his colonels reportedly said to him.

He would not blow the bugle. He would take care that no word he spoke could be taken as a call to resist the realities of defeat. Soon many Southerners would flee the country — to Mexico, to Canada, to Brazil. Some would be going to avoid possible arrest and trial for treason; others would simply refuse to live again under the Stars and Stripes. Lee sensed all this coming. He would stay and meet whatever fate awaited him. When he spoke to the young staff officers riding with him now, he told them that when they got to their homes they should stay there, behave peaceably, and take any kind of job that offered.

Like young Marshall and Taylor, he did not know what the Federal government might impose upon the South, but as they rode along he urged them to do whatever would be required to enable them once again to vote and to hold office.

II

Their third day on the road brought them to the house of Charles Carter Lee, his oldest brother. He dined with him that night, but insisted on sleeping in his tent. It was a continuation of his practice during the war; he wished always to share the field conditions his soldiers must experience. With a literary shake of the head, his aide Taylor wrote of Lee's doing this even now: "This continued self-denial can only be explained upon the hypothesis that he desired to have his men know that he shared their privations to the very last."

The next morning, this remnant of headquarters was up and about at dawn. Soon enough Lee's deep voice was heard — "Strike the tent!" — and the wagons moved off. People living along the road somehow knew that Lee was coming, and from cabins women appeared with food they handed to the men on the wagons. Little girls dashed into the road, half-hiding their faces with aprons, and presented him with bouquets of hyacinths and daffodils.

Lee could not bear it. He turned to Taylor and burst out, "Colonel, these people are kind — too kind. Their hearts are as full as when we began our campaigns in Eighteen Sixty-One. They do too much — more than they are able to do — for us."

Although the flowers were a tribute to Lee, many of these women, those living in cabins and those in larger houses, were constantly bringing out whatever food they had, to give to passing soldiers. White Southerners regarded these tired, limping boys, from whatever state, as being part of their families. A soldier from Kentucky, forced to surrender many hundreds of miles from home, said that he set off without a penny and was never asked to pay for a meal or a night's lodging on the way.

Chapter 6

T HE DAY OF APRIL 15 would see Lee into Richmond. Just six days
before, he had met with Grant to sign the surrender agreement.
Three days ago, his regiments had laid down their arms in the surrender ceremony. Now, stopping for breakfast along the road at the house
of a family named Gilliam, Lee showed the lighter side of his nature.
Always he enjoyed the conversation of ladies and of children; above all,
he enjoyed his teasing encounters with little girls. This day his entrance
into Richmond as a paroled prisoner of war would cause many to
weep, but the man who symbolized this despair took ten-year-old Polly
Gilliam on his knee, smiled at her, and said, "Polly, come with me to
Richmond and I will give you a beau."

On the road, later in the morning, Lee was joined by a huge man on
a horse. This was Rooney, his second son, William Henry Fitzhugh
Lee, all six feet three inches of him. He had the same flushed skin as did
his father, but, while Lee was five feet ten and a half inches tall, with
graceful hands and notably small feet, his towering son had hands and
feet that a contemporary called "immense." A man who had rowed
stroke oar on the crew at Harvard, he had left before graduation to
take a commission in the United States Army, resigning from the service two years before the war. Now twenty-seven and a major general
of cavalry, Rooney was catching up to his father's shabby caravan after
bidding farewell to the last of his troopers at Appomattox.

Of Lee's three sons, Rooney had given him much the greatest concern. Lee was a loving, strict, demanding father. He always worried
that one of his sons might turn out to be like his own father, "Light-
Horse Harry" Lee, a noted soldier, once governor of Virginia, who had

tarnished his reputation by disastrous speculation in western lands — a practice that twice landed him in debtor's jail and contributed to a self-exile in the Caribbean that had resulted in his dying far from home when Lee was eleven. His father's irresponsibility, extravagance, and marital infidelity had broken his mother's heart, and caused her endless humiliation and years of financial hardship. Lee named none of his three sons for his famous father. When he learned that Rooney's grades were bad and that he was getting into debt at Harvard, he wrote to Mary from Texas, "It is time he began thinking of something besides running about amusing himself. I wish him to do so at once."

Whatever Rooney's undergraduate flings, the war brought him and his family a full measure of agony. During the first two years of the war, Rooney and his frail young wife, Charlotte, lost their two children — Robert E. Lee III, who died of illness at the age of two, and Annie Agnes Lee, who died as an infant late in 1862. At the great cavalry battle of Brandy Station in June of 1863, Rooney was wounded; his younger brother Robert, then a lieutenant, supervised moving him to the house of his mother-in-law, in an area thought to be safe from the enemy. There he was joined by Charlotte and his mother and three sisters.

Two weeks after this devoted circle began their determined nursing of Rooney, a Federal raiding party rode up. The women had the horrifying experience of watching this seriously wounded man — son, husband, brother, son-in-law — carried flat on his back into captivity. Charlotte never recovered from the shock and died later in the year while Rooney was still in a Federal prison waiting to be exchanged. Before Charlotte died, Lee wrote to his beloved daughter-in-law: "In the lone hours of the night I groan in sorrow at his captivity and separation from you." He had yet another grief to deal with as he lay on the cot in his dark tent: in October of 1862 Lee's daughter Annie, for whom Rooney's dead daughter had been named, had died of typhoid fever in North Carolina.

A spring rain was pouring as Lee rode through the town of Manchester, opposite Richmond on the south side of the James River. A Baptist minister was on his porch and saw Lee pass.

> His steed was bespattered with mud, and his head hung down as if worn by long travelling. The horseman himself sat his horse like a master; his face was ridged with self-respecting grief; his garments

were worn in the service and stained with travel; his hat was slouched and spattered with mud . . . Even in the fleeting moment of his passing by my gate, I was awed by his incomparable dignity. His majestic composure, his rectitude and his sorrow, were so wrought and blended into his visage and so beautiful and impressive to my eyes that I fell into violent weeping.

Both bridges across the James River had been destroyed by Lee's army when it evacuated Richmond. Now he crossed on a pontoon bridge the Union forces had thrown across the river after they captured the city. On the far side, Lee and his wagons rode into what another returning soldier called "the grinning ruins" of downtown Richmond. Tall brick chimneys and jagged, blackened walls stood above charred wreckage. This large area of devastation, with seven hundred structures burnt, was caused by fires the retreating Confederates had set to destroy tobacco warehouses and military supplies, fires that had gone out of control.

The rain had stopped now. Most of the black bricks and scorched timbers were not as high as Lee's eye as he rode Traveller; after the fire, everything that could be pulled down was leveled to keep the ruins from collapsing on those walking through. The former streets were mere trails through rubble. Above this waste, intact, rose the capitol building of the Commonwealth of Virginia. It was Thomas Jefferson who had selected as the model for this structure the Roman temple known as La Maison Carrée at Nîmes in France. It was made of brick covered by white stucco, and had tall modified Ionic columns supporting the roof of its portico. For the past four years this handsome classic building had served as the legislative seat of the Confederate States of America, a government that had levied taxes, run a postal service, sent missions to foreign countries, raised armies, waged war. Many of its legislators, making speeches in the hall of the House of Delegates, had seen themselves as heirs of 1776, a latter-day Continental Congress under a flag of thirteen stars, breaking away from an exterior power that was forcing its will upon them.

Lee had a less flattering opinion of the Confederate Congress that had met in this building. He said to General John B. Gordon, "It is enough to turn one's hair gray to spend one day in that Congress." A month before the end of the war, he said to his son Custis, "I have been up to see the Congress and they do not seem to be able to do anything except to eat peanuts and chew tobacco, while my army is starving."

All that was past. Above the long roof of the capitol, the Stars and Stripes hung placidly in the damp afternoon; soldiers in blue were in charge.

Where the wreckage began to give way to houses still intact, groups gathered along Main Street, brought there by little boys racing up from the river to say that Lee was coming. In a few minutes, there he was, erect on his horse. Behind him was his son Rooney and his aides Marshall and Taylor. All still had their swords at their sides, silent testimony of the honorable terms with which Grant had released them from Appomattox. Behind these horsemen came the muddy wagons.

The crowd grew. Men cheered; women cried out and waved their handkerchiefs. Muddy though he was, Lee was incapable of cutting a poor figure; a Northern newspaper reporter who now saw him for the first time described him as "a most splendid specimen of a soldier and a gentleman."

Off-duty Federal soldiers were along the sidewalk, watching. Better than the Southern civilians among whom they stood, they knew just how great a general was passing, and what it had taken to bleed his army to death. These soldiers in blue, block after block, raised their little visored caps and held them high, honoring the man they wished had ridden with them instead of against them. To all the exclamations from the crowd, Lee raised his muddy wide-brimmed hat, inclining his head each time he did so, his face composed. It was his last, unscheduled parade, and he wished it over.

They turned off Main Street, went over to Franklin, and stopped in front of Number 707, the red-brick, three-story house that Custis had rented for the family during the war. The fire had come so near that a neighboring house was damaged. Here the crowd was thickest. It was the outpouring at Appomattox all over again. Civilians who revered him, wives of his soldiers, children to whom his name was magic, all crowded about him, reaching up their hands to Lee, touching his boots, his sword.

One of the enlisted men came forward from the wagons to hold Traveller's head while Lee dismounted. A woman thought that Lee was so emotionally affected that his body would scarcely obey him, and he had difficulty getting off his horse. People packed around him on the sidewalk in these last seconds that he would wear the sword of a soldier, grasping his hand, each trying to tell him something. Lee shook hand after hand, nodding to blurted utterances of admiration and good wishes and thanks for his services. He opened the iron gate that separated the sidewalk from the stone front steps, climbed those eight steps, and turned under the little portico. Lee took off his muddy hat and bowed once more. Then he opened the door and disappeared.

Chapter 7

BEHIND THAT DOOR were the two things he needed most, the chance for some sleep and his family. The Lees were a devoted group, sharing his love for sunsets and trees, horses, dogs, cats. His wife and three surviving daughters had been living here during the latter part of the war. Rooney had just come home with him, and Custis, taken prisoner at Sayler's Creek, had been released and had arrived home three days before. Young Robert was still missing.

These grown children surrounded their father with love. Ranging in age from thirty-two-year-old Custis to nineteen-year-old Mildred, to them the battlefield leader was also the man who invariably forgot his shaving brush when traveling, the father who loved buttermilk and thought it could cure almost anything. When he took off his hat, they saw that their father's deep tan stopped abruptly where his hat brim had rested above his eyes. They saw something else, a touch of vanity remarked on by a man who first saw him at Appomattox: "He is growing quite bald, and wears one of the side locks of his hair thrown across the upper portion of his forehead, which is as white and as fair as a woman's."

Lee's wife, Mary, was confined to a wheelchair as a result of arthritis and complications from her numerous childbirths. Although they had seen each other with some frequency during the war, they had been apart at the moments of family tragedy — the deaths of Rooney's two children, the death of their daughter Annie, the death of Rooney's wife. It was Christmas Eve of 1863, the year that had seen victory at Chancellorsville and failure at Gettysburg, when Lee opened his wife's letter that told him that Charlotte was dying. Replying quickly to

Mary, and referring to Rooney by his given name of Fitzhugh, Lee wrote, "That you may know my sorrow in all its breadth & depth, as far as I know my own heart, I feel for her all the love I bear Fitzhugh. That is very great . . . She was so devoted to Fitzhugh, seemed so bound up in him, that apparently she thought of and cared for nothing else. They seemed so united that I loved them as one person."

It was across memories such as these that Robert Edward and Mary Custis Lee were reunited as the Confederacy shuddered to its close. Like her husband, Mary had been opposed to secession, but once Virginia was committed to the war, there was no more ardent rebel than this woman. From her wheelchair she had superintended what was virtually a sock-knitting factory for Confederate soldiers, conducted daily in her large downstairs bedroom. As the Army of Northern Virginia withdrew from Richmond in the retreat that was to end a week later at Appomattox, an astonishing scene ensued at 707 Franklin Street. The fire that swept the city set the house next door ablaze, and sparks were striking 707, having no effect on the bricks but threatening to ignite the front door. Friends rushed into the house, urging Mary and her daughters to flee, but she posted her oldest daughter, Mary, on the top step with a bucket of water to throw on the front door if it should catch fire. Through all this, "she sat in her chair, calmly knitting away on her soldier sock."

Then a Federal officer dashed up, followed by four horses pulling an ambulance. He felt there was so little time to lose that he ordered his men to save the Lees' possessions by filling their trunks and throwing them out a window. Mary told the well-meaning enemy soldiers to get out of the house, and refused to be carried out. There she sat — flames in the house next door; Union soldiers standing by in the street; Mary Lee in her wheelchair beside the window inside her threatened house, knitting a sock for an army from which she was now cut off. The fire came no nearer.

In the next days Mary was to look out that window, see more Union soldiers in the streets, and still say to her friends, "The end is not yet. Richmond is not the Confederacy." When they brought her news of Appomattox, she said, "General Lee is not the Confederacy; there is life in the old land yet." Now that even she knew that the remaining Confederate forces to the south must soon collapse, she wrote a cousin, "For my part it will always be a source of pride and consolation to me to know that all mine have perilled their lives . . . in so holy a cause."

Of her husband she wrote, "He is wonderfully well considering all that he has endured."

Lee's nature was to forgive, in matters large and small. Mary bore the North a cold hatred for taking her beloved Arlington and destroying so much of the South. Nonetheless, it was not in her to ignore courtesy, and she understood that from the moment the United States Army had entered Richmond and that ambulance dashed to her house, a protective arm had been constantly about her. Federal rations were delivered to the house every day. "It is impossible," she said, "to describe the kind attention of the Union soldiers to me."

Whatever the civilian authorities in Washington might do to Lee, it was obvious that the United States Army considered him an erring but brilliant son whose big mistake had been to fight in defense of his homeland. A sentry in blue stood in front of the house at all hours, not to hinder the family's coming and going, but to protect them from looting or unwanted intrusions. Mary Lee was an army wife; in those young soldiers taking turns on guard on the sidewalk she saw not the enemy, but homesick boys doing their duty, just as boys in grey had done theirs. Each morning she sent breakfast on a tray out to the Union soldier who had stood with his musket while she and her family were sleeping. As for the reaction of her prominent neighbors, who thought that this was "uncalled for," she was a law unto herself, and had been long before she married Robert E. Lee.

II

So Lee was home, wanting only to rest and leave aside the enormous responsibilities that had partly destroyed his heart. It was not to be that simple. The world outside this brick house was instantly in added turmoil; in Washington, only hours before Lee rode into Richmond, President Abraham Lincoln died from the bullet of an assassin who was a Southerner. LINCOLN MURDERED! Lincoln, whose policy toward the toppling Confederacy was, from his own lips, "Let 'em up easy."

As the news spread, some in the South rejoiced that the leader of their enemies had been struck down. Lee's reaction was "It is a crime previously unknown to this Country, and one that must be deprecated by every American." The North was wild with vengeful grief. The new President was Andrew Johnson, a pro-Union Democrat from Tennessee who had been made Vice-President on a wartime coalition ticket, and a man who nobody had ever imagined would be President. The Republican-dominated Congress and a political hybrid of a President who was a Southerner were setting forth on an uneasy march that would end in an impeachment trial. As the curtain fell on war, the ruins of the South were visible, but the tragedy of future years waited off-stage.

Any number of people felt that they had immediate, legitimate business with Robert E. Lee. Two days after his arrival in Richmond, the famous photographer Mathew Brady appeared at the door. Brady, who was an old acquaintance, had spent the war with the Union armies. This was his first chance to enter the recent Confederate capital. "It was supposed," Brady said, "that after his defeat it would be preposterous to ask him to sit, but I thought that to be the time for the historical picture."

Lee certainly thought it was preposterous. "It is utterly impossible, Mister Brady. How can I sit for a photograph with the eyes of the world upon me as they are today?"

Brady beat a tactical retreat to the house of his friend Judge Robert Ould, who agreed to ask Mrs. Lee to intercede in the matter. Word soon came from Franklin Street that Mr. Brady could come back and bring his camera with him. Lee appeared on the back porch, accompanied by his son Custis and his aide Walter Taylor, and said, "Very well, Mister Brady, we are ready for you." He was wearing one of his grey sack coat uniforms with no braid on the sleeves, and he was without a sword. Brady set to work, and came up with remarkable pictures. In some, Lee is flanked by Custis and Taylor, but the most arresting ones are of Lee facing the camera alone. The light of battle is still in his eyes; on his face is written sorrow and determination. He is a man who has surrendered but is not defeated.

Mindful of his solitary conversation with Grant on that knoll near Appomattox, Lee now tried to bring an end to further futile Confederate military resistance, most of it being put up in North Carolina by his old West Point classmate Joseph E. Johnston. On April 20, Lee wrote to President Jefferson Davis. Before leaving Appomattox, Lee had sent Davis a formal report of his final operations, losses, and surrender. Now he wrote in broader terms, trying to make the still-resisting Davis understand that the South had lost both the ability and the will to make war.

Sensing that he was dealing with a desperate leader who might be considering a guerrilla war if all else failed, Lee tried to forestall Davis with these words: "A partisan war may be continued, and hostilities protracted, causing individual suffering and the devastation of the country, but I see no prospect by that means of achieving a separate independence." At Appomattox, Lee had rejected the idea of letting his army fight on as small roving bands; now, polite as always, he told Davis to face facts: "To save useless effusion of blood, I would recommend measures be taken for the suspension of hostilities and the restoration of peace."

His effort was in vain; Davis and a handful of his officials were moving south through North Carolina, still avoiding Federal capture, clutching the wild hope that somehow they could start to win again.

III

Since an appearance on the streets of Richmond would draw more attention than he wished, Lee waited for night to get exercise by walking through this neighborhood bordering the silent ruins. The pipes that fed the city's gaslights were cut and the streets were black, the silence broken only by the tread of Federal patrols.

On these walks Lee was accompanied by his youngest daughter, Mildred, whose vivacity had years before caused him to give her the nickname "Life." Lee was possessive of his daughters, speaking of "little Agnes," who was twenty-four, and on one occasion writing Mary of these three young women, "Tell the little creatures that they must work like beavers and get a supply of eggs and chickens." Mildred, good-hearted, enthusiastic, and the greatest cat fancier in a family of animal lovers, was Lee's favorite. She had dark hair and a plain, intelligent face. During the harsh siege of Petersburg, a city whose citizens had stood behind Lee to the end despite suffering and sacrifice that were to haunt him, he had written to Mildred in Richmond. He had urged her to get her ailing mother some buttermilk, and closed, "I think of you, long for you, pray for you. It is all I can do. Think sometimes of your devoted Father, R. E. Lee."

One evening, Lee and Mildred decided to call unannounced at the house of General R. H. Chilton, his adjutant general, who had also come home after Appomattox. When the candle was lighted in the hall, there in the shadows was Chilton's nephew Channing Smith, a young cavalry scout from Mosby's Rangers, a celebrated unit that had not yet surrendered. He had slipped into the city to find out for his daring commander whether they ought to surrender or fight on.

When the young soldier asked General Lee for instructions, a lifetime of military protocol dictated his answer: "Give my regards to Colonel Mosby," Lee said in the candlelight, "and tell him that I am under parole, and cannot, for that reason, give him any advice."

The scout took this in and then asked, "But, General, what must *I* do?"

That was a different matter. Lee looked at this youth he had known from before the war and said, "Channing, go home, all you boys who fought with me, and help to build up the shattered fortunes of our old state."

☆ ☆ ☆

The ebbing tide of war to the south uncovered another survivor — Lee's missing youngest son, twenty-one-year-old Captain Robert E. Lee, Jr., known to the family as Rob. Of his reception by his mother, father, brothers, and sisters, he said with understatement, "They were all much relieved at my reappearance."

Missing for nearly a month, Rob had quite a story to tell. Early in the final retreat from Richmond to Appomattox, he had been cut off from his cavalry unit when his horse was wounded during a skirmish. By the time he was able to borrow another horse from a friendly farmer, there were thousands of Union soldiers between him and the

Army of Northern Virginia. He spent nearly a week trying to ride un-
detected around the heads of the Federal cavalry columns that were
moving to encircle his father's army. When he finally got all the way
around to the west of Appomattox Court House and headed east in the
expectation of meeting the retreating army, he encountered some Confederate cavalrymen who had gotten out before the surrender and were
on their way to continue the fight in North Carolina. Rob had thrown
in his lot with them.

At Greensboro, North Carolina, he and another officer were in the
room when his father's official report of the surrender at Appomattox
was delivered to Jefferson Davis. "After reading it," Rob wrote, "he
handed it to us; then, turning away, he silently wept bitter tears."

In determining what to do next, Rob had the advice of his uncle
Sydney Smith Lee, a commodore in the Confederate Navy who had
carried on the fight as far as this inland point. It was Smith Lee, a former United States Navy officer, who had given a breezier explanation
of his decision to serve the Confederacy than his brother Robert's "I
could take no part in an invasion of the Southern States." Smith had
said, "Virginia comes first with us all, you know, so here I am." After
consulting with his uncle, Rob said, "It was decided to go back to Virginia to get our paroles, go home, and go to work."

Certain that the war was over, whatever Jefferson Davis might
think, Rob had headed for Richmond. He arrived shortly after the
news that on April 26 General Johnston had surrendered to General
Sherman in North Carolina. This left little organized resistance, although Davis, now fleeing through South Carolina, still had hopes of
continuing to fight west of the Mississippi.

It was strange for Rob and his father to talk to each other without
the sound of cannon, or at least shouted orders, in the background.
They had seen each other a number of times during the war, but, as
with Custis and Rooney, Lee had felt that to have any of his sons on his
staff would smack of nepotism. Each of the three had made his own
way in the Confederate service, and all of them had seen violent action.

One instance stood out in the memories of Rob and his father. He
had been an eighteen-year-old private in the Rockbridge Artillery
when it fought at Sharpsburg, Maryland, on September 17, 1862. Attacked by a larger force on that bloodiest day of the war, the Army of
Northern Virginia had eleven thousand men killed or wounded near

the Antietam Creek — one Texas regiment started the day with two hundred and twenty-six men, and had forty-two left by night. Three of the four cannon in Rob's artillery battery had been knocked out of action by one o'clock in the afternoon, and many of his comrades, and their horses, were dead or wounded. The unit was ordered to pull out of the fighting; as the remnants of the battery withdrew from the left flank they came to a knoll where Lee and his staff were gathered.

When his captain rode over to ask Lee for instructions, Rob and some of the other young enlisted men, sweating through black powder stains, trailed along on foot. Lee was dismounted, an orderly holding his horse. He had bandages and splints on both hands; his wrists were sprained and several bones in his right hand broken. At the recent Second Battle of Manassas, he had been standing beside Traveller when the horse shied, and Lee, lunging to regain control of the bridle, had fallen, sprawling. The commanding general could not dress himself these days, and when he was astride Traveller a courier had to take the reins and lead the horse.

As the injured Lee listened to the artillery captain's report of what was left of his unit, he looked at the battle-stained artillerymen, "his eyes," Rob said, "passing over me without any sign of recognition." Then Lee told Rob's captain to reorganize what serviceable men, horses, and ammunition he had, and take the one functioning cannon back into the desperate fight that was raging a few hundred yards away.

> I went up to speak to my father. When he found out who I was, he congratulated me on being well and unhurt. I then said:
> "General, are you going to send us in again?"
> "Yes, my son," he replied, with a smile; "you all must do everything you can to help drive these people back."

Home now, this fairest of the dark-haired Lees found that 707 Franklin Street had become even more of a dormitory than it had been during the war. Referred to as "the Mess," from the long period when Custis and other officers had used the rented house as a bachelor officers' quarters before the arrival of Mary Lee and her daughters, the house was now packed. Not only were there Rob's mother and father, his three sisters and two brothers, but cousins and friends were sleeping on straw-filled mattresses all over the house, until they could find out where their families were and discover which of their distant homes had been destroyed or abandoned and which had not.

The initial procession of callers, including Mathew Brady, had now become a stream. Rob observed, "All sorts and conditions of people came to see him; officers and soldiers from both armies, statesmen, politicians, ministers of the Gospel, mothers and wives to ask about husbands and sons of whom they had heard nothing."

In the midst of all this, a reporter from the *New York Herald* named Thomas M. Cook presented himself to General Lee. The people of the North, he said, wanted to know how Lee viewed the present state of affairs. What with the increased Northern hostility ablaze since Lincoln's assassination, and the fact that Jefferson Davis was still at large and some sporadic fighting continued, a statement by Lee might have a good effect. Although the reporter did not say so, he was one more Northerner who was making an interesting discovery: the only thing that white Southerners were repentant about was that they had lost the war. Wouldn't somebody please say that they were sorry?

Lee wanted to avoid public statements, but he saw this as an opportunity to say something that would be conciliatory without being apologetic. The reporter paraphrased much of the conversation, quoting directly only a few times. Regarding Lincoln's assassination, "the General considered this an event in itself one of the most deplorable that could have occurred. As a crime it was unexampled and beyond execration. It was a crime that no good man could approve from any conceivable motive. Undoubtedly the effort would be made to fasten the responsibility of it upon the South; but, from his intimate acquaintance with the leading men of the South, he was confident there was not one of them who would sanction or approve of it."

Reviewing the origins of the war, Lee explained the Southern belief that secession had not been unconstitutional, and that participation in that secession was not treason. It was a position that he had come to believe in during the war. Referring to the Constitutional Convention of 1787, he said that "in the convention that formed the organisation of the land, the question of defining the relative power of the States, and their relation to the general government, was raised, but after much discussion was dropped and left unsettled. It has remained unsettled until the present time. The war is destined to set it to rest. It is unfortunate that it was not settled at the outset; but as it was not settled then, and had to be settled at some time, the war raised on this issue cannot be considered treason."

Speaking of the war itself, Lee reminded the reporter that the South had been putting out peace feelers for the past two years, "looking for some word or expression of compromise or conciliation from the North upon which they might base a return to the Union, their own political views being considered."

"Their own political views." This led Lee and the reporter straight to the enormous subject of slavery. Just as Mary Custis had brought land into Lee's adult life, so she had brought him into a working relationship with slaves: at his father-in-law's death, three and a half years before the war, there were one hundred and ninety-six slaves of all ages on the three Custis farms. At no moment did they belong to Lee, but as executor of his father-in-law's will, he had the task of trying to put the farms back on a paying basis and still carry out his father-in-law's provision that all the slaves should be freed within five years of his death. True to his father-in-law's word, Lee had freed the last of them in 1862, during the war. Among those he had freed before the war he had sent to Africa those who wished to settle in Liberia, and some of the letters that slipped through the Federal naval blockade had been from them, telling him of their new lives.

Lee had a low opinion of black abilities, and thought that Virginia would be better off it its freed black population now migrated south into the Cotton States. On the other hand, four years before the war he had written, "Slavery as an institution, is a moral and political evil in any country," and in a postwar conversation he was to say, "I am rejoiced that slavery is abolished." He now said to the reporter from New York, adding to his statement that the South had been looking for a way out of the war, that "the question of slavery did not lay in the way at all. The best men of the South have long been anxious to do away with this institution, and were quite willing to see it abolished. They consider slavery forever dead."

As the reporter reconstructed the conversation, Lee went on to say that the great problem, not simply now, but even before the war, for those like himself who believed in a long period of gradual emancipation, was "What will you do with the freed people? . . . unless some humane course is adopted, based on wisdom and Christian principles, you do a gross wrong and injustice to the whole negro race in setting them free. And it is only this consideration that has led the wisdom, intelligence and Christianity of the South to support and defend the institution up to this time."

Some Northerners might exasperatedly respond that it was an odd form of Christianity that would keep anyone in slavery for any reason, or that Lee was naïve if he believed that many slaveholders were keeping their blacks in bondage to protect them from a cruel world outside the plantation. But now Lee left the subject of the blacks and returned to the theme of his desire for "the restoration of peace and tranquility to the country." Lee was in transition; less than a month before, "the country" had meant only "the South" in his vocabulary. The reporter noted that he said "we" in speaking of North and South together, and added, "It was a most noticeable feature of the conversation that General Lee, strange as it may appear, talked throughout as a citizen of the United States. He seemed to plant himself on the national platform, and take his observations from that standpoint." Only once did Lee betray what the reporter called "an evidence of painful sadness at heart that prompted the added expression that he would have been pleased had his life been taken in any of the numerous battlefields on which he had fought during this war."

Lee might feel that the war, the role that his loyalty to Virginia had compelled him to play in it, and the war's wreckage, all made him wish that he were one of its six hundred thousand dead, but in this same interview he said that the South was "anxious to get back into the Union and to peace," and that the vital question in the South's mind "was the treatment to be accorded to the vanquished." Had Lee been more expansive, he could have added that the reporter was looking at the guarantor of peace. Lee had rejected the idea of turning his Army of Northern Virginia into guerrilla bands; he had written Jefferson Davis pointing out the bloody folly of continued resistance. In conversation and by letter, he was urging every Confederate to forget the war and to take a constructive role in the peace. Mr. Cook of the *New York Herald* duly noted that Lee promised "to make any sacrifice or perform any honorable act that would tend to the restoration of peace," but neither he nor his readers understood the value to the nation of that vow.

Chapter 8

A<small>S</small> M<small>AY OF</small> 1865 began, the last guns were falling silent throughout the South. It was a time of wildly different experiences, all
stemming from the same national convulsion. Dazed white Southerners nursed the wounds of their defeat. In the North, the funeral
train carrying the body of Abraham Lincoln made its way from Washington to Springfield, Illinois, as grieving crowds along the tracks sang
"The Battle Hymn of the Republic."

In these first weeks of a most uneasy peace, the four million former
slaves of the South were experiencing their new freedom. Hundreds of
thousands of them flocked to the shattered cities, believing that a glorious life awaited them. In Richmond's Capitol Square they sang and
danced for hours each day, thrilled and exalted by the thought that
they were no longer the property of white masters, to be punished as
someone else dictated, to be sold as someone else wished, to be listed
along with furniture and cattle in someone's will.

There were excesses. Reports of freed slaves wearing the stolen finery
of whites, racing about in stolen carriages pulled by stolen horses, con-
founded the North. To justify the deaths of three hundred and sixty
thousand Union soldiers who had died in the war to end slavery,
Northerners wanted to think of blacks as manacled saints who wanted
only a few days of vacation after centuries of slavery, and would respect
the property of those who had held them in bondage for generations.

As for white Southerners, the North kept eyeing the prostrate South
as if it were a rattlesnake that might strike again. Across this chasm,
some men of good will attempted to learn each other's views. Twelve
days after Lee had talked to the reporter from New York, he opened
the door of his house to Major General George Gordon Meade of the

United States Army, who at Appomattox had smilingly said that Lee was responsible for his grey hair.

The contrast in the situation of these two West Point graduates could not have been greater. Lee knew that he might be arrested at any time on orders from Washington; recently, when a delegation of dis- banded Confederates had asked him to come home with them to their mountain passes, where they could defend him against all comers, he had answered them, "You would not have your General run away and hide. He must stay and meet his fate."

Meade, on the other hand, was passing through Richmond at the head of his Army of the Potomac, which had for so long opposed Lee's Army of Northern Virginia. Meade's mighty force was now marching to Washington, where it was to be demobilized after a Grand Review. Northern civilians might be worried about a resumption of serious fighting, but the professionals were taking most of their forces out of the South while there was still some scattered shooting going on and while Jefferson Davis was still at large.

It was Meade who had sought this interview with his old army friend, for the good of the nation. Confederates were being put under pressure to take an oath of allegiance to the United States, thereby for- mally disavowing their recent allegiance to the Confederate States of America. Meade, whose thoughts were so far from arresting Lee that he hoped Lee might eventually become governor of Virginia, told his former comrade that he should take the oath. This would presumably re-establish his civil status and set an example for all Confederates.

Lee explained that he might take the oath, but not until he saw how the Federal government intended to treat the South. As he spoke, Lee was wearing his Confederate uniform, which had recently undergone a change. The authorities of the military occupation of the South had decreed that all Confederate insignia must vanish, including the crests and CSA initials on uniform buttons. Because even buttons were scarce in the South, and their old uniforms were all that most veterans had to wear, wives and mothers covered the offending buttons by sewing black cloth over them—some said that the buttons were "in mourn- ing."

Meade thought about Lee's answer that he would not take the oath until he could better judge the victors' intentions, and replied that Lee was putting the cart before the horse. This very matter that Lee wished to study before acting, this future Federal policy toward the South, would be favorably affected if Confederates were willing to sign a document saying that they would obey the laws of the United States. Was that asking so much?

Lee said that he would wait and see. The two professional soldiers then spent a long time talking about the needy and chaotic situation of the newly freed blacks, which a Federal relief agency, the Freedmen's Bureau, was attempting to alleviate by establishing offices, bread lines, and black schools throughout the South. Meade departed; the two generals who had faced each other at Gettysburg would never see each other again.

II

Lee was trying to concentrate on the future, but the past thronged to his door. The number of visitors had outstripped his ability to see them. Lee's sons and nephews, and their friends, formed a screening committee to turn away those who had little claim on the general's time.

One morning, when Lee had decided that he must write some letters without interruption, Custis opened the door to find a tall Confederate soldier standing outside, in rags, with his arm in a sling. The reserved, dignified Custis explained that his father was not receiving.

The soldier nodded, but remained standing at the top of the outside steps. He said that he had spent four years in the Texas Brigade, was about to start walking home to Texas, and would like to see once more in his life the man he had followed through so many campaigns.

Major General Custis Lee knew that his father admired the Texans above all other Confederate soldiers; indeed, the bond between Lee and his Texans was almost mystical. On May 6, 1864, during the fighting in the Wilderness, soon after sunrise Lee had found himself almost alone, with veteran Confederate regiments streaming past him to the rear, breaking in the face of a powerful Federal assault. The advancing blue lines were only two hundred yards away. Then, out of the drifting battle smoke into which others were retreating, twenty men in nondescript clothes ran forward with muskets at the ready, entering the field at the end of a forced march to reach the front.

"Who are you, my boys?" Lee shouted to these scarecrows, as scores more dashed up to form a line of battle.

"Texas boys!" they yelled. In a few more seconds, there were hundreds of them.

"Hurrah for Texas!" Lee stood in his stirrups and waved his hat. "Hurrah for Texas!" He rode to the left of the line, and the Texans realized that he intended to lead the counterattack, straight at the blue lines.

"Go back, General Lee!" they shouted, "go back! We won't go on unless you go back!"

"Texans always move them!" Lee roared, about to spur Traveller right into the enemy. A sergeant grabbed Traveller's rein, holding Lee back. Brigadier General John Gregg of the Texans blocked Lee's horse with his own, arguing that this was no place for the commander of the entire army. Only when Lieutenant Colonel Charles Venable galloped up and pleaded with him did he subside, still waving his hat and cheering as the Texans prepared to charge. Taken to the rear virtually under guard, Lee was soon helping to form up an Alabama unit for the counterattack. "Alabama soldiers!" he shouted, his eyes glittering as he pointed in the direction from which he had been tugged, "All I ask of you is to keep up with the Texans!"

And this was one of those Texans, at the door of 707 Franklin Street on a still, hot morning. Custis told the man to wait and he would see what he could do.

While Custis went upstairs to see his father, his place as a volunteer doorkeeper was taken over by Colonel Clement Sullivane, who had been Custis' aide.

> I offered the old soldier a seat and entered into a friendly conversation with him about his wounds, etc. Presently I heard the stately step of General Robert E. Lee descending the stairway. As we both arose on his entrance into the room, he bowed gravely to me and then advanced to the Texan, with his hand extended. The poor fellow grasped it, looked General Lee straight in the eye, struggled to say something, but choked and could not, and, wringing Lee's hand, he dropped it as he burst into tears; then, covering his face with his arm, he turned away and walked out of the room and the house.
>
> General Lee gazed after him for a few moments motionless, his fine, deep dark eyes suffused with emotion, and then, again gravely

bowing to me, he left the room and returned upstairs. Not a single word was spoken . . .

In this month after Appomattox, letters of sympathy came from all over the South, written as if to a family that had suffered a death. The underpinning of religious thought that was shared by Lee and Mary, as well as his greater warmth, emerged in their answers to two such letters, written on different days to different correspondents.

Mary Lee: "Tho' it has not pleased Almighty God to crown our exertions with success in the way & manner we expected, yet we must still trust & pray not that *our will* but His may be done in Heaven & on earth."

Robert E. Lee: "I know you sorrow for us, but you must not be too distressed. We must be resigned to necessity, and commit ourselves in adversity to the will of a merciful God as cheerfully as in prosperity. All is done for our good and our faith must continue unshaken."

In his early classics studies, Lee had been much taken by the Stoics; one of his favorite maxims, singularly appropriate now, was that of Marcus Aurelius: "Misfortune nobly borne is good fortune." Nonetheless, there were moments when he was swept by self-pity. One day a lively young girl who lived nearby, and was frequently in and out of the house, came upon Lee in an unguarded moment. The expression on his face caused her to exclaim "Why *will* you look so heartbroken?"

"Why shouldn't I?" Lee answered. "My cause is dead! I am homeless — I have nothing on earth."

"Yes, you have," the girl said. "You have got a plenty of love and admiration!"

To another young woman who later asked him why he was so sad, Lee said, "I'm thinking of the men who were lost after I knew it was too late."

"Why didn't you tell them?" the girl said.

"No," Lee replied, "they had to find it out for themselves."

As for Mary Lee, her bitterness momentarily turned her against many of her fellow Southerners. Writing to her nephew Edward Lee Childe, who lived in France, she said:

> The sad truth is that our people got tired of the war, and proved unworthy of the noble blood that had been shed for their liberty. Virginia will rue the day that her sons ever laid down their arms . . . I cannot describe to you the agony of mind we have endured.

Chapter 9

O N MAY 10, a month and a day after Lee surrendered at Appomattox, Federal troops caught up to Jefferson Davis near Irwin-
ville, Georgia, and took him into custody. On the same day, President
Andrew Johnson issued a proclamation stating that "armed resistance
to the authority of this Government in the said insurrectionary States
may be regarded as virtually at an end."

Davis was taken to Fort Monroe, on the Virginia Peninsula, and
placed in solitary confinement in a cell located at the water line of a
wall that rose from Chesapeake Bay; at high tide the salt water came
almost to his barred window. In this damp cell, there were two armed
guards just inside a grated door, and four more sentries and two officers
on duty at all times just a few yards away. The general commanding
the fortress had received orders from Washington that gave him dis-
cretion as to whether to place the prisoner in irons; the implication was
that Secretary of War Edwin M. Stanton would not be displeased if
this was done. The morning after Davis arrived, an officer entered his
cell, accompanied by a blacksmith and his assistant, who were to place
a heavy iron chain on him, an end locked to each of his ankles so that it
would hobble him as he moved around his cell. Davis protested, and
then struck at those advancing on him with the chain. Four soldiers
held him down while the blacksmith and his assistant riveted and
locked the shackles into place. After five days these were removed at
the insistence of an army doctor, but Davis went on in the damp cell,
with few changes of clothes, and a bright lamp that was kept burning
at night in such a way that it was hard for him to sleep. He was allowed
no newspapers, no mail, no word from his wife — even his lawyers
could not get in to see him.

There were echoes of this treatment, postwar statements that in no way resembled the behavior of the combat veterans at Appomattox. Congressman George W. Julian of Indiana, who had never come near a battlefield, cried out in a speech that he would hang Jefferson Davis "in the name of God," and that it was an outrage that Lee was at liberty. Lee should be hanged, too: "I would hang liberally, while I had my hand in." The lands of prominent Southerners should be divided among the blacks; a former plantation owner should not be left even enough land "to bury his carcass in." An orator at a public meeting at the Customs House in New York City whipped the crowd into a chant: "Hang Lee! Hang Lee!"

Ulysses S. Grant knew the realities. He wrote his wife, "The suffering that must exist in the South . . . will be beyond conception; people who speak of further retaliation and punishment do not conceive of the suffering endured already, or they are heartless and unfeeling."

Richmond slowly began to move again. The railroads, repaired by the victors, started to deliver supplies. From the passenger cars there alighted a variety of Northerners. There were dedicated men and women schoolteachers, some sent by missionary societies and some employed directly by the Freedmen's Bureau. Their job was to open schools for the black children, who previously had received no education; indeed, a Virginia statute of 1831, sometimes enforced and sometimes not, made it a crime to teach a black to read. These teachers would be besieged by newly freed adult blacks, begging to be taught how to read and write.

The trains also brought less idealistic Northerners. Although the great influx of "carpetbaggers" was not to come for another two years, itinerant promoters traveled south to exploit both whites and blacks. Some bought up the land of whites who were hungry and helpless; others sold worthless deeds to gullible blacks who wanted to own the land they had been forced to work as slaves.

Tourists thronged to see the surrendered Confederate capital, coming down on the train from Washington in the morning and returning in the late afternoon. Although they might not catch all the nuances, their walks around the city included sights such as a young Confederate colonel, leader of one of Lee's best regiments only a few weeks before, now supporting himself and his family as a taxi driver, using an old

ambulance pulled by two cavalry horses. Majors, captains, and lieutenants were working as laborers rebuilding the burnt-out commercial
district. A returned lieutenant saw them "sitting in the sun with their
trowels, jabbing away in awkward fashion at their new and unaccustomed tasks, covered with dirt and plaster . . . With all the hardship of
such unaccustomed work, it was the best and most comfortable and
least dangerous employment that they had been engaged in for years."

Lee's house was one of the high points for the Northern tourists.
They clustered in front of it, staring at its windows and the sentry at his
post on the sidewalk. Shabby veterans of Lee's army would pause here,
too, standing apart from the crowd, taking off their hats and gazing at
the house, seeking the strength and leadership they had relied on in
days of battle.

The man inside the house knew that he was marking time. Rooney
and Rob had departed to try their luck at working the farms their
grandfather Custis had left them. Rooney's was the White House. He
had lived there briefly before the war; since then, Union troops had
burnt down its house. Rob was taking over Romancoke, near Rooney's
farm along the Pamunkey River, but they were both sleeping in a
lean-to at the White House and using their cavalry horses to pull
plows. Even this harsh challenge was denied to Custis. He was heir to
Arlington, the heart of the Custis holdings, but his inheritance was in
Federal hands.

Like his sons, like those veterans who paused across the street, Lee
wanted to rebuild his life. He was out of the army and looking for a job.
He could not afford the cost of continuing to maintain his family at
Franklin Street. Living there was like living in a goldfish bowl, and
he wanted to get Mary out of the coming summer heat and into the
country.

Despite the difficulties he had encountered in his prewar bout of
farming the run-down Custis lands, Lee had always toyed with the
idea of being a full-time farmer. It was in many ways just a dream;
again and again he had chosen to go on with his army career, when at
any time during the thirty years before the war the entire family would
have been delighted if he had resigned and devoted himself to life at
Arlington. Now there was no army career.

Lee decided to leave Richmond for several days to see if he could find some farm undestroyed by the war that might be for sale at a modest price. "I am looking for some little quiet house in the woods," he wrote to one of his former artillery generals, "where I can procure shelter and my daily bread if permitted by the victor."

If permitted by the victor. In his letters, Lee sounded like a man who was waiting for the other shoe to drop. Nonetheless, he set off on Traveller and rode some twenty miles northeast from Richmond, to consult with his cousin Colonel Thomas H. Carter, an artilleryman who had also surrendered at Appomattox. Here, at Carter's farm with its rambling house, he found the relaxation that so eluded him in Richmond. He relished the sight of Traveller turned loose on the spacious lawn, eating the early June grass, rather than the corn that had been such a part of Confederate rations for man and beast.

For the first time since his surrender, Lee's spirits soared; he even had the pleasure of playing with his favorite people, little girls. Rob, who rode over from his new farming tasks to visit, gave this picture of the dignified recent commander of the Army of Northern Virginia: "There were three children in the house, the two youngest little girls of five and three years old. These were his special delight, and he followed them around, talking baby-talk to them and getting them to talk to him."

It was while he was at his cousin's house that Lee picked up a newspaper and saw President Johnson's proclamation of May 29 concerning amnesty and pardon for Confederates. This was a statement of Federal policy, just the thing that Lee had told General Meade he wished to know before committing himself to take the oath of allegiance.

Lee studied it closely. For the great majority of those who had sworn to uphold the Confederacy, taking this oath of loyalty to the United States would reinstate them as citizens. For fourteen special categories of Confederates, including civil and military officers, it would be necessary to apply for a special pardon, but even for these more prominent men, "clemency will be liberally extended as may be consistent with the facts of the case and the peace and dignity of the United States."

II

Riding the twenty miles back to Richmond on Traveller, Lee had much to consider. His talks with his cousin had narrowed the geographical area in which he would look for a farm. He had loved his days in the country, and he was enthusiastic about bringing his wife and daughters to some quiet retreat.

As for the presidential proclamation, Lee would call some aspects of all this oath-taking "absurd," but he was satisfied that these conditions of the victor were within what he was prepared to accept. His conclusion was to emerge in talking to Custis, who wrote that his father said, "It was but right for him to set an example by making formal submission to the Civil Authorities." If he regained his citizenship, Lee told Custis, he might be able to help other Confederates who had not, "especially Mr. Davis."

Thus, as he rode back into the city, the two matters — a farm, and taking the oath — had twined. It would be better to clear up his status before buying a farm; indeed, there was some question as to whether he could legally own property in his present situation. If he could apply for a pardon and get it over with, along the lines held out by that encouraging proclamation, the quiet rural life he wanted might be his.

Arriving at Franklin Street, Lee was greeted by the news that a Federal grand jury in Norfolk had just indicted him for treason, a crime whose punishments included death by hanging. The other shoe had dropped.

The news of this formal accusation and prospective trial rocked the South, producing anger and fear. Although no move was made to arrest him, many thought it was only a matter of time. Mildred was sitting with her father in the back of the front hall when the doorbell rang. Lee opened the door and faced "a long, tall, lean man dressed in homespun and his shoes and lower part of his trousers covered with dust."

As Mildred told it, this man "grabbed the General's extending hand" and said, "General Lee, I followed you four years and done the best I knowed how. Me and my wife live on a little farm way up on the Blue Ridge Mountains. We heard the Yankees wasn't treating you right, and I come down to see 'bout it. If you will come up thar we will take care of you the best we know how as long as we live."

The veteran had taken both Lee's hands as he said this, and tears were running from his eyes. Lee was so startled and moved by this appearance of a self-appointed protector who had hurried more than a hundred miles to shield his old commander, that tears suddenly started down his cheeks.

At a loss for once, Lee looked around the front hall, which was often filled with little presents that were delivered at the front door by admirers. He knew that a box near the door contained a man's suit. Taking one of his hands from the mountaineer's grip, Lee lifted the box and said, "My friend, I don't need a thing. My friends all over the country have been very kind and have sent me more clothes than I can possibly use, so I want to thank you for coming and give you this new suit."

Mildred described what happened next.

> The man snatched his hand from General Lee, crossed his arms, straightened himself, and said, "General Lee, I can't take nothin' offen you." After a few moments he relaxed, put one hand on the box and said, "Yes, I will, General, I will carry them back home, put them away and when I die the boys will put them on me."

Offers of assistance came in from both Northern and Southern lawyers, but Lee first had to decide what stance to take. While he spoke of his problem in a philosophical manner — "Well!" he said to one group of friends, "it matters little what they do to me; I am old, and have but a short time to live anyhow" — he moved swiftly to ascertain the views of Ulysses S. Grant. Lee and his army had surrendered on Grant's terms, the last words of which were that they could "return to their homes not to be disturbed by United States authority as long as they observe their paroles and the laws in force where they may reside." It was Lee's belief that "not to be disturbed by United States authority" meant just that: Grant had promised Lee and his men that surrendering was enough, and that no further action would be taken against any of them, including Lee.

To reach Grant's ear, Lee used his friend Senator Reverdy Johnson of Maryland, a man who had supported the Federal government during the war but who was strong for reconciliation. The senator spoke to one of Grant's aides, Colonel Adam Badeau. An oral message from Grant was quickly relayed to Lee: Grant was in complete agreement. He was determined that Lee should be protected from the treason charge by the terms reached at Appomattox, and urged Lee to go ahead and apply for his pardon, which Grant would endorse. Although Lee did not know it, Grant went further than that: he let it be known in Washington that he would resign from the army in protest if Lee were arrested.

Thus, on June 13, 1865, just six days after he was indicted for treason, Lee enclosed in a letter to Grant his application to President Johnson for "the benefits and full restoration of all rights and privileges" of citizenship. In his letter to Grant, Lee stated a personal position that was important to him. Having made up his mind to apply for pardon and make "formal submission to the Civil Authorities" before he heard of the treason indictment, he did not want it thought that he was asking for a pardon in order to escape trial:

> I am ready to meet any charges that may be preferred against me, and do not wish to avoid trial; but, if I am correct as to the protection granted by my parole, and am not to be prosecuted, I desire to comply with the provision of the President's proclamation, and, therefore, inclose the required application . . .

Grant immediately wrote President Johnson, not only giving an "earnest recommendation" that Lee be pardoned, but going on to ask that John C. Underwood, the Federal judge having jurisdiction in Virginia, "be ordered to quash all indictments against paroled prisoners of war, and to desist from further prosecution of them."

This appeal to the President by Grant on Lee's behalf produced a split result. The government prosecutors did not want to argue with the victorious commanding general of the United States Army about the immunity conferred by a military parole. They quietly halted the treason proceedings, without formally dismissing them. On the other hand, no pardon was forthcoming from President Johnson, despite Grant's intercession. Lee had no way of knowing from day to day whether the government might reopen its case against him or whether a pardon might be issued. He was free, but in civil limbo.

☆ ☆ ☆

The South was united in its condemnation of the Federal indictment of Lee for treason, but the news that he had applied for a pardon was another matter. Among Southerners, it became the most controversial act of his life. To some Confederates, this was a betrayal of men scarcely cold in their graves. By his asking for a pardon, these hard-liners felt, Lee was kneeling before the enemy and was admitting that everything — secession, creation of the Confederacy, fighting the Northern armies that had marched into the South — had been wrong. For the realistic Lee, it was the only way for a Confederate to secure his civil rights and to pave the way for white Southerners once again to elect their own leaders.

Critics fumed, but Lee's act produced the result that he, and for that matter Grant and Meade, hoped it would. Grant was right when he wrote, even before this, that Southerners "will be guided to a great extent by his example." Those who had followed Lee in war believed that if *he* applied for a pardon, they ought to go ahead, sign the oath of allegiance, and be done with it. Tens of thousands of them grimaced and signed, and were immediately restored to their rights in a manner that the authorities were withholding from Lee.

For many, this act of swearing allegiance to the government that had so recently sent Sherman on the marches that disemboweled the South produced an agony of conflicting feelings. Captain George Wise, son of the former Virginia governor and Confederate general who said, "We hate you, sir," to a Federal general at Appomattox, was so upset by the choice that he went to the house at Franklin Street.

Mary Lee had known the young captain since he was a boy. She told him that her husband was sick but would see him nonetheless.

The veteran entered the parlor to find Lee lying on a couch, pale and tired, wearing one of his old uniforms from which the insignia had been removed.

"They want me to take this thing, General," Wise said, holding out a copy of the oath. "My parole covers it, and I do not think it should be required of me. What would you advise?"

"I would advise you to take it," Lee said quietly, and went on to agree that their paroles should have made all this unnecessary.

The young officer burst out, "General, I feel that this is submission to an indignity. If I must continue to swear the same thing over at every street corner, I will seek another country where I can at least preserve my self-respect."

Lee lay silent for a long time. "Do not leave Virginia," he finally said in a sad voice. "Our country needs her young men now."

Wise took the oath. When he told his firebrand father what he had done, the former governor and general exclaimed, "You have disgraced the family!"

"General Lee advised me to do it."

"Oh, that alters the case. Whatever General Lee says is all right, I don't care what it is."

Lee's application for a pardon drew attention in the North as well as the South. Henry Ward Beecher, the famous preacher, antislavery figure, and brother of Harriet Beecher Stowe, the author of *Uncle Tom's Cabin,* issued a statement strongly commending what Lee had done. Other Northerners took the view that this was asking very little of a principal leader in a traitorous rebellion that had, North and South, cost six hundred and twenty thousand Americans their lives.

III

On Sundays, Lee attended services at St. Paul's Episcopal Church in Richmond. It was a church with a long history and a distinguished congregation. It had been during the service on the Sunday morning a week before Lee's surrender that a messenger had come up the aisle to give Jefferson Davis a dispatch from Lee. Opening it as he sat in his pew, Davis had read Lee's warning that his army might have to evacuate the city that night. The Confederate President had left quietly to organize the departure of officials and the removal of important papers.

On this warm June Sunday, the sermon was preached by Dr. Charles Minnigerode, the rector. Lee sat in his pew on the left side aisle. As the service progressed, there was no indication that anything unusual might happen.

Colonel T. L. Broun, of Charleston, West Virginia, had come to Richmond on business and was in the congregation. "When the minister was ready to administer the holy communion," he wrote, "a negro in the church arose and advanced to the communion table. He was tall, well-dressed, and black. This was a great surprise and shock."

The congregation froze; those who had been ready to go forward and kneel at the altar rail remained in their pews. "Dr. Minnigerode was evidently embarrassed."

Here was the South's worst nightmare. There was a section in the western gallery that was for blacks; if they wished to receive communion, they could come forward after the last of the whites returned from the altar to their pews. The white South could endure defeat and poverty, could accept the fact that slaves were free, but this black man had come to the front of the church as if he were a social equal. Three months before, if a black man had dared to do this, he would have been hustled from the church, jailed for disturbing the peace, and quite possibly flogged. Now, in a city under Federal military occupation, the black man knelt at the altar rail while the congregation remained in their pews and the minister stood dumbfounded.

"Gen. Robert E. Lee was present, and, ignoring the action and presence of the negro, arose in his usual dignified and self-possessed manner, walked up the aisle to the chancel rail, and reverently knelt down to partake of the communion, and not far from the negro."

The other communicants went forward to the altar, and the service continued.

Chapter 10

DESPITE THE POSSIBILITY that the government might reopen its case against him, Lee had not for a moment lost his hope of getting his family to the country. He was thinking about buying a farm he had seen near the Rapidan River. Only his amorphous status, with the treason proceedings against him suspended but not dismissed, kept him from a decision.

At this moment a letter came from a friend, Mrs. Elizabeth Randolph Cocke, offering the Lees the use of a small vacant house on her estate fifty-five miles west of Richmond.

The Lees accepted, although with differing degrees of enthusiasm. Lee was delighted; this would take them out of the hot Richmond summer, so hard on Mary in her invalid condition, and into a serene countryside. It would allow him to avoid, for the time being, making a commitment to buy a farm, and still give him the private life he craved.

For Mary, at the age of fifty-six, it was another breaking of ties. With the war's onset she had been forced to leave the house at Arlington — the place where she had been born, was married, and gave birth to seven children. She became a refugee, an honored one, but a homeless person nevertheless. For two and a half years she had visited relatives and friends in parts of Virginia. This rented house at Franklin Street, into which she had moved early in 1864, was the nearest thing to a home she had possessed since Arlington. She and her Richmond friends had become wartime comrades, knitting hundreds of pairs of socks for her husband's soldiers as they listened to the cannon in the distance. Together, they had read the lengthening casualty lists and coped with the dwindling food supplies. Now she was leaving these friends, for a place still farther from Arlington.

At the end of June, the Lees and their daughters Agnes and Mildred, with all their trunks, valises, hatboxes, and crates, boarded one of the boats that plied the James River and Kanawha Canal. The Lees' daughter Mary was visiting friends in Staunton; Custis had left two days before, riding Traveller to their destination.

This canal boat would be pulled by a team of three horses that moved along the towpath beside the canal. The team was kept in order by the towman, who rode another horse. A man on the bow used a pole to fend the boat off the bank when necessary, and a black helmsman steered the vessel. There was a cargo hold, and a long cabin that served as both lounge and dining room; when a partition was put up after supper, it became two sleeping compartments, the women having regular berths at their end, and the men making the best of the couches and chairs.

It was late afternoon when the Lees came aboard. A crowd of friends arrived to wish them bon voyage. Presents of flowers surrounded Mary; in this light that was soon to be sunset, there was "a catch in her voice" as she said good-bye to her wartime friends.

Cousins and friends went ashore. Lines were cast off, and the horses pulled forward in their harness, lifting the towrope from the water. The boat began to move; handkerchiefs waved, on shore, on the boat. The Lees glided toward the sunset.

When it was time to go to bed, the canal boat's captain "had the most comfortable bed put up that he could command," and this was offered to Lee. Wishing no special treatment, and knowing that every man in the lounge would insist on his taking the best couch, Lee went up on the deck. He lay down, pulling over him his old military overcoat, which he had once called his "house and bed in the field."

It was the last night he would sleep under the open sky. Lying there, looking up at the stars, he could hear the water passing beneath the boat. There was an occasional snort from one of the horses on the towpath, and sometimes a sudden curse from the mounted towman as he moved his team through the darkness. The black helmsman hummed a monotonous song; when the man at the bow cried, "Vi-ach!" it meant "viaduct," and was a warning that those on deck should duck their heads because the boat was nearing a low bridge. When they neared one of the canal's locks, the towman blew the horn he carried, signaling the lock-keeper to open his downstream gates.

Heading west through the night on the James River, Lee was leaving behind most of his past. Each step these horses took pulled him farther from the scenes of his early childhood at Stratford Hall, his boyhood in Alexandria, his married life at Arlington, his defense of Richmond and Petersburg. The scenes of his biggest battles receded in the darkness. Tonight he was severing himself from constant contact with many who had been close to him during the war, or had reason to seek him out in its aftermath. The shooting and dying were over, but as he lay looking at the stars, his wife and daughters asleep in the cabin below, he had no idea of what lay ahead for him, for them, for Virginia, for the nation.

The canal boat slid under the stars.

Chapter 11

A FTER STAYING for a week at Oakland, the handsome house of
their hostess, Mrs. Cocke, the Lees moved into Derwent, the
small house two miles away that she had offered them. Custis had
fallen sick and was to stay on at Mrs. Cocke's for the time being.

What the Lees found was a simple frame house of the type used by
tenant farmers. It had two rooms upstairs, two rooms and a shedlike
kitchen downstairs, and in the yard a run-down structure that had
been used as a farm office. Mrs. Cocke had put furniture from Oakland
into it, giving it some comfort, but Mary Lee spoke plainly about Derwent in a letter to a friend: "You would suppose from the title of this
retreat that we were in sight of cool lakes and romantic scenery but it is
a retired little place with a straight up house and the only beauty it
possesses is a fine grove of oaks which surround it. Thro' the kindness of
a friend who has given us the use of it it has been rendered habitable,
but all the outbuildings are dilapidated and the garden is a mass of
weeds . . ."

Lee saw it in positive terms, writing Rob: "We are all well, and established in a comfortable but small house, in a grove of oaks . . . It
contains four rooms, and there is a house in the yard which when fitted
up will give us another." He loved being in the country, but still hesi-
tated to buy a farm until his legal status was better defined: "I can do
nothing until I learn what decision in my case is made in Washington."

Three months had elapsed since Appomattox; Lee was finally in a
place where he could rest, away from men of affairs, away from admirers, away from the curious.

Only once was there an echo of the attention he had constantly received in Richmond. All about Derwent there lived members of a family named Palmore. This clan of farmers provided the vegetables, butter, meat, and ice for the Lees, and Mrs. Spencer Palmore made a new pair of trousers for the general. Mr. Palmore ran a country store that also served as a post office, and Lee rode there to see if any mail had arrived at this new address.

With the mail in his hands, Lee began talking with Palmore about the local crops. The word flashed through the neighborhood that General Lee was in the store, and soon the place was packed with many times the usual number of customers.

For a while, chatting with the proprietor, Lee did not see what was happening. Finally he looked around and realized that all these people were not here to buy anything or to pick up their mail or to gossip among themselves, but were standing silently, almost reverently, watching him.

How to extricate himself was a challenge to which Lee was equal. "Ah, Mister Palmore," he said, "pardon me for keeping you talking about corn and tobacco so long, for I see I am detaining you from your many customers." And with that, he took home the mail.

Each day, Lee rode Traveller along these country roads. Many an old farmer who never dreamed that he would meet Lee found himself standing by a fence, talking to the grey-clad man on the grey horse, discussing the merits of the cattle within view. Dropping by Palmore's store one day, Lee found a letter that annoyed him. It was from the Union general David Hunter, whose clumsy withdrawal from a major raid on the Valley of Virginia had given Lee a chance to thrust Jubal Early and his men into Maryland. To Lee's amazement, Hunter was writing in the hope that Lee would agree that his movements on that occasion had been skillful and wise.

Was it not true, Hunter asked, that his raid had forestalled Lee from sending forty thousand men to the aid of Joseph E. Johnston? Further, did not Lee agree that Hunter had chosen the best line of retreat?

When Lee answered Hunter, he chose polite accuracy for his weapon. "I had no troops to spare General Johnston, and no intention of sending him any," he said, and then courteously demolished Hunter's hopes of justifying his bungled retreat: "I would say that I am not advised as to the motives which induced you to adopt the line of retreat you took . . . but I certainly expected you to retreat by way of the Shenandoah Valley, and was gratified at the time that you preferred the route through the mountains to Ohio — leaving the Valley open for General Early's advance into Maryland."

Not all the letters penned at Derwent afforded their writers this much satisfaction. Writing a friend in Kentucky, Mary Lee said, "Our future will be guided by circumstances, all seems so dark now, that we are almost tempted to think God has forsaken us." As if recoiling from her words, she went on, "Yet we have many blessings . . ." Of these days at Derwent, she was to remember "a quiet so profound that I could even number the acorns falling from the splendid oaks that overshadowed the cottage."

It was just this silence, these simple summer days, that Lee was enjoying so much. "My dear Bertus," he wrote Rob, using a childhood nickname; "We have a quiet time, which is delightful to me" — then, thinking of Mildred and Agnes — "but I fear not so exhilarating to the girls."

In this last he was correct. Their tall and angular daughter Mary, always independent, had no intention of joining her sisters in this enforced idyll, and stayed on with her friends in Staunton. As for Mildred, she wrote a friend, "I am sometimes lonely here, but that is not often the case. I read almost all day long. I don't know what I should do without books. I am ashamed to say principally novels." This was the Victorian age, when a young woman was supposed to be reading something spiritually uplifting or domestically self-improving. In fact, most educated young women with some time on their hands were likely to be doing just what Mildred was, although in her case she was risking her father's strong disapproval. Six years before, when she was thirteen, her father had written her from the stark Texas plains, "Read history and works of truth — not novels and romances." It was not a new thought with him; worrying about Rooney, he had, years before that, written Mary, "Let him never touch a novel. They print beauty more charming than nature, and describe happiness that never exists. They will teach him to sigh after that which has no reality, to despise the little good that is granted us in this world and to expect more than is given."

Under this quiet roof in the country were four individuals capable of powerful emotions. Agnes, the prettiest of the Lee sisters, had lived some chapters that were harsher and more dramatic than anything in the Victorian romances Mildred was reading. In October of 1862, when their sister Annie was stricken with typhoid, Agnes had nursed her through to the hour of Annie's death, risking her life to do it. Then, two months later, she had come to the parting of the ways with Orton Williams. Although she was not present at some of the scenes in his tragedy, it was her tragedy too; in a way, she became a permanent casualty of the war.

Mildred's novelists might have found the raw material of the story a bit too melodramatic: two brothers, Lawrence and Orton Williams, both officers in the United States Army, Lawrence choosing to fight for the North, and Orton resigning to fight for the South. Orton, in love with Agnes, coming home on leave from the Army of Tennessee to propose to her, but making a detour to serve as a volunteer aide to Agnes' father at the Battle of Fredericksburg; Orton, his uniform smelling of powder smoke, arriving at a house named Hickory Hill, where Agnes and her mother were staying, bringing as presents for the Southern belle he loved "a pair of ladies' riding gauntlets and a riding whip."

Before the war, the Orton of 1860 had been of such excellent character that Lee had written a glowing recommendation when Orton applied for the commission he received in the United States Army. That did not mean that Lee wanted Orton, or anyone else, as a son-in-law; he wanted his sons to marry, but, speaking of his daughters, he had once written a friend, "I know it will require a tussle for any one to get my children from me, and beyond that I do not wish to know."

Two years of war had changed that estimable Orton of 1860; now a Confederate colonel, the man who arrived to propose marriage at Christmas of 1862 drank too much and had killed a private on the spot for a disciplinary offense — something that had made Orton's men so wild against him, despite his bravery in combat, that his superiors had been forced to transfer him to a command in a different area. In the hope that his reputation would not come along with him, he changed his name from Orton Williams to Lawrence Orton — borrowing the first name of his brother, who was to end the war as a Union brigadier general and was the man who sent word to Lee at Appomattox that Custis was captured but safe.

For several days, Orton's visit seemed to be going beautifully; a little boy at Hickory Hill said, "I remember about the horses being brought out and their cantering off from the gate . . . It was the first romance of our lives. He was the Prince Charming and she the Sleeping Beauty that our fairy tale book had made us acquainted with, and we became excited partisans of Prince Charming, and believed the Sleeping Beauty would awake, and they would ride away together and live happily ever after."

What Lee thought about all this would be a matter for conjecture, but Mildred wrote, "He was apt to be critical on the subject of our young men visitors and admirers." Fond as Lee had been of Orton, whom he could remember even as a little boy, he had plenty of equally brave colonels who did not drink to excess or shoot privates out of hand. Whether Lee expressed his disapproval, or whether Agnes decided entirely on her own, the little boy at Hickory Hill saw his fairy tale blasted: "We could not understand it at all when one day after a long session in the parlor (from which we children had been warned to stay away) he came out, bade the family good-bye and rode away alone. We could not understand it."

The next and final part of Orton's life soon exploded. Within weeks, another woman accepted his proposal of marriage — a rebound complicated by the fact that the woman already had a husband, was living with him, and was thought to be "deranged." Then, on the night of June 8, 1863, two men in Federal uniform, on beautiful horses, rode up to a Union Army headquarters at Franklin, Tennessee. The senior in rank introduced himself as Colonel Lawrence Orton of the United States Army and produced a most impressive set of credentials, including instructions signed by Lincoln's secretary of war, Edwin M. Stanton. The two men said that they were on an inspection tour of the Union front.

The Federal colonel in charge at Franklin decided to make sure that his higher headquarters knew about these distinguished visitors. He sent off a telegram and received the chilling reply "There are no such men . . ." The communication was signed by Brigadier General James A. Garfield, future President of the United States. Shown this, Orton admitted that he was a Confederate colonel, and his companion identified himself as a Confederate lieutenant. Another telegram was sent to Garfield, who answered, "Call a drumhead court-martial tonight and if they are found to be spies, hang them before morning, without fail."

Within hours, Orton and his fellow Confederate officer were swinging dead from a gallows, but even those who convicted them kept thinking that they were not "spies in the ordinary sense." There was that seemingly authentic pass from the secretary of war, and Orton's statement that they had entered Federal territory as a means to start a mission that was to take them to Canada and to Europe. Orton would say no more; what his mission was, no one on the Confederate side ever revealed. In the hours before he was hanged, he wrote his sister "Markie," one of Agnes' closest friends, "Do not believe that I am a spy; with my dying breath I deny the charge." He did not write Agnes; to the married woman who had accepted his proposal of marriage he wrote, "When this reaches you I will be no more. Had I succeeded I would have been able to marry you in Europe in a month . . . I have been condemned as a spy — You know I am not."

Lee was horrified that Orton had been executed. He admitted that Orton's life was "forfeited under the laws of war" for wearing a Federal uniform inside Federal lines, but felt that there should have been clemency: "My blood boils at the thought of the atrocious outrage against every manly and Christian sentiment, which the great God alone is able to forgive."

As for Agnes, a lifelong friend said, "The terrible death of Orton Williams was a shock to Agnes from which she never recovered. She became very quiet and pensive in after life. I do not recall hearing her laugh . . ." In addition to grief, she may have felt that if she had accepted Orton, he would not have volunteered for the fatal mission. Some people who met her after the war were offended by her "haughtiness and reserve." They were seeing not pride, but a mask for sorrow.

II

Before coming to the country, Lee had received, among other visitors in Richmond, a publisher from New York named C. B. Richardson. This enterprising man was the first of many publishers to recognize that if Lee wrote a book about the war, it would have a tremendous sale in both the North and South, and he approached Lee on the subject.

Lee had indicated interest in the idea, but wished to write only of the campaigns in which his Army of Northern Virginia had engaged. His motives, he said, were not "to vindicate myself, or to promote my own reputation. I want that the world shall know what my poor boys, with their small numbers and scant resources, succeeded in accomplishing."

Richardson now reinforced their meeting with a letter urging Lee to set to work and promising every sort of cooperation. He was sending Lee "by Express a sett [sic] of the *Rebellion Record*" and some other books, and promised to secure an important Union report on Lee's great victory at Chancellorsville, some letters and diaries of Mosby's Rangers, and a copy of the manuscript of a forthcoming life of Stonewall Jackson. "I shall at once make an effort to get access to the captured documents in the hands of the Govt. If I am successful the reports you desire shall be rapidly copied. Nevertheless, I would renew my suggestion that you make application directly to Genl Grant."

As a master of strategy, Lee must have enjoyed seeing a man advance on so many fronts at once, but there was more. In a combination of flattery and practicality, Richardson enclosed a gold pen, "trusting it may lighten the labor before you and prove faithful to the end."

Then Richardson's letter turned to a matter that plunged into Lee's family history. "Perhaps you will remember my remarks with regard to your father's 'Memoirs' ..." This was the two-volume work on the southern campaigns of the American Revolution written fifty-three years before by Light-Horse Harry. Most of it had been written while Henry Lee was in jail for debt, and dealt with that earlier, promising period in the life of the dashing cavalryman who, as governor of Virginia, said of his former commander, George Washington, "First in war, first in peace, first in the hearts of his countrymen." This extraordinary historical span — that Robert E. Lee, commander of an army in 1865, should be the son of a man who had been at Yorktown in 1781 — was explained by the fact that Light-Horse Harry, married for the second time to a woman much younger than he, was fifty when Lee was born, in 1807.

"The copyright expired several years ago," Richardson told Lee about his father's book, "but can be renewed by the addition of new

matter. I should be happy to accomplish this for you, if you will prepare an introduction of a few pages." Put simply, the public would buy
anything that had something written in it by Robert E. Lee. "I desire
to issue that at the same time and in uniform style with the new volume from your own pen."

Richardson's timing was perfect. Lee wanted to do something along
these lines, and he now had time in which to begin. He started sending
letters to his principal officers whose addresses he knew, explaining the
difficulty that faced him in getting what he most wanted: the reports of
troop strength that would show the odds against which his regiments
had fought. In the wreck of the Confederacy, most of his headquarters'
papers pertaining to the last year of the war had been lost, or burnt to
prevent capture. He hoped that some of his generals could track down
duplicates of what they had submitted to headquarters or could recon-
struct some reports from memory.

It was a difficult request, but many of his generals went to work with
a will, eventually forwarding what they could find or remember. They
accompanied these documents with news of their efforts to rebuild
their lives as civilians, and sent warm wishes to Lee and his family.

Just fifteen weeks after Appomattox, Lee's postwar course seemed
set. His intention was to continue a country life; he wrote Rooney that
if the Federal government would leave him alone, he would go ahead
with his plan to buy a farm: "I shall endeavour to procure some humble, but quiet, abode for your mother and sisters, where I hope they can
be happy." He would farm; he would write his account of the campaigns through which he had led "that array of tattered uniforms and
bright muskets." Now that he was finished with the punishing tempo
of commanding an army, and the demands of those weeks in Richmond, he had time to take stock of his health. Although he felt well, he
knew that something was wrong; he did not know how damaged his
heart was or that his arteries were hardening. Still, with his daily ride
on Traveller for exercise, no people to see for other than social pleasure,
and a life in which he could control the pressures on him, he might
belie what he had said: "I am old, and have but a short time to live
anyway."

Chapter 12

WHILE LEE was enjoying his quiet life, peacefully riding about on the horse that had carried him through the bloodiest scenes of the war, some men he had never met held a meeting in a little town in the Blue Ridge Mountains.

These were the trustees of Washington College, a small school that had been nearly destroyed by the war, and whose postwar survival was in doubt. In the first wave of enthusiasm in 1861, its students had gone off to fight. In the 1864 raid that General David Hunter had written Lee about, this town of Lexington, Virginia, had suffered severely. Subsequent occupation of the college by Federal troops had damaged the buildings, scattered the library, and destroyed the laboratory equipment. The troops of a Pennsylvania regiment were still using some college buildings for offices and barracks. During the chaotic past spring, the college had been kept open "chiefly as a Preparatory School," with four professors as faculty. The student body consisted of some forty boys under military age who attended sporadically while their scattered families were engulfed in the final disaster.

The trustees of the college were meeting on the evening of August 4, four days after Lee had sent out his first batch of letters starting the research for his book. These were stubborn men, the resolute Scotch-Irish Presbyterians of the Valley of Virginia, determined to nurse back to health the school entrusted to their care.

The treasurer's report now put before them was an example of how the South's financial heart had stopped beating. "The following investments may be considered as worthless," the Committee on Finance wrote, and listed holdings of Confederate 7 percent bonds, Confederate 4 percent bonds, Bank of Virginia stock, and $2458.20 in Confederate currency. There was some hope for such securities as a block of Virginia state canal stock, valued at twenty thousand dollars, that George Washington had donated in 1796, causing the school to change its name from Liberty Hall Academy to Washington College, but even this was paying no income. "No provision has been made by law for the payment of the interest on the State debt and no provision can be made until the meeting of the Legislature in December, and the revenues of the state will not then be sufficient to meet the interest on all the debt."

The school was in an odd form of bankruptcy. Ninety-four thousand dollars of its prewar endowment was nominally intact, but in the form of securities that in almost every instance were not paying interest, and that could not be sold because no buyer could be sure of their worth. In the meantime, the professors had to be paid something, and there was no money. There were other bills, as well.

The trustees were undaunted. Having failed in an earlier effort to borrow five hundred dollars to open the college this coming September, they now resolved to try to borrow forty-six hundred, on the theory that it might be easier to get a big loan than a small one. While they were at it, they passed this motion: "Resolved, that a committee of three be appointed to wait upon the Commandant of the Federal forces now at Lex. & ask that the college buildings be at once vacated by the troops."

Because the prewar college president had been a Union sympathizer who was driven from the campus, it was necessary to name a new leader. Several names were placed in nomination, and a vote was about to be taken, when one of the board members rose and told his colleagues that he had heard something he felt they should know. A friend in Staunton had recently been talking to Miss Mary Lee, daughter of General Lee, while she was visiting there. Miss Lee had said that, although the people of the South stood ready to *give* her father everything he might need, what he really needed was a job by which he could earn a living for himself and his family.

The idea shone in the room. "Then various members of the board said what a great thing it would be for the college if the services of General Lee could be secured, and wondered if there was any chance of doing so."

They could not resist. A few minutes later, Robert E. Lee, who knew nothing about it, was unanimously elected president of Washington

College, by men who had no reason to suppose that he would accept. They were thinking of Lee as a famous battlefield leader, but they had just named a former superintendent of the United States Military Academy at West Point who knew more about educational administration than they did.

"Then there was a pause, and silence prevailed for some moments. The board seemed oppressed with the gravity of the situation, and seemed to feel that they had acted rashly." A participant later said that it suddenly struck them as a great presumption to have elected Lee head of a "broken-down college."

They had done it; they plunged on. The committee appointed to draft a letter to Lee agreed that such a proposal could not drift in through the mail; they asked Judge John Brockenbrough, the head of the board, to carry this invitation to General Lee, wherever he was, and urge him to accept.

The tall, heavyset judge stood, looking down at his threadbare clothes, and said that he did not have a suit that was in good enough condition for a man who was supposed to call on General Lee. He had no money for clothes or travel expenses, and neither, he reminded them, did the college.

Men who could elect Lee were not going to be stopped by that. One man loaned Brockenbrough a suit, and another arranged to borrow fifty dollars from a Lexington woman who had recently sold some tobacco from her farm. That fifty dollars — new United States greenbacks that were slowly coming into circulation among those who were so fortunate as to have any money — was all the cash at the disposal of Washington College. It was about to be used as venture capital.

And so it was that Judge John Brockenbrough, wearing a borrowed suit and representing a college that borrowed the money to send him, arrived unannounced at the tenant house in which Robert E. Lee was living through the courtesy of a friend. The worldly fortunes of both men, and of the college one represented, were at their lowest.

Lee listened. The college's offer included the use of a house and garden, and a plot of land on which vegetables could be raised. He would receive a percentage of the tuition fees. The salary would be fifteen hundred dollars a year — dollars the college did not have, but hoped to take in.

II

At length Judge Brockenbrough departed, and in the days that followed Lee considered the matter. He still wanted a private farming life; his personal inclination was not at all for a college presidency. He knew it would mean that his days would be packed with people, and his desk piled with problems. Lee detested public speaking; this job would involve presiding over all manner of occasions. It was clear that Washington College was struggling to survive, at a time when most Southern families were worrying about food for their stomachs rather than college educations for their sons. Leading the effort to save Washington College would put his body back under the strains he had just removed.

Although Lee respected education, the interests of his career had always lain elsewhere. In 1852, when he had received the orders assigning him as superintendent at West Point, he had within hours written a request that the job be given to someone else — anyone else. When that failed to move the War Department, he did his usual meticulous job, and after the three-year tour moved on as soon as he could to his next assignment, with the Second Cavalry in the West.

On the other hand, that had been in another life, when he was a professional soldier, trying to practice his profession rather than to prepare cadets for it. Now, with his profession barred to him and his beloved South slumped in defeat, the idea of educating young men to be useful peacetime citizens was a different matter. Even during the war, the future of the troops who would live through it was on Lee's mind. Near the climax of the Battle of Chancellorsville, Lee had sat astride Traveller, watching his men advance to the chilling high-pitched sound of their Rebel Yell, and had spoken quietly to a German military observer. He talked not of the battle, but of what the survivors among those grey-clad troops would do after the war, and of the educational needs of the South.

And here was this unsought offer. As in the lives of all persons, Lee's essence was to be found not in what he said, but in what he did. There were other dimensions to Lee, but his life was one long response to whatever struck him as being the call of duty. For thirty-five years, as cadet and officer, he had given himself unsparingly to the United States Army. When he believed that his duty as a Southerner required that he "take no part in an invasion of the Southern States," he had resigned from the United States Army. Knowing that his native Virginia was soon to be attacked by the United States Army, his sense of duty led him to accept when he was offered the command of Virginia's forces. Now here was a new responsibility that perhaps he should undertake.

On one of these hot August days, Lee rode more than thirty miles over to Albemarle County to discuss the matter with his old friend Reverend Joseph Wilmer, an Episcopal clergyman. Wilmer's initial reaction was this: "I confess to a momentary feeling of chagrin at the proposed change (shall I say revulsion?) in his history. The institution was one of local interest, and comparatively unknown to our people. I named others more conspicuous which would welcome him with ardour as their presiding head."

Lee was not worried about the relative prestige of various Southern universities and colleges. As Wilmer discovered within a few more minutes, Lee felt "that this door and not another was opened to him by Providence, and he only wished to be assured of his competency to fulfill his trust." Leaving Wilmer's house the next day to ride back to Derwent, Lee was still concerned about some other factors, things that he wished were irrelevant, but were not. It seemed to him that, with his name anathema to so many in the North and the chance that he might still end up behind bars like Jefferson Davis, he might prove to be Washington College's biggest and final liability. It was a point that he had raised in talking with Brockenbrough. There was his health, which would limit what he could even try to do. Finally, he was an Episcopalian, and Washington College had until now been in practice a Presbyterian school.

Lee was not left to ponder these matters unassisted. Judge Brockenbrough wrote, again urging him to accept. He assured Lee that, far from hurting the college by associating his name with it, "you have only to stretch forth your powerful arm to rescue it," and went on to express what was certainly the hope in Lexington: "You alone can fill its halls, by attracting to them not the youth of Virginia alone but of all the Southern and some even of the Northern States."

There were two other letters from men Lee knew well, residents of Lexington who could judge some aspects of the situation better than he could. One was from John Letcher, a wartime governor of Virginia who had been imprisoned for six weeks at the war's end, and a man whose judgment Lee greatly valued. Lee and Letcher had already been in correspondence about the postwar fate of the South; both were optimists in a dark time. Letcher wrote: "You can do a vast amount of good in building up this institution, and disseminating the blessings of education among our people."

The other letter was from William Nelson Pendleton, the rector of the small Episcopal church in Lexington, and a man whose life had embraced both religion and the military. Graduating from West Point a year behind Lee, he had eventually recognized a religious calling and had resigned from the army to enter the ministry. Not without soul-searching, he had entered the Confederate Army as an artillery officer rather than as a chaplain, and had risen to be one of Lee's generals. Now he was back in his prewar position at Lexington's Grace Church. While acknowledging in his letter to Lee that "Lexington is, as you are aware, a place of no great importance," Pendleton pointed out the attractions of its mountain scenery, and added that "the house & appliances provided for the President would present many comforts."

It was not on these grounds, however, that he put his case to Lee. He knew his man, and he said the magic words, expressing "my hope that it might accord with your views of duty & with your tastes to accept the important trust." Pendleton explained why he thought this was such a significant opportunity:

> One great reason why I hope you may judge favorably of this invitation is, that the destiny of our State & country depends so greatly upon the training of our young men. And now our Educational Institutions are so crippled that they need the very best agencies for their restoration and the revival of high aims in the breasts of Virginian & Southern youths.

An old soldier was calling a comrade to arms in the cause of peace. The general and doctor of divinity summed up his view with the words, "I have thought Dear General while thus doing an important service to the State & its people you might be presenting to the world in such position an example of quiet usefulness & gentle patriotism, no less impressive than the illustrious career in the field."

III

After considering the matter for close to three weeks, during which he received private assurances that Washington College would favor no particular Christian denomination, Lee wrote the trustees a conditional acceptance. He stressed that they must weigh the fact that he had not received a pardon and might never receive one. "Being excluded from the terms of amnesty ... and an object of censure to a portion of the Country, I have thought it probable that my occupation of the position of President might draw upon the College a feeling of hostility." Previous presidents of the college had taught classes, but Lee did not feel that his health was up to that. "I could not, therefore, undertake more than the general administration and supervision of the institution."

He was explicit about what this Southern school, in the town that proudly claimed the Virginia Military Institute, might expect his political views to be:

> I think it the duty of every citizen, in the present condition of the Country, to do all in his power to aid in the restoration of peace and harmony, and in no way to oppose the policy of the State or General Government directed to that object. It is particularly incumbent upon those charged with the instruction of the young to set them an example of submission to authority ...

The trustees met and on August 31 sent him a letter, assuring him that they believed he would be an asset and not a liability, and agreeing that he would have no classes to teach. Since Lee had made it clear that if these matters were acceptable he would take the job, he became the president of Washington College, a school he had never seen, in a place he had never been.

☆   ☆   ☆

Five months after Appomattox, all had changed for him again. It was not to be a quiet life in the country. Efforts on his book would have to be squeezed in among new and pressing matters; in fact, his projected history of his campaigns would never get beyond his collecting of materials for it, although eventually he would write an introduction for the new edition of his father's Revolutionary War memoirs. Lee would leave Derwent and go to Lexington ahead of his family, sending for them when the house he had been promised was ready.

Twenty weeks since Appomattox. The man who had said, "Then there is nothing left me but to go and see General Grant, and I would rather die a thousand deaths," was now writing, "The decision of war, having been decided against us, it is the part of wisdom to acquiesce in the result, and of candor to recognize the fact." He was urging "the healing of all dissensions."

Of those dissensions between North and South, some were more obvious now than in the hours after the guns fell silent. White Southerners accepted the fact that slavery had ended, but they had their own ideas about what should come next where the blacks were concerned. Northerners who heard of it were staggered to learn that many former slaveholders believed that the victors should compensate them financially for the loss of those blacks, formerly their property under Southern laws, who had walked out on them when they received their freedom. From the Southern point of view, the slaves had indeed been property — one estimate placed their collective value at two billion dollars — and it was common practice to use slaves as collateral for loans, just as a man might take a mortgage on a house. In purely economic terms, to strip two billion dollars' worth of property from its former owners overnight was to create an entirely new class of paupers.

Dimly, many white Southerners perceived a truth. Unless the North was even richer than they thought, the blacks were still dependent on the whites of the South for their livelihood. Throughout the South, labor contracts were entered into between white employers and black workers, and at the same time vagrancy laws were enacted. The blacks believed that the labor contracts were to put them into their old bondage under a new guise, and that the vagrancy laws were to keep them from leaving the areas where they had been exploited as slaves. Soon there would be an entire set of "black codes," drawn up by Southern whites to limit the rights of blacks.

From Washington, President Andrew Johnson was trying to implement a moderate policy toward the recent Confederacy. As Lincoln had, he believed that the Southern states had been out of their "proper practical relation" to the Union while in rebellion; now that the rebellion had failed and there was no longer a nation known as the Confederate States of America, those Southern states, whether they liked it or not, were once more part of the United States. In Johnson's view, there was nothing else that they could be. Under the plan that he had proclaimed and was almost single-handedly enacting, the former Confederate states were in the process of electing new governors, legislatures, and congressmen. Johnson's plan required, among other things, that these postwar legislatures should declare their secession in 1861 to have been illegal, and that they must ratify the Thirteenth Amendment to the Constitution, which outlawed slavery. Those matters accomplished, the former Confederate states could send their senators and representatives to Washington when the Congress convened in December. Once they were seated, the President would revoke martial law in the South, the Federal occupation troops would be withdrawn, and the South would be fully restored to the Union on an equal political footing.

Although they remained bitter about their defeat and the presence of Federal garrisons among them, Southerners were inclined to view President Johnson as the best friend they had in Washington. This was doubtful. By leading them to believe that he was in sole control of the process of reinstating them in the Union, he was causing them to think that all of their recent enemies endorsed his program and saw the South's compliance with it as evidence of sufficient political rehabilitation.

That was an immense misconception. In the dominant Republican Party, even moderate congressmen were upset that the President was dealing with the Southern states as if readmission were a matter for the executive branch alone, something to be presented as a fait accompli to the Congress when it convened. As for Southern compliance with Johnson's plan, most Northerners had not expected blacks to have a part in reorganizing the Southern state governments, but they did expect the whites to give them equal protection under the law. Now they saw that, despite military occupation and the presence of Freedmen's Bureau offices and agents throughout the South, white Southerners were enacting black codes to ensure that there would be one law for the whites and one for the blacks. Until this moment, the idea of a vote for the blacks had been entirely secondary in Northern thinking, with many opposed to the idea. The war had been fought to end secession and to abolish slavery, rather than to extend the franchise to blacks, but now increasing numbers of Northerners began to think that giving blacks the vote would be the best way to help them defend themselves.

If the black codes were disturbing to moderates, they were infuriating to the Radical wing of the Republican Party. Representative Thaddeus Stevens of Pennsylvania, the House leader of this steadily growing faction, held that the Southern states should be treated as "conquered provinces" that were on a lengthy period of Federally supervised probation. Some Radicals wanted to confiscate the land belonging to former slaveholders and redistribute it among the blacks. The Radicals unceasingly told the Northern public that the sacrifices of war were being negated by a policy that was putting Southern state governments back into much the same hands that had guided them into the war.

Five months since Appomattox. As Lee prepared to go to Lexington, new emotional battle lines were being drawn. Suffering, resentful, and unrepentant, eight million white Southerners believed that if all this oath-taking meant that they were American citizens again, then they should be represented in Washington and should be granted a free hand in running their state and local governments, in which they felt that blacks were not qualified to participate. Twenty million Northerners were determined that the deaths of three hundred and sixty thousand Union soldiers should *mean* something, and that four million blacks should not have their fate decided for them by those who had held them in their absolute power for generations.

In his little borrowed house in the country, Lee cleared up his correspondence before leaving. He wrote, "I believe it to be the duty" — that word again — "of everyone to reunite in the restoration of the country, and the reestablishment of peace and harmony." To his friend John Letcher, who agreed with him, he outlined what he thought public-spirited Southerners should do. It was just what he had told his young staff officers, on the road from Appomattox to Richmond. "They should remain, if possible, in the country; promote harmony and good feeling; qualify themselves to vote; and elect to the State and general legislatures wise and patriotic men, who will devote their abilities to the interests of the country." The definition of what was "wise," what was "patriotic," and what were the best "interests of the country," would be the source of endless contention between North and South.

In answer to letters from those in despair, Lee counseled patience, moderation, and hope. "I look forward to better days," he said, and meant it.

IV

As Lee packed the baggage that was to be sent ahead of him, the nation was reading about his new position in its newspapers. In the South, approval, and one more lesson by example from Lee — go to work, do something, even if it's not what you did before, and let's get things going again. In the North, the *New York Independent* said of Lee's future relationship with his students, "As president, he must look after the morals of his young men. If he desires to impress upon them the obligations of truthfulness, he can remind them of the oath he took to support and defend the Government of the United States, and how he has kept that oath the last four years ... the bloodiest and guiltiest traitor in all the South, that man we make president of a college."

Mail descended on Washington. Among the letters that President Johnson received, he read this: "Aren't you ashamed to give Lee the privilege of being President of a college? Satan wouldn't have him to open the door for fresh arrivals."

For his family, however, he was husband and father, going somewhere. On September 14, 1865, Mary Lee wrote a friend, "He starts tomorrow *en cheval* for Lexington. He prefers that way, and, besides, does not like to part even for a time from his beloved steed, the companion of many a hard-fought battle." As for the job itself, "I do not think he is very fond of teaching, but he is willing to do anything that will give him an honorable support."

So a rapidly aging man with a clear head and a bad heart swung up on the horse he loved, and headed west into the hills.

Chapter 13

A T THREE O'CLOCK in the afternoon of a mid-September day, a
nine-year-old boy named Jimmie was in the front yard of the
Mountain House, an inn built into a slope at the crest of the Blue
Ridge Mountains at Rockfish Gap. Jimmie lived there with his parents
and older brother. He went to school in the mornings, and in the afternoons he followed around his hero, Uncle Mose, a black man who took
care of the stables.

A gentleman rode up to the front gate on a handsome horse and
asked Uncle Mose if there was a room available for the night. Told that
there was, the man came along to the stables to see what kind of stall
would be provided for his mount.

As the three of them stood around the unsaddled horse in the stable yard, they saw a small raw surface on one shoulder. Jimmie spoke
right up:

> I told him that I knew what would heal it (Uncle Mose's lore) and
> that was the moss from a nearby chalybeate spring. The gentleman
> said that the moss was an astringent, and something of an antiseptic
> was useful; and leading the horse by the halter we all went to the
> spring.

At the spring, the boy plunged his arm into the icy water and
proudly came up with a big handful of the moss, which the man care-
fully applied to his horse's sore. Then the three of them started back
toward the stable, with Jimmie wistfully looking up at the horse.

> Probably he noticed the longing expression on my face, for he said,
> "Jimmie, don't you want to ride back to the stable?" Grabbing the
> clothing about the back of my neck with one hand he took hold of

the seat of my trousers with the other and threw me on the horse's back, and we took the horse to the stable and returned to the Inn.

When Jimmie and his new friend came up to the hotel, "there was no one around, and we seated ourselves on the steps which led to a porch the length of the house, and talked of anything that came to my mind."

As they chatted on the steps of the rustic inn, Jimmie's hound, Donder, was sounding a cry as he ran through the woods, "trailing some small animal — a rabbit or fox." Jimmie explained that he could not tell from his dog's cry which animal he was after. The man said that when the cry was continuous, it meant the hound was after a fox, but when it was broken, the dog was chasing back and forth trying to regain the scent of a rabbit.

They talked on about other things, with the man showing no interest in going into the hotel. Jimmie's older brother appeared, coming home from school; he had made a detour through the stables to see what new horses and carriages might have arrived. The older boy nodded as he passed them on the steps, but seemed in a state of suppressed excitement. In a moment there was "peeping and whispering" from inside the hotel. Jimmie's brother had seen the silver initials R.E.L. on the back of the newcomer's saddle.

Down the steps came "two elderly maiden ladies," one of whom broke into the conversation between Jimmie and his friend.

"We once met Colonel Lee at the White Sulphur Springs," she said, referring to a prewar summer, "and I believe that our friend of the White Sulphur is none other than General Lee."

Lee rose and came back to the world. "Yes, I am General Lee, but am sorry to have been recognized as such, for I am now simply a citizen of the United States, on my way to Lexington to arrange with the authorities of Washington College as to my becoming associated with that institution."

Lee went on to make himself agreeable to the guests, but at supper Jimmie found that his friend had arranged to be seated near him, and they went on talking.

II

On the morning of September 18, Lee and Traveller entered Rockbridge County, heading south up the Valley of Virginia to their new
home in the county seat of Lexington. This was a world different from
the flatter, long-settled Potomac River country that had for two centuries nurtured the Lees, the Custises, the Fitzhughs, and their myriad
cousins and friends. Here was a vast upland valley, its floor studded
with hills. To Lee's left was the chain of the Blue Ridge Mountains; off
to his right, thirty miles to the west, the valley's opposite wall was
formed by the Alleghenies. A century before, this had been the frontier,
with log-cabin settlements amid forests and great meadows where buf-
falo then ran.

The people, too, were different from those of coastal and lowland
Virginia. Like the trustees of Washington College, these were the
Scotch-Irish, hard-working Presbyterian farmers, mechanics and trades-
men, plain and sober. Their valley was a land of lovely views and
homely names — Chalk Mine Run, Hog Back Mountain, Nettle
Creek. Lovers of liberty who had crossed the Atlantic to escape religious persecution, these Calvinists had provided many of the frontier
riflemen of the American Revolution; the Lexington toward which Lee
and Traveller were heading had been named in honor of the Massachusetts village where that war began. This was the home of a hardy,
God-fearing people.

Despite their thirst for political freedom, the citizens of this high
country exacted great conformity within their own society. Arriving in
Lexington just before the Civil War, a young man from Lee's part of
Virginia expressed this reaction to them:

> Their impress was upon everything in the place. The blue lime-
> stone streets looked hard. The red-brick houses, with severe stone
> trimmings and plain white pillars and finishings, were stiff and for-
> mal. The grim portals of the Presbyterian church looked cold as a
> dog's nose. The cedar hedges in the yards, trimmed hard and close
> along straight brick pathways, were as unsentimental as mathemat-
> ics. The dress of the citizens, male and female, was of single-breasted
> simplicity; and the hair of those pretty Presbyterian girls was among
> the smoothest and flattest things I ever saw.

There was all that, but Lee knew of Rockbridge County in quite another way. His son Rob had served in the Rockbridge Artillery, a unit
that named its four cannon Matthew, Mark, Luke, and John. Among
the four infantry companies from Rockbridge County that had entered
battle before his eyes as part of the Stonewall Brigade, there was the
Liberty Hall Volunteers. This unit, originally composed of the Class of
1861 and other students and alumni, had maintained its character as
the Washington College company through the entire war. Fighting in
thirty-two major battles — at Chancellorsville it lost nineteen killed
and wounded, of twenty-eight who started the day — this brave unit's
survivors had marched to the end with Lee at Appomattox.

That would have been enough of a military record for any commu-
nity, but Lexington was also the home of the Virginia Military Institute, whose graduates led troops on all of Lee's battlefields. Even the
Institute's youngest, beardless cadets, still in classes at Lexington during the war, had suddenly been ordered to march down this valley to
meet the enemy. So small, so neatly uniformed, and so well-drilled that
their Federal opponents thought they were encountering foreign mer-
cenaries, the cadets dashed into action at the Battle of New Market,
their valor forever silencing those fellow Confederates who had stood
beside the road singing "Rock-A-Bye, Baby" as they watched these
boys march up for battle.

And there was the memory of Stonewall Jackson, the eccentric instructor at the institute, preoccupied in manner, who was unexpectedly
brilliant when war came, and never more so than in his great campaign
in the north of this valley up which Lee was riding. A contemporary
wrote, "Probably the last people in America to believe in Jackson's genius were his old fellow-citizens."

Riding toward the town of twenty-five hundred where Jackson had
lived and now lay buried, Lee was a man who had from their first
meeting understood this man with the bright pale eyes. Lee and his
greatest lieutenant communicated almost without speaking. In the
chilly morning before Jackson's epic flanking movement in Lee's great
victory at Chancellorsville, the shabby Jackson and the ever-neat Lee
sat beside each other on a crate, studying a map. Lee had intended
some sort of turning movement on his left, but now Jackson made a
stunning proposal: he would take his entire corps, twenty-eight thousand men, and slip them around the right end of the Union line, leav-

ing Lee with only fourteen thousand to face the fifty thousand Federal soldiers across the way. Lee looked down at this diagram of an enormous gamble and authorized it with "Well, go on."

As Traveller stepped down the road, Lee could see on both sides of him the results of war. The forest mountains were beautiful in the sunshine, but in the foreground were untilled silent fields, empty of cattle, hogs, or sheep. The Union Army had brought to the Valley of Virginia the same war of attrition that Sherman had practiced farther south in his march to the sea. Fences were gone, bridges were burnt, mills were destroyed. Mile after mile, chimneys stood where houses had been. General Philip Sheridan of the Union Army had said that a crow flying across this devastation would have to carry its own rations.

Lee came down the road on one side of the valley, a man in grey, wearing a brown slouch hat, alone in the landscape with the horse that was his friend. In his saddlebags were the extra clothes he had brought for this trip; symbolically, he was also carrying with him the brutally beaten pride and hope of the South. The civilian leaders of the Confederacy had never captured their people's hearts or their imagination; the dwindling popularity of Jefferson Davis had been restored only by the severity of his treatment when he was captured. It was its generals that the South loved, and Lee stood first among several great names. Stripped of wealth and strength, the South could comfort itself only with the recent bravery of its soldiers and the skill and character of some of its generals. Lee had not produced victory, but his prodigious effort in staving off defeat for so long on its main northern battlefront was the best success story the South had. Whatever Lee did next, the South had a need for it to go well. So did the North. Even men like Grant and Meade did not understand it fully, but Lee was the only man who had a chance to do it all — save the South's pride, give the South the calm example that would guide it in a stormy postwar period, and do it all in a way that the North would first approve and then applaud.

But would it go well at Lexington? Lee's admirers were looking to a man whose health was in a precarious state — a fact unknown to them and only partially recognized by Lee. He could easily turn out to be the Invalid of Lexington, or simply die. As the Radicals gained influence in Congress, it was certain that he would have to face something more at their hands.

There were problems subtler than that. Here came a general whose entire experience with American college education had been at West Point, first as a cadet and then as its superintendent. Here was the man who had said, regarding his own son, "Let him never touch a novel." Four years of ordering men to their deaths might not be the best background for dealing with a homesick seventeen-year-old freshman who had not served in the war. Lee was used to transferring incompetent officers; all it took was a stroke of his pen. How was he going to deal with the members of the faculty, each of whom knew more about his subject than did Lee? No matter what he did, was it realistic to expect Washington College to survive? The University of Alabama had just opened its doors for this first postwar session; only one student had appeared, and the university had closed again.

III

At one o'clock in the afternoon Lee crossed the North River and entered the town of Lexington. On a ridge above him were the ramparts of the Virginia Military Institute, broken and blackened by the raid conducted by General Hunter the year before. Surprisingly, the Federal military occupation authorities were allowing this hatchery of Confederate officers to open for the autumn term, just a few months after Appomattox. The only curb on this extension of professional courtesy among military colleagues was that the cadets were to wear civilian clothes and not carry muskets. Because the barracks were destroyed, the cadets would be living at boarding houses or with families in town.

Coming up the main street, riding slowly, Lee raised his hat to those who recognized him. Several out-of-work veterans of the Army of Northern Virginia were aimlessly talking in front of the Lexington Hotel when their former commander reined up on Traveller. They snapped to attention. One of them saluted before placing a hand upon Traveller's bridle and another on the stirrup, waiting for Lee to dismount.

At this moment another man on horseback appeared, slimmer than Lee and much younger, and hastily introduced himself. This was Professor James J. White of the faculty of Washington College. He told Lee that he must not think of staying at the hotel; a room was ready for him where White and his wife and children were living at the house of his father-in-law, Colonel S. McD. Reid, the senior member of the college's Board of Trustees. Lee looked at this capable horseman who had been the original captain of the Liberty Hall Volunteers, leading them with great distinction at First Manassas before illness forced him from the service, and accepted the invitation. A small crowd had gathered; unseen by Lee, a youth acquired a souvenir by slipping behind Traveller and plucking some hairs from his tail.

By the time that Lee and Professor White arrived at the house, Lee had elicited from White not only the record of his brief but gallant Confederate service, but had learned that he was one of the four professors who had kept the college open during the conflict as a preparatory school for youths under military age. Having the choice of addressing him as "Professor" or "Captain," Lee was calling him "Captain White" by the time they dismounted. At the first introductions, the family was somewhat tongue-tied in the presence of this eminent figure who was to preside over the college, but then Lee was introduced to the children. In a matter of minutes, he was playing with them, and there was young laughter in the house. Lee had arrived in Lexington.

Chapter 14

BEFORE BREAKFAST the next morning, Lee went downstairs and wrote Mary a letter. There was something they had not told him, and now he had to convey it to his wife. The house normally assigned to the president of the college had been rented for some time to a doctor, and in the postwar shortage of livable houses, the doctor had not yet been able to find another. So Lee had to write Mary, who was back at Derwent expecting to join him soon, "I do not know when it will be vacated."

Lee told her that Lexington was truly in the mountains. It was only September 19, but "last night I found a blanket and a coverlid rather light covering, and this morning I see a fire in the dining room."

A new place, new people, a new job. In these minutes before any of his host's family came downstairs, before a day in which he must meet many people and be pleasant to them all, Lee found himself missing his family. For the moment he simply told Mary that "I have thought much of you all since I left," but before the week was out he would write, "I wish you were all with me. I feel very solitary and miss you all dreadfully."

The next three days proved as busy as Lee had expected. He was shown the college buildings, on a slope of what a local wit called "the outsquirts" of town. Lee found them "beautifully located," with the white pillars in front of the rank of brick classroom buildings forming a handsome classic colonnade, but every structure was in terrible condition, with some undergoing repairs and all of them needing attention. The grounds were so torn up and neglected that there were more patches of bare soil and weeds than there was grass. "The scarcity of money everywhere embarrasses all proceedings," Lee reported to Mary; the doctor who occupied the house that was promised to Lee might be moving from Lexington because his patients could not pay him. The *Lexington Gazette,* after commenting that there was no bank in this remote town, told a joke about dollars being so scarce that their owners had to introduce them to each other when they met on Main Street.

Beneath the battered but seemingly peaceful surface of this town that was Lee's new home, passions were still burning. William Nelson Pendleton, the Episcopal clergyman and recent artillery general who had urged Lee to come to Lexington, was in trouble with the officers commanding the Federal military garrison. In his services at Grace Church, he had omitted the prewar prayer for the President of the United States, using instead a prayer for "rulers and all in authority," the wording of which he compiled from various parts of the Book of Common Prayer. He also delivered some sermons that were deemed "very inflammatory" by the same men who were prepared to see the Virginia Military Institute reopen.

Retribution was not slow. Pendleton was arrested as he walked off the altar and into the vestry room at the close of a Sunday service, and was confined in the garrison's guardhouse until late that night; after his release, his church was shut until further notice. Pendleton had some old gloves from his days in the United States Army after graduating from West Point, and one day soldiers of that army stopped him on the street and cut the United States brass buttons from his gloves. The temporary wooden marker at the grave of his son "Sandie," a young lieutenant colonel who had died as a Confederate hero, was mutilated by knives and had insults penciled on it in an act of vandalism by Federal troops. When Pendleton asked for permission to reopen Grace Church, and in the same letter attempted to justify his omitting the prayer for the President, he received this reply, without salutation:

> Your quibbling would be impertinent were it not contemptible. When you are prepared to use the prescribed form of prayer — not a garbled quotation from another part of the Prayer-Book — I will request the proper authorities to permit your church to be opened.
>
> Robert C. Redmond
> Major Commanding

It was during this autumn that a Northern woman who had come to Lexington to teach black children in a new Freedmen's Bureau school said that the students of Washington College habitually greeted her on the street with "Damn Yankee bitch of a nigger teacher."

II

Lee met with the trustees twice during his first four days in Lexington. All was cordial and constructive, but there were things that he did not know. The trustees were immensely proud of Lee and honored to have him among them, but their difficult stewardship of Washington College moved them to think of him as a magnet for attracting both students and financial gifts. Even as they discussed other matters, the trustees were considering a fund-raising campaign that would center on the idea that the Southern public would be contributing money to pay Lee's salary. When he finally learned of it, Lee angrily forbade this tactic, but the notion was to appear again in several guises.

On one matter, Lee and the trustees quickly collided. They wished to make a great occasion of his installation as president, two weeks hence, just before the college opened for the new session. "It was proposed . . ." a contemporary wrote, "to send invitations far and wide, to have a band of music play enlivening airs, to have young girls, robed in white and bearing chaplets of flowers, to sing songs of welcome; to have congratulatory speeches, to make it a grand holiday."

Lee would have none of it. He detested this type of attention, but there were graver reasons than that. In just these four days there had already been an incident that worried him. As he rode Traveller down the street, a crowd had gathered in an outburst of cheering and the Rebel Yell that had so disconcerted him that he rode straight back to his host's house. With the town under martial law, the last thing he wanted was to become the focus of random, unpredictable public demonstrations. He was not a martyr; what he wanted to do had to be done outside the Federal garrison guardhouse. Lee knew that the Confederacy was dead, even if others saw it suddenly alive in him as he rode by; it was the South he wanted to help, and he knew that had nothing to do with brass bands and speeches that inevitably would allude to his recent past.

The trustees gave in. At nine o'clock on the morning of October 2, recently returned from a few quiet days at the nearby Rockbridge Baths, a hot-springs resort, he was ushered into the physics classroom on the second floor of what was then known as South Hall. It was filled with early-arriving students, the faculty, local officials, and the ministers of Lexington's churches. Lee had enough news value for the *New York Herald* to send a staff correspondent to Lexington for this moment, and the reporter described Lee as being "dressed in a plain but elegant suit of gray" — one of his uniforms, stripped of insignia; he had no other suits at this time. To the reporter's surprise, when the assemblage rose for the invocation given by the minister of Lexington's Presbyterian church, "he prayed for the President of the United States." This was followed by a short speech of welcome addressed to Lee by Judge Brockenbrough. Then Lee took the oath of office, administered by Squire William White, justice of the Rockbridge County Court.

After Lee had signed a copy of this oath, Judge Brockenbrough handed him a metal ring from which hung the keys to the college buildings. The simple ceremony closed with Lee, the trustees, and the faculty all passing into the next room, which was to be his office. This immediate procession into the place where Lee would work was more symbolic than any of them then knew. It was from this office — "a good-sized room," the reporter noted, "but very plainly and tastefully furnished" — that Lee was to exert his singular influence on everything from the drinking habits of a boy from Georgia to the reconciliation of North and South.

This same day Lee signed another document in addition to his oath as president of the college. In June he had petitioned President Johnson for the restoration of his civil rights. Although he had then counseled others to take the controversial oath of allegiance, he had not included such a signed oath in his application for pardon, because word had not yet been received in Richmond that such a document must be among the papers required in special cases such as his.

Now, to perfect his appeal and to do all that he could to protect the college, he signed the oath of allegiance to the United States. Being a meticulous man, Lee sent this vital document to Washington through reliable channels, but no Federal authority acknowledged its receipt. Believing that this indicated the government's desire to keep him just where they had him — neither pardoned on the one hand, nor brought to trial under the treason indictment on the other — Lee did not pursue the matter.

What in fact happened to this piece of paper was bizarre. It came to the desk of Secretary of State William H. Seward, the man who was soon to buy Alaska from Russia. Apparently thinking that the routing of this document to him guaranteed that it had already been recorded on Lee's behalf, he gave it to a friend for a souvenir. The friend put it in a pigeonhole in his desk and forgot about it. It was found in a bundle of papers in the National Archives one hundred and five years later.

Chapter 15

THE DAY AFTER he was inaugurated, Lee sat down in his office and came to grips with an enormous correspondence that was not to stop until his life ended. The entire nation knew where Lee was; a large wicker laundry basket overflowing with letters of every sort awaited him. This correspondence was to be a seamless web; letters written to him on one subject nevertheless touched on others, and in even the smallest matters, Lee was in effect offering a lesson to those he answered, by what he did and did not say. In this bare office next to a classroom that in three days would be filled with young men's voices answering questions, Lee was meeting by mail the vast constituency that considered him the unelected but undoubted leader of the South.

He tried to answer some of the most important letters during the seventy-two hours before classes began. One of the first to which he gave his attention was from Major General Pierre Gustave Toutant Beauregard, the proud and fiery professional soldier from Louisiana whose varied service had included fighting under Lee in Virginia. Egotistical and given to planning military operations too ambitious for the supplies and transport available, Beauregard had sometimes failed to cooperate with Lee, but now, in these complicated postwar months, he again turned to him as a leader.

Beauregard was one of the principal officers from whom Lee was hoping to receive records and reports for his projected history of his campaigns. Lee now read that Beauregard's papers were missing and, for the moment at least, unavailable.

Then Beauregard addressed the question that so many recent Confederate leaders, both civilian and military, were asking themselves:

What position should I take in relation to defeat? Beauregard and Lee had both heard from Confederate generals who had left the country. These recent comrades were writing from Havana, from Mexico City, from Canada, from England. Before long there would be an entire colony of Confederates and their families in Brazil, a nation in which slavery was still legal; wanting enterprising immigrants who knew how to work with slaves in clearing land for new farms, the Brazilian government would offer them free transportation and free land. Matthew Fontaine Maury, the internationally known oceanographer and recent commodore in the Confederate Navy, was in Mexico, trying to start a settlement of his fellow Virginians. Confederate officers would enter the military service of the Khedive of Egypt, the Prince of Rumania, the Emperor of Korea.

And what, Beauregard respectfully asked Lee, did Lee think of all this, and, by implication, what did Lee think that he, Beauregard, should do?

Sitting next to a silent classroom on the first working day in his office, Lee picked up his pen and wrote a famous letter to a famous man. Beauregard was not Lee, but what he did would have great influence with many thousands of veterans and with a Southern public that held his name in esteem.

"I am glad to see no indication in your letter," Lee wrote, "of an intention to leave the country. I think the South requires the aid of her sons now more than at any period in her history. As you ask my purpose, I will state that I have no thought of abandoning her unless compelled to do so."

Lee reviewed for his Napoleonically inclined lieutenant who had suddenly become humble his own efforts to regain full United States citizenship. His concluding passage was to be quoted for generations:

> I need not tell you that true patriotism sometimes requires of men to act exactly contrary, at one period, to that which it does at another, and the motive which impels them — the desire to do right — is precisely the same. The circumstances that govern their actions, change, and their conduct must conform to the new order of things. History is full of illustrations of this: Washington himself is an example of this. At one time he fought in the service of the King of Great Britain; at another he fought with the French at Yorktown, under the orders of the Continental Congress of America, against him. He has not been branded by the world with reproach for this, but his course has been applauded.

II

As classes got under way in October, Lee made a point of meeting every student in the college. Only fifty had been on hand when he was inaugurated; drawn by the knowledge that he was in Lexington, a few more arrived each day from different parts of the South, until a hundred and forty were enrolled. The *Lexington Gazette* made a point of stating that there was still plenty of room so that qualified applicants would not think all places filled, but in the desperate condition of the South, a hundred and forty young men able to pay their way in one form or another was a sizable number.

Many of these young men were veterans of Lee's Army of Northern Virginia; some had been wounded on battlefields only a few yards from Lee. The war had made some into libertines and some into serious, sober men, but it had left its mark on all of them. Givens B. Strickler, coming back as a sophomore, had joined the Liberty Hall Volunteers at the end of his freshman year and had risen to be its twice-wounded captain before being captured when he led a charge into the Union lines at Gettysburg. Strickler was the soul of responsibility; it was shocking to think of all that he had experienced between his freshman and sophomore years, an interval usually bridged by one pleasant summer.

Most of the veterans were serious about their studies, but some found the saloons and billiard parlors of Lexington more congenial than the classroom; others, used to sleeping on the ground and walking endless miles, spent their days hunting foxes afoot, with hounds. Many had shotguns for birdshooting; others had pistols with them because their travels to Lexington had taken them through parts of the South where gangs of highwaymen were robbing travelers. A student said, "At times we were a wild and excitable bunch of youths. War and race prejudice still ran high, and more than once some of our number were guilty of indiscretions."

In their meetings with Lee in his office, these bearded veterans did not always know whether they were talking to the college president or the general. Speaking freely to Lee of his plans, one of them said, "I am so impatient to make up for the time I lost in the army — "

He got no further, because Lee turned red and his deep voice said loudly, "Mister Humphreys! However long you live and whatever you accomplish, you will find that the time you spent in the Confederate army was the most profitably spent portion of your life. Never again speak of having lost time in the army."

"And," recalled that veteran, who went on to take a doctorate at Leipzig and have a long career as a classics professor at three American universities, "I never did."

With the boys who had been too young for the war, Lee took a gentler tone. One of these "yearlings," as the nonveterans came to be known, fearfully approached Lee's office for his first meeting. "My heart cut all kinds of capers, and my knuckles could make but a very gentle rap on the office door. I was not sure what would happen when I really stood face to face with the General . . . But I did at last timidly rap, and the voice which told me to come in seemed to bring with it a sort of strengthening and sustaining power. Within two minutes, I was seated in a chair, talking to the General as if I had known him and played at his feet since childhood."

One of these incoming younger students was so taken aback by Lee's gentleness that he thought he was in the wrong office and that this was not the recent Confederate commander: "He was so gentle, kind, and almost motherly, that I thought there must be some mistake about it." Once this boy was convinced that he was indeed talking with Robert E. Lee, he saw something more. "It looked as if the sorrow of a whole nation had been collected in his countenance, and as if he were bearing the grief of his whole people. It never left his face, but was ever there to keep company with the kindly smile."

Lee met all of his students individually in his office, and to their astonishment he was able to remember their names from then on. "If he met one or two of the students walking on the street," an undergraduate from South Carolina recalled, "it was his custom to call each by name. If he had had no other gift for the college presidency, this would have gone far towards qualifying him."

Even as the students settled into their classroom work, they were thinking of their president as something more than an educator. "It was a general belief in all the Southern States," a young man from Maryland said, "as expressed by the students therefrom, that the example of General Lee would weigh far more in the restoration of normal conditions and true peace than any other factor in a war-torn country."

III

If the trustees and faculty thought that Lee might be an esteemed figurehead rather an active president, they instantly learned otherwise. This was a man who had commanded a field army five hundred times the size of this student body; now, despite a bad heart, he focused his energy and attention on this smaller group.

Within a few days, Lee had arranged his daily schedule. At the Lexington Hotel, where he was living until his house was ready, he breakfasted at seven o'clock. At a quarter to eight, he was in the college room that served as a chapel, ready for the brief morning devotions that were conducted in rotation by the ministers of Lexington's churches.

At eight in the morning he entered his office and did not leave it until two in the afternoon, when he would go to the hotel for his midday dinner, which he took at that hour. These six hours were Lee's great resource in dealing with the river of paperwork that never ceased flowing through his office. He seldom returned to his office after his midday dinner; after a brief nap, if there was no faculty meeting or other college business, he would go for a long ride on Traveller, returning to the hotel in the early evening. After a light supper at seven-thirty, he would read the newspapers or the pocket Bible he had carried for many years. At ten o'clock he went to bed; it was Lee's belief that every hour of sleep before midnight was worth two afterward.

His output in the office was prodigious. During the war he had always had able staff officers and at least four clerks to whom he could dictate; here, he wrote everything himself. In addition to answering the tremendous flow of correspondence from the general public, from former officers, from family and friends, he replied to every letter that came to his office concerning every aspect of the college. He answered every inquiry about admission; after a while, parents of Washington

College students would cease to be startled by the frequency with which Robert E. Lee was writing them about their sons' progress, or lack of it. An admiring professor wrote of his attention to college administration, "He audited every account; he presided at every faculty meeting; studied and signed every report."

Lee's working relationship with his faculty soon resembled the one he had developed with his generals. It was up to him to evolve or to approve the overall plan; they must execute their parts of it as circumstances dictated. They were teachers; let them teach. From time to time he would appear in the back of a classroom, listen to the recitation in progress, and depart. It was enough.

IV

Lee was sitting in his office when his door swung open without anyone knocking. A little boy, his cheeks blazing, marched in and stood in front of his desk. Lee took off his reading glasses and asked him what he wanted.

Indignantly, the boy said that his father had been killed in the Confederate Army, but because his mother was originally from New York, his playmates kept taunting him by telling him that he was a Yankee. He had decided to come to headquarters for justice.

"The next boy that calls you 'Yankee,' " Lee growled, "send him to me."

The boy nodded and departed, armed with a threat that "struck such terror into the hearts of his small comrades that the offense was never repeated."

No one, not even Lee, knew just what was going to happen next in his office. He had sent word that he wanted to see a young Kentuckian whose behavior was causing bad reports. The student appeared chewing tobacco.

"Chewing is particularly obnoxious to me," Lee said. "Go out and remove that quid, and never appear before me again chewing tobacco." The young man went into the hall, and came back into Lee's office, still chewing.

Lee took one look, wrote briefly on a piece of paper, and told the student to read what was on it, because it would be posted on the college bulletin board in ten minutes. The boy saw that the first thing on it was his name, followed by "is dismissed from Washington College for disrespect to the President."

As Lee took hold, each day some miscreant found himself called in. Veterans of savage wartime fighting emerged from Lee's office with their eyes red because Lee had spoken to them of their mothers, and told them how pained their families would be by their riotous behavior and inattention to studies. Lee was acting out what he had said to his general A. P. Hill: "You'll have to do what I do: when a man makes a mistake, I call him to my tent, and use the authority of my position to make him do the right thing the next time."

The approach was tailored to the offender and the offense. One young man simply disappeared before classes one morning and was not seen again until dark. When called in to explain himself, he readily admitted that he had spent the entire day fox-hunting.

Lee looked at him for a minute, and then said softly, "We did not come here to hunt foxes."

"That boy," one of his friends said, "never even *wanted* to go after foxes any more."

Lee's verdicts were seldom harsh, but they were final. Although they did not know it, these students felt as had a private of the Second Cavalry, before the war, when brought before Lee for a minor offense. Seeing that the young soldier was scared, Lee said gently, "You shall have justice."

The boy answered, "That is what I am afraid of, sir!"

☆ ☆ ☆

Remote as Lexington was, there were unannounced callers who came just to see Lee. A book salesman had sent Lee a copy of a hastily compiled volume about the war, and now appeared in his office. He began, "I sent you the other day, General, a copy of this book which I am engaged in selling."

Lee promptly answered, "Yes, sir, I received it, and am obliged to you for your kindness."

Mistaking politeness for encouragement, the salesman pressed on: "I called this morning to get you to give me a recommendation of the work. A line from you would be worth a great deal to me."

"You must excuse me, sir," Lee said in his formula for indicating that a meeting was at an end. "I cannot recommend a book which I have not read, and never expect to read."

On another of these autumn mornings the agent of an insurance company called on Lee and told him that he was authorized to offer him its presidency. He mentioned a salary of ten thousand dollars, more than six times what Lee was making.

Lee explained that he was unwilling to resign the college presidency he had just begun, and said that he could not do both jobs at once.

"But, General," the insurance salesman said, "we do not want you to discharge any duties. We simply wish the use of your name; *that* will abundantly compensate us."

"Excuse me, sir," Lee said. "I cannot consent to receive pay for services I do not render."

Always there was the silent pile of letters. Even an inquiry about admission could be a ghastly footnote to the war.

Knoxville, Tenn.
Nov. 5, 1865

Gen. R. E. Lee

Dear Sir,

I offer my best respects and well wishes for the prosperity & happiness of yourself and kind family — I have to say to you that I am a wouned soldier of the Confederate Army I lost my right arm at Vicksburg Miss and was taken prisoner and remain in prison until last Feb. I then volteered in the 7th S.C.C. as courier I remain there until the surrender at Appomattox Court House Va.

I have neather father nor mother living so you must excuse me for this time. I have no body near me but a granmother and she says that she will give me a good education and I am not fit for this life with out I have a good education Will you be so kind as to inform me what my tutition and board will be for twelve month I am twenty years old. I am indited here for treason and my trial does not come up until the fourth Monday in this month so if you will attend to this for me I will thank you very much This is written with my left hand I have been in the service for four years so please excuse me.

John H. Finley

V

Even before Lee had been offered the presidency of Washington College, his son Custis had applied for a position as a professor of mathematics at the Virginia Military Institute. He had been appointed to the job at V.M.I., and Lee was happy when Custis arrived to take up his work and joined him in living at the Lexington Hotel. Although the handsome, cigar-smoking Custis was so silent that some found him morose, Lee enjoyed his son's company. Sometimes Custis would join him on his late afternoon rides, but near four o'clock, with or without Custis, Lee and Traveller would set off on one of the roads that took them through the beautiful hills surrounding Lexington.

The students at Washington College, many of them out for long walks between the end of classes and supper, now saw their president as the veterans among them remembered him. The afternoon ride was for exercise and to clear his mind, but Lee wore virtually what he had dressed in for battle — cavalry gauntlets, top boots, spurs, grey uniform, now without insignia, and "a large light-colored hat with a military cord around it."

These students doffed their hats as Lee went by. They thought he looked splendid, and it was not Confederate sentiment that made them think that: Lee on Traveller was a genuinely magnificent sight. The former commander of the Second Cavalry was a lifelong professional horseman, and in Traveller his expert eye had picked a superlative mount. At a review in the summer of 1863, the occasion had called for Lee and a number of other mounted officers, most of them far younger than he, to ride a distance of nine miles around a major part of his army, drawn up at attention on a plain. Lee's son Rob described how the reviewing party set off. "Traveller started with a long lope, and never changed his stride. His rider sat erect and calm, not noticing anything but the gray lines of men he knew so well." After a few minutes of this pace, horses and riders began to drop out. At last, as the troops waited with their eyes to the front, only one horse and rider came galloping out from behind the drawn-up divisions: Lee on Traveller, blazing toward the reviewing stand. "Then arose a shout of applause and admiration from the entire assemblage, the memory of which to this day moistens the eye of every old soldier."

A seven-year-old boy who watched Lee heading out of Lexington on Traveller later put it this way: " 'Traveller' was a mighty proud horse. I've seen him many a time coming up the street, and he wouldn't look to right or left. He looked like just the horse for General Lee."

There were moments, however, when Traveller did indeed stop. A man standing across the street watched Lee bring Traveller to a halt as he stopped to greet two pretty Lexington girls. As Lee sat astride his mount with his hat in his hand, chatting with his blushing admirers, the man noticed that Traveller was prancing handsomely and pawing the ground with his forehooves. This striking effect was secretly being produced by Lee with what the man across the street noted as a "dextrous and coquettish use of the spur."

On the country roads far from town, Lee found the serenity that was not to be had in his office. Gazing over the beautiful valleys with their brilliant autumn foliage, he would talk quietly to Traveller as he patted him, but even in the most peaceful setting, their thunderous past occasionally faced them. Riding Traveller through a forest north of Lexington, Lee saw a plainly dressed countryman riding toward him. The stranger reined in and responded to Lee's usual pleasant greeting by identifying himself as one of his veterans. Then the man said, "General Lee, I am powerful glad to see you, and I feel like cheering you."

As Lee told it, he replied that there was no point in that; there were just the two of them here in the forest.

The man who had followed him in battle said he just had to do it. Waving his hat, he began shouting, "Hurrah for General Lee! Hurrah for General Lee!"

Lee rode off; the veteran kept cheering until he and Traveller were out of sight.

VI

In the definition of intelligence that calls it the ability to decipher the environment, Lee had scored brilliantly as a soldier; now he demonstrated a peacetime application of meeting challenges by maneuvering one's resources. From his first postinaugural meeting with the trustees, held when he had been president for only three weeks, there emerged a new and practical vision of education at Washington College.

The trustees had been greatly impressed by Lee's energetic leadership, and the faculty had found him eager to listen to the ideas they put forth at their weekly meetings with him. The result, almost immediately after Lee took over, was a synthesis in which plans were made to reorganize and expand the curriculum while the trustees, believers now in Lee's ability as well as his reputation, set out to raise the money to do it.

Lee saw the need to give students an education that would prepare them for postwar realities. No one wished to abandon Latin or Greek, but the shattered South needed men who could design bridges, develop chemical compounds for fertilizers, restore the railroads and canals, and work up blueprints for factories.

The trustees' minutes of a meeting on October 24, 1865, three weeks after Lee took over, were a shopping list of the South's needs. Five new professors were needed to open up these new fields, and money must be found to hire them. The proposed professorship of practical chemistry would include metallurgy and chemical aspects of mining. There would be a separate chair for mechanical and civil engineering, an area completely understood by Lee, who had spent most of his United States Army career in the Corps of Engineers. There would be three additional chairs. Practical mechanics was to embrace subjects ranging from architecture and building materials to thermodynamics. Modern languages were to have a department of their own. English literature and composition, and modern history, were moved as a group away from the classics, so that a student need not see English history, or Shakespeare, through the lens of ancient Greece or Rome.

The proposed new curriculum was the fusion of many minds, but one idea was entirely Lee's. His experience in the Mexican War and in Texas had convinced him of the need for Americans to understand the Spanish language and the Latin American civilization. At a time when only a few of the nation's largest universities offered Spanish courses, Washington College would join their number.

What was emerging from all this in the months following Lee's installation was one of the first elective systems in the country. It was a sharp and conscious departure from the classics-steeped prewar education of Southern gentlemen, all of whom were expected to take exactly the same courses in college, no matter what they planned to do in life. Lee had deciphered the environment; seeing that most of his West Point experience was not applicable here, and never having been through a rigid liberal arts curriculum, he was ready to experiment. He had created a climate in which his faculty was encouraged to suggest new things.

When these plans took their larger form at Washington College, they would attract national attention, and praise in the Midwest and North as well as the South. Under Lee's guidance, the thrust of this reorganization would result in ten new departments, expanded graduate studies, and a range of special programs and offerings, including a proposed course in photography, that would make the school one of the most innovative in the nation.

All this lay ahead in the autumn of 1865; there would be moments of crisis for Lee and the college, but it was he who created the climate of hope, the feeling that all things were possible for Washington College. By the time he died and the school was renamed Washington and Lee University, Robert E. Lee was entitled to a position in the first rank of American educators, without reference to his military past.

☆ ☆ ☆

Even a modest start on all this was going to take money, and an idea formed in the mind of Judge Brockenbrough. Three clergymen were acting as fund-raisers for the college, two soliciting by mail from Lexington and one traveling about the nation, but Brockenbrough wanted to try for a large gift from Rockbridge County's most prominent son. This was Cyrus H. McCormick, the inventor of the mechanical grain reaper. Nineteen years before, McCormick had moved from Lexington to Chicago, then a small city, to build his revolutionary machines near the vast Midwestern wheat fields where they would be used. Ironically, this Virginian's horse-drawn invention had helped to defeat his native South by freeing for military service huge numbers of farm boys who would otherwise have been swinging scythes to feed the North.

To approach this rich inventor and manufacturer, Brockenbrough and Lee devised a masterful combination of what a later generation would call the "soft sell" and the "hard sell."

Lee went first. On November 28, he wrote to McCormick, whom he had never met, a chatty letter about new developments at Washington College. A contribution was not mentioned, but the proposed new curriculum was. Lee told this mechanical genius that the college was increasing its science courses "to meet the present needs of the country" and to enable its graduates "to enter at once upon the active pursuits of life." He was sure that McCormick would see "the benefit of applying scientific knowledge and research, to agriculture, mining, manufacturing," and other business fields.

Lee then pointed out that the people of Rockbridge County, "notwithstanding their impoverished condition," were generously responding to the need for "funds" — that was as close as Lee came to speaking of a donation — "for the execution of this project." Having conjured up the picture of McCormick's poverty-stricken former neighbors gallantly digging into their pockets to support science courses that would rebuild the shattered South, Lee bowed himself out of his letter with this: "Their efforts, I am sure, will be strengthened by your sympathy; and your influence will cheer them in their meritorious work."

The hard sell was provided a few days later by Judge Brockenbrough, who wrote McCormick that what was needed was a classroom building — to be named after him, of course — to house these new and useful departments. "Can you come down with a *good round sum* to build up a school with which your name will be associated in all time to come?"

McCormick decided that ten thousand dollars was a round number, and sent along a check for this amount — a princely gift for the time — with indications that more would follow. The school was on its way.

Chapter 16

T HERE WERE WHARVES for shallow-draft vessels on the North River east of Lexington, and on the morning of December 2, Lee and Traveller were at the canal-boat landing. Up the river came a horse-drawn vessel similar to the one the Lees had used to go from Richmond to Derwent. This particular boat belonged to the president of the James River and Kanawha Canal Company, and had been put at the disposal of Mary Lee so that she could have a comfortable trip to her new house, which was at last ready.

The vessel tied up, and Mary was carried ashore by Rob, who was recovering from malaria he had caught while working with Rooney at their farms in the lower country this past summer. Mildred bustled about, superintending the landing of the baggage, which included some of her cats and kittens, and three chickens she had raised at Derwent. Agnes and Mary were to come later; Rooney was at his farm. Custis could not be here to greet them because he had classes to teach at V.M.I.

Lee installed Mary, Mildred, and Rob in a carriage; the mountain of baggage, the cats in their baskets, and the chickens in their cages were to follow on a wagon. He rode Traveller beside their carriage, a happy glow on his face as they traveled the mile and a half to their new home, a house of dark brick and white trim on the slope near the colonnade of the classroom buildings.

Lee was no believer in ghosts, but of all the houses in the South, he and his family had moved into one with most unusual associations. As one entered and walked down the hall, on the right at the rear there was a small apartment that had been built onto the house. The prewar president of the college, the Reverend George Junkin, had lived in this house, and his daughter Eleanor had married a V.M.I. professor named Thomas Jonathan Jackson, later known as Stonewall. Young Captain Jackson had courted Eleanor in the garden, now bare in December; when they married, they had moved into the little apartment at the back. They were a happy, loving couple; then, fourteen months after their marriage, Eleanor died. Even after her death, the grieving Jackson stayed on in this apartment, until eventually he married again and moved elsewhere in Lexington. Now he lay buried within a mile of this house, Lee's greatest general, the man who thought so nearly as he did that they could plan for large battles with few words.

There was another sort of memory associated with the house. Jackson's father-in-law, President Junkin, had been a Union sympathizer and was hounded from the campus by his students at the onset of the war. He devoted himself to visiting both Federal and Confederate wounded in Union Army hospitals; after Gettysburg, he found a dozen of his former students lying wounded within a few yards of each other. It was the saddest of reunions, but he was glad to see them, and they were glad to see him.

The house was a symbol of the problems facing Lee. The past must be put into a respected but not inflammatory perspective. The last president of Washington College had been driven away as the nation cracked in two; this president intended to work for conciliation.

II

Now, at just the moment when the Lees were settling into their new life in Lexington, the Thirty-ninth Congress convened in Washington. Having reconstituted their state governments under President Andrew Johnson's plan, the former Confederate states sent to Washington the men they had elected to represent them in the United States Senate and House of Representatives. All that was needed was for the legislators from the other states to accept them, and they would be seated.

In a combination of naïveté, defiance, and an unfortunate reliance on President Johnson's representation of himself as guarantor of their readmission to the Union, the Southern states had elected their prewar leaders, and these were in many cases the men who had led the Confederacy just eight months earlier. As one of its United States senators, Georgia sent Alexander H. Stephens, Vice-President of the Confederate States of America under the now-imprisoned Jefferson Davis. Four Confederate generals, eight colonels, and various recent civilian officials of the Confederacy presented themselves in the expectation that they would be made full partners in writing the laws of the United States of America.

Washington exploded. The Southern representatives were told to go home. All factions of the powerful Republican majority now agreed that a thorough study must be made before the South could be permitted to re-enter the national political process. On December 13, at a time when Lee and his family were looking forward to their first peacetime Christmas in five years, the Senate and House created the Joint Committee on Reconstruction. The term "Reconstruction" was one of those optimistic slogans that governments invent, meant in this case to conjure up the image of a successful effort to reshape the political institutions and racial attitudes of the South. The committee was directed to hold hearings "to inquire into the condition of the States which formed the so-called Confederate States of America, and report whether they or any of them are entitled to be represented in either house of Congress."

Reflecting the size of the Republican majority, this committee had twelve Republicans and three Democrats. One of its important members was Thaddeus Stevens, the increasingly influential Radical leader. Others of this growing Republican faction shared his belief that the South should be treated as a group of "conquered provinces," but Stevens was in a class by himself when it came to hating white Southerners. He believed that the ends justified the means, and thought that neither the President nor the Supreme Court should block any legislative action affecting the South. His view of the traditional balance of power among the executive, legislative, and judicial branches was that the Constitution of the United States was whatever the Congress said it was. In time, the position of the two major parties would be reversed, but in this turbulent postwar era the Republicans were the liberals who believed in a strong Federal government, and the Democrats were the conservatives who wanted the state governments to retain as much power as possible.

Ironically, the forthcoming hearings were to be conducted as a virtually all-white forum. The committee began summoning Confederates as well as Freedmen's Bureau agents, United States Army officers serving in the military occupation, white Northerners living as private citizens in the South, and a host of other categories. One hundred and thirty-six white witnesses were called, but only eight of the four million blacks whose status was one of the principal subjects of this inquiry were asked to testify.

This was not an oversight. Thaddeus Stevens had a passionate concern for the situation of the blacks in the South, but his Radical faction, in its efforts at Reconstruction, needed as many congressional votes as possible. Therein lay a problem. While increasing numbers of Northerners were perturbed about the postwar treatment of blacks in the South, the North was itself divided concerning its own treatment of blacks. Although the Northern and Midwestern states had sent their sons to shed blood to preserve the Union and to end slavery, many of them had their own state laws that prohibited blacks from voting or severely qualified their right to do so. These were not old laws that Northern state legislatures had forgotten to repeal; on the same day that Lee was sworn in as president of Washington College, Connecticut's voters cast their ballots to reject a measure that would have given the vote to the two thousand blacks living within their state. A month later, Michigan and Wisconsin did the same thing. Nearly two years after this beginning of the Reconstruction Committee's hearings, when Thaddeus Stevens was having his way and seven hundred thousand blacks were registered to vote throughout the South, twelve Northern and Midwestern states would still sharply limit or prohibit voting among their small black populations. There would indeed be few black witnesses at these hearings; one of them might say something that would be a political embarrassment to a legislator whose vote was needed.

The subcommittee appointed to inquire into the loyalty and suitability for readmission into the Union of Virginia, North Carolina, and South Carolina was headed by Republican Senator Jacob M. Howard of Michigan. Although many of his fellow Radicals believed in black suffrage as a matter of principle, Howard, whose own state had just rejected a vote for the blacks, felt that a black vote in the South was desirable chiefly for the strength it would add to the Republican Party. Howard's really strong feelings were on the subject of loyalty to the Union. He and his colleagues sent for Robert E. Lee to appear before them.

For Lee, it was a singularly painful return to Washington. Until the war, this area had been the place of many of his happiest memories. Across the river was his boyhood home in Alexandria. Also south of the river, just opposite the city, was Arlington, majestic on its great bluff, the Custis mansion in which he had married Mary, and the place where they had lived for so many years and where their seven children had been born. At the time of Appomattox, Lee had hoped that he could recover Arlington, despite its Federal wartime occupation and the use of some of its acres as a military cemetery. It was only now that he was learning of the manner in which the government had confiscated Arlington without facing the issue of confiscation. In January of 1864, more than a year before Appomattox, the United States Treasury Department had quietly sold Arlington to itself at a tax sale of which Lee was unaware, and under circumstances that would have made it impossible for anyone representing the Lee family to have appeared to pay the tax delinquency that was the pretext for the sale. Lee would continue his efforts to recover the house and all or part of Arlington's eleven hundred acres, but as far as the Federal government was concerned, Lee and his wife and children had no claim to their former home. The darkened, empty house loomed on its hill across the river — in happier days Lee said of its heavy-columned façade that it was "a House that any one might see with half an eye" — and on the late afternoon of February 16, 1866, Lee checked into the Metropolitan Hotel.

On this Washington side of the river, all was different too. Not far from his hotel was the War Department, where he had served at several points in his career; as a carefree lieutenant riding a horse home to Arlington one afternoon, he had spotted his friend Lieutenant John Macomb on foot and told him to swing up behind him on the horse. Directly in front of the White House, the two young officers in uniform, both on one horse, encountered the Honorable Levi Woodbury, secretary of the treasury, and bowed solemnly; it was said that "a more astonished gentleman has not been seen before or since." In later years, Colonel Lee was brought back from Texas to Washington as the nation moved to the climax of the secession crisis. Systematically freeing the Custis slaves under the terms of his father-in-law's will, Lee had nevertheless been opposed to war as a means of bringing the practice of slavery to an end. Far from being a military man who in some corner of his heart hopes for a war, Lee wrote, as North and South came to the precipice, "War is a terrible alternative and should be the very, very last resort."

Now, having had their war, millions of Northerners and Southerners would agree with him. Ten months after Appomattox, Lee was back in the city that had been the enemy capital. Although many friends came to see him at his hotel — among those who called at a moment when he was out was Amanda Parks, one of the former Arlington house slaves, who wanted to see him and to hear the news of the family — he was aware of the anger that the mere mention of his name created in much of the city. Lee decided not to call at the houses of old friends, for fear of causing them difficulty. To Markie Williams, sister of Orton and Lawrence, he wrote, "I am now considered such a monster, that I hesitate to darken with my shadow, the doors of those I love lest I should bring upon them misfortune."

The day after he arrived in Washington, wearing a grey suit that had been one of his uniforms, Lee entered a large, high-ceilinged room that was crowded with spectators. Reporters were present. He was called forward, asked to place his hand upon a Bible, and swear that he would tell the truth. It was indicated to him that he should sit in a chair facing those who were to question him.

Not since the guns stopped firing had Lee faced the enemy in such hostile form. The room was silent. Here was the chief military officer of the rebellion, dressed in grey. This was not a trial, but in effect Lee was on trial, brought here by the Republican majority as part of its effort to demonstrate that the South was not ready for readmission to the Union. Lee's testimony would not be protected by any form of immunity; every word was to be transcribed, and if the government chose to reopen its treason case against him, this record could be a principal source of potentially damning statements by Lee about his activities in opposition to the United States government.

The tension felt by Lee and the spectators was fully shared by the congressmen who were about to question him. Thousands of their constituents had died at the hands of soldiers led by the man who faced them. Their desks were heaped with letters from widows asking for pensions. They knew little girls and boys who were growing up without fathers.

When the questioning began, it was a fencing match. Lee was asked if the South would submit to the taxes that would pay off the costs of the war that had destroyed the South. Lee answered that the South would pay the taxes levied upon it. He was asked if Southerners were willing to mix socially with Northerners who had come to live among them. Lee answered that most would prefer not to do so.

Soon the committee got something they wanted. Asked the opinion of the Southern white population concerning President Johnson's program, Lee replied, "So far as I know the desire of the people of the south, it is for the restoration of their civil government, and they look upon the policy of President Johnson as the one which would most clearly and surely re-establish it." Since the Radical Republicans were even now laying the groundwork for accusations against Andrew Johnson as a traitor to the best interests of the nation as a whole, nothing suited them better than an endorsement of his policy by the South, in the person of General Robert E. Lee.

Senator Howard turned to the Radical faction's intention to confer the vote on the black adult male population of the South.

QUESTION: How would an amendment to the Constitution be received by the secessionists, or by the people at large, allowing the colored people or certain classes of them to exercise the right of voting at elections?

ANSWER: I think, so far as I can form an opinion, they would object.

QUESTION: They would object to such an amendment?

ANSWER: Yes, sir.

QUESTION: Suppose an amendment should, nevertheless, be adopted, conferring on the blacks the right of suffrage, would that, in your opinion, lead to scenes of violence and breaches of the peace between the two races in Virginia?

ANSWER: I think it would excite unfriendly relations between the two races. I cannot pretend to say to what extent it would go, but that would be the result.

Now the committee made a mistake. They tried to link Lee with the sufferings and deaths of Union soldiers in Confederate prisons.

With the first in this new line of questions, Lee went on the offensive. In the original indictment of Major Henry Wirz, the commandant of Georgia's Andersonville prison, where twelve thousand captives had died, Lee and Jefferson Davis had both been named as co-conspirators in an effort to murder Northern prisoners by abuse and neglect. President Johnson had stricken the names of Lee and Davis from that indictment, as being far too removed from the matter. Wirz had been hanged in Washington; Davis was behind bars on other counts; Lee was not going to let this committee smear him on a matter of professional military honor.

His task, Lee pointed out to the committee, had been to send captured prisoners to the rear, to Richmond, where they passed out of his control. Nonetheless, he thought that they might suffer because of the shortages of food and blankets and tents that his own men were experiencing, so he had "urged the establishment of the cartel which was established" — the mechanism for the exchange of prisoners.

The committee stirred uneasily; they saw what was coming. "I offered to General Grant, around Richmond, that we should exchange all the prisoners in our hands." Lee cited another case, when, during the long Union siege of Petersburg, even the Southern civilians were close to starving, and he had offered to send all prisoners back to the North, "provided they returned an equal number, man for man."

There was the rub; these senators and representatives knew that the policy determined in Washington during the war had been to drain the South of its lesser manpower by allowing few Confederates to return to their army in prisoner exchanges. Inevitably, this had meant that Union soldiers had languished in prisons, where the Federal authorities knew they might die because the South was starving.

Senator Henry T. Blow of Missouri abandoned this line of questioning after nine increasingly embarrassing answers. The committee decided to concentrate on its most politically potent topic. Blacks, prisoners of war, Lee's opinion of President Johnson's policy — all these were secondary to the question of the South's current loyalty to the Union. If it could be shown that white Southerners were less than loyal to the

Federal government, then the committee had their answer to "whether they or any of them are entitled to be represented in either house of Congress."

Lee was not going to tell the committee that the South was pleased with its ever-more-severe treatment. "The feeling, so far as I know, now is that there is not that equality extended to the southern States as is enjoyed by the north."

That was an immense, politely worded understatement. Three weeks before this, Lee had written to Senator Reverdy Johnson, one of the South's few friends in Congress: "To pursue a policy which will continue the prostration of one-half the country, alienate the affections of its inhabitants from the Government, and which must eventually result in injury to the country and to the American people, appears to me so manifestly injudicious that I do not see how those responsible can tolerate it."

Much as Lee had just scaled down his feelings in giving his answer, the committee were not pleased with it.

QUESTION: You do not feel down there that while you accept the result, we are as generous as we ought to be under the circumstances?

Lee answered drily, "They think that the north can afford to be generous."

Senator Howard now got down to brass tacks. There was still the fear that somehow the South might again attack the North, and here was the leader who had done so much with so little.

QUESTION: I understood you to say, generally, that you had no apprehension of any combination among the leading secessionists to renew the war, or anything of the kind?

ANSWER: I have no reason in the world to think so.

QUESTION: Have you heard that subject talked over among any of the politicians?

ANSWER: No, sir: I have not. I have not heard that matter even suggested.

The committee began wishing that they had left Lee in Lexington. If the object was to exhibit to the nation an example of threatening rebel mentality, this calm, reasonable man was not the right choice.

Failing to get an ominous syllable out of Lee, Senator Howard began

hypothesizing. If there should be a chance of renewing the war, of seceding, of attacking the North with the help of some powerful foreign
ally, "what in such an event, might be your own choice?"

ANSWER: I have no disposition to do it now, and I never have
          had.

At this moment Lee and his questioners were looking at each other
across a gulf of misunderstanding. In saying that "I never have had" a
disposition to attack the United States, Lee was thinking of his repeated prewar statements against secession, and the fact that it was not
some hypothetical foreign alliance, but the certainty that the North
was going to march into his native Virginia, that had led him to resign
his Federal commission and put on Confederate grey.

The committee, on the other hand, were looking at a man who had
sworn to defend the United States, who had been taught his profession
at the United States Military Academy, who as cadet and officer had
worn the uniform of the United States Army and been paid by it for
thirty-five years, and who had then accepted the command of Confederate forces that killed hundreds of thousands of men wearing the uniform of that army. The legislators were finally ready to call him a traitor guilty of treason, but they went at it obliquely.

QUESTION: You understand my question? Suppose a jury was em-
           panelled in your neighborhood, taken by lot, would it
           be possible to convict, for example, Jefferson Davis, for
           having levied war against the United States, and thus
           having committed the crime of treason?

ANSWER: I think it is very probable that they would not consider
           that he had committed treason.

QUESTION: They do not generally suppose that it was treason
           against the United States, do they?

ANSWER: I do not think that they so consider it.

No more hypotheses; Senator Howard was talking about actions
taken by Jefferson Davis, by Robert E. Lee, by every Southerner who had
carried a gun or driven a wagon or knitted socks for soldiers, and the
point he was making was that a people who still did not think they had
committed treason had no right to be represented in Washington.

Senator Howard finally asked the question about secession that
could hang Lee if he were tried for treason. In effect, it was: What did

you think you were doing? Howard realized that he might be leading Lee into fatal self-incrimination, and he gave him a way out.

> QUESTION: State, if you please — and if you are disinclined to answer the question, you need not do so — what your own personal views on that question were?

Lee would not take the proffered retreat. His answer came from a view of states' rights and state citizenship that had died at Appomattox.

> ANSWER: That was my view; that the act of Virginia, in withdrawing from the United States, carried me along as a citizen of Virginia, and that her laws and acts were binding on me.

The legislators were through with Lee, but he was not quite through with them. He had never cared for politicians, including Confederate congressmen; clarifying an answer, he let go with this quiet condemnation of the role that elected officials of both North and South had played in bringing on the war:

> I may have said and I may have believed that the position of the two sections which they held to each other was brought about by the politicians of the country; that the great mass of the people, if they had understood the real question would have avoided it . . . I did believe at the time that it was an unnecessary condition of affairs and might have been avoided, if forbearance and wisdom had been practiced on both sides.

Lee had been on the stand for two hours. A frustrated and disappointed committee excused him, and he headed for home.

Chapter 17

BACK IN LEXINGTON, Lee thankfully slipped into the domestic life that had been so dramatically interrupted by his summons to Washington. Although he had lived through catastrophe and change, he was a creature of habit. Each morning he expected Mary, his daughters, and any guests to be at the table at seven for the prayers he led before breakfast. From the school's chapel service he would go to his office, and at two he would return to the house for a midday dinner that was removed from the oven when the cook saw him coming. A rest after dinner, a ride on Traveller in all but the worst weather, and supper at seven-thirty. When there was an afternoon faculty meeting or a long meeting of the vestry of Grace Episcopal Church, the ride on Traveller might have to be sacrificed.

The evenings were given to the Lees' version of an open house. After eight-fifteen, friends were free to call, and every night a number of them did. Each student received at least one invitation to call on a specific evening during the school year, and many came often. Food and drink were seldom served, and it would seem that this was no loss for the guests. Of all the thousands of admiring words written about Robert E. and Mary Lee by those who stayed at their house or were invited to dinner, the sole compliments about food concerned some pecans from Georgia and some raw oysters on ice from Maryland.

Social life revolved around the Lee daughters: Mary, who was known to Lee as "Daughter," and Agnes and Mildred. Mary now was thirty-one, Agnes twenty-five, and Mildred twenty, so the gentlemen on hand ranged from bachelor professors through returned veteran students down to the "yearlings." Some young married couples from the faculties of the college and V.M.I. also appeared, and there frequently were young women house guests, friends from other places.

The custom was for the Lee daughters to greet each guest at the door; if the man was a frequent caller or seemed well able to take care of himself, he was turned on into the house without further specific introductions to other guests. A shy undergraduate would find himself taken under one wing after another, introduced to everyone with words that it was hoped would establish something in common, and never neglected as the evening progressed. The entertainment was the world's simplest — sitting or standing around, talking, with an occasional gathering about the piano when Mildred played.

All of this took place in the front parlor. Back in the dining room, Mary Lee would sit on one side of the fireplace, invariably doing some kind of needlework. Guests were surprised to find her mending the underwear of the Hero of the South, or darning socks for her son Custis. As Mary Lee worked, Lee would read to her in his rich voice, either excerpts from the *Lexington Gazette* or one of the newspapers that arrived by mail or from some book of her choice. If a young man new to the house arrived, one of the daughters would bring him back here for a few words with her parents.

At ten o'clock the general would appear in the front room and begin closing the shutters. Wise young men would have left before that, first bowing to General and Mrs. Lee; the shutters were the last call. A "Captain W.," informed that Lee had a high opinion of his character, replied that this was because he always got out of the house before the first shutters closed.

It was a scene that appeared to be a happy one, and for Lee it was. For the women of the family, life was not that easy. Mary Lee was frequently in agony from her arthritis. The house had no porch; once a good horsewoman and an avid gardener, she had to be carried down the steps to enjoy an hour of spring sunlight in the yard. Mary Lee seldom went anywhere; when she did, she had to be placed into a carriage. Most hours of most days she was confined to her "rolling chair" inside the house. As she saw all these youths dashing about while she became more of an invalid, she wrote a friend, "It often seems to me that my affliction is peculiarly trying to one of my active temperament." She noted that much was happening at Washington College and V.M.I., "but I am unable to mix in anything that is going on & am often very sad and lonely." She wished that one of these boys would call on her rather than pay his respects to the general or spend the entire evening in the front room with her daughters. "There are so many students. I suppose they are studying very hard, as they never seem to find time to visit me." Always she thought of Arlington, empty, Union graves in the garden where she had spent so many hours. The house, the garden, the pine groves were to her like children crying for her, but she could not go to them. The ladies of Lexington were kind, she wrote a friend, but "with the exception of my own immediate family I am entirely cut off from all I have ever known & loved."

The situation of the South was an even greater sorrow for her. Before the war, she had written against secession in terms as eloquent as her husband's, "Secession is nothing but revolution." As she saw the crisis overtaking the nation she said, "I would lay down my life could I save our 'Union,' " and to a friend she wrote that no evil could be "greater than the Division of our glorious Republic into petty states."

War had changed her. Arlington had been taken from her. Friends had been killed. Friends of her sons and daughters had been killed. Early in the war, Rooney's house had been burnt to the ground by Union troops. Later, she had watched a Federal raiding party carry him flat on his back into captivity, seized while he was convalescing from a wound at a supposedly safe place behind the lines. Rooney's wife, Charlotte, never in good health, had died from the shock of that moment and her subsequent terror that Rooney would die in a Federal prison.

Mary Lee was through with the North, but from Washington there now came a stream of news that she regarded as salt in her wounds. In the weeks after her husband returned from his interrogation, the Congress had hardened and had passed, over President Johnson's veto, legislation strengthening Federal control of the South for the purpose of protecting the blacks. A message was being sent to white Southerners: You are on probation for an indefinite period. If you want to rejoin the Union, show us a willingness to treat your former slaves as equals under the law. To make sure that Confederates got the point, on April 9, 1866, the first anniversary of Lee's surrender, the Congress passed a Civil Rights Act. This conferred citizenship on blacks and strengthened their status in legal proceedings and property rights, but did not touch the question of a vote for blacks.

The body before which Lee had appeared, the Joint Committee on

Reconstruction, was now putting forward the recommendations that would be the basis for the Fourteenth Amendment to the Constitution. Among this amendment's several provisions was a measure to reduce the representation of states that refused to extend the vote to blacks, and a section controlling the re-entrance of former Confederates not only into the Federal government, but into the government of their own states. At the same time that Congress was studying these resolutions, it overrode President Johnson's veto and passed a bill that authorized funds as part of an indefinite extension of the Freedmen's Bureau beyond the time it had been scheduled to cease its activities.

Mary Lee's reaction to all this was:

> I think the last resolutions of the committee exceed all that has yet been done or said for the injury & oppression of the South & what do you think of their appropriating 11 millions for the support in idleness of lazy negroes who throng the Capitol & are now robbing the South quite as much as the Yankees ever did. Even in this little place Every House has been robbed & even the spring plants pulled up out of our garden ... There has been lately a Yankee store set up here which is strongly suspected of receiving these stolen goods tho' as yet there is no proof. If our people could have realised all they were to suffer at the hands of the ungenerous & unprincipled party who are unfortunately now in power they would never [have] relaxed their efforts to obtain their independence. It is too late now to say what might have been.

☆   ☆   ☆

The problems of the Lee daughters were of a social nature. Lexington was part of a culture that was alien to them. Until the war, their lives had been spent among the landed Virginia aristocracy, in a mansion high on a bluff that looked straight at the Capitol dome in the distance. To their table had come lively, sophisticated men and women from all over the United States and from foreign countries. In their society there was nothing unusual, let alone suspect, about wine with dinner, or dancing the waltz, in which the man's arm was about the woman's waist.

They were making the best of Lexington, but the beginning had been a disaster. Soon after arriving, Mildred wrote a friend, "I believe it was you who told me Lexington was such a delightful place. I disagree with you in toto. I am dreadfully lonely, know no one well in the whole town . . . Lucy do you know what starvation of the *heart & mind* is? I suffer, & am dumb!" In a reminiscence, she complained of "the provincial society," and on another occasion called Lexington's permanent residents "Saints."

As for the Saints, they were less than enchanted with the Lee girls. A young professor who himself was none too fond of Lexington balanced it out thus:

> I have recently been to call on the Miss Lees, and found them exceedingly agreeable. They don't seem to like Lexington much, think the people stiff and formal, which is very much the case. I only saw Miss Mary and Miss Agnes. Miss Agnes I like very much, her seeming haughtiness and reserve which offend the Lexingtonians so much, I particularly admire.

Miss Mary Lee's reaction to Lexington was to spend a lot of time away from it, on an almost endless round of trips and visits to friends. Her mother said of her, "We rarely hear from Mary; she is a bad correspondent." When she was in Lexington, Daughter startled everyone by taking long walks by herself through a countryside where robberies sometimes occurred. Men seemed to have a nearly identical reaction to the tall, angular Mary: one called her "wholly devoid of fear," with a "strong, but somewhat eccentric character"; another called her a "very masterful type, not afraid of anything or anybody." In the family she was known for her sharp tongue. It was of her as much as anyone that Lee was thinking when he wrote to Rooney on his farm, "We are all as usual — the women of the family very fierce and the men very mild." Agnes, whose "haughtiness and reserve" concealed the grief and shock she felt over the death of Orton Williams, visited away from Lexington with some frequency, but became part of the domestic scene. Mildred, sweet and enthusiastic, crazy about cats, her father's favorite child, was home most of the time.

Soon enough, Mary and Agnes were in the company of professors from the college and from V.M.I. Ice was on the river. "No lady skates," the Lexingtonians said. "If she does, it is a Yankee lady." All three sisters loved to skate; they skated, and found plenty of young men joining them on the ice. Mary and Agnes went for a sleigh ride through the darkened winter countryside with two professors from V.M.I. With spring, the Lee daughters had a skiff on the North River. Mary and Agnes and Mildred founded the Reading Club, a group of twelve young women who met at different members' houses, with male guests invited. Lee wrote of this organization, "As far as I can judge, it is a great institution for the discussion of apples and chestnuts, but is quite innocent of the pleasures of literature."

Some of these young men declared themselves to be seriously interested in Mildred, who was described by a friend as "not beautiful, but had a bright, interesting face and a pleasing personality, and fine literary taste and culture." A student from Arkansas, a nonveteran younger than Mildred, became a good friend of hers, with "no romance in our relations." She confided in him. "Miss Mildred was much sought after by men whose alleged love, she knew, was 'mingled with respect that stood aside from the entire point.' "

That was half the problem. To be a daughter of Robert E. Lee was to be in the position of an heiress who does not know whether professions of love are genuine. By the same token, Lee was held in such reverence that many a Southern man would no more have seriously approached one of his daughters than he would have embraced a statue at a shrine.

There was more than this to complicate the emotions of Mary, Agnes, and Mildred. Lee wanted his sons to marry but was possessive of his daughters. He appeared to exert no control over his daughter Mary, but he was constantly writing Agnes and Mildred to come home whenever they were visiting friends and particularly when they were off at weddings. One letter to Mildred said: "Experience will teach you that, notwithstanding all appearances to the contrary, you will never receive such a love as is felt for you by your father and mother. That lives through absence, difficulties, and time. Your own feelings will teach you how it should be returned and appreciated." He wrote to Agnes, who was in Baltimore for the wedding of a friend, "I miss you very much and hope that this is the last wedding that you will attend."

Mary, wherever she was, did not seem to form any serious attachments, and Agnes and Mildred could hardly be expected to admire their father less than did eight million other white Southerners. Here was the military leader of the Lost Cause, striding into the house in his riding clothes, boots, gauntlets, and campaign hat, cheerfully calling out in his deep voice, "Where is my little Miss Mildred? She is my light-bearer; the house is never dark if she is in it." Seventeen years after his death, Mildred wrote, "To me he seems a Hero — and all other men small in comparison!" Rob, who came up from his farm on the Pamunkey to visit when he could, described part of the daily routine: "After his early and simple dinner, he usually took a nap of a few minutes, sitting upright in his chair, his hand held and rubbed by one of his daughters."

What did their mother make of all this? The modern study of personality was in its infancy. A later generation might speculate that, married to an invalid, Lee was sublimating his feelings in an innocent but smothering relationship with his daughters. "As to the girls," Mary Lee wrote a friend, "they seem to be in the condition of 'poor Betty Martin' who, you know the song said, could never 'find a husband to suit her mind.' I am not in the least anxious to part with them; yet think it quite time, if they intend to change their condition, that they were taking the matter under consideration."

None of them ever married — not Mary, not Agnes, not Mildred. Lee would have been dismayed if he had understood the degree of his possessiveness and his daughters' acquiescence in it. He just did not want them to marry *now*. Long after his death, Mildred wrote, "Most women when they lose such a Father, replace it by husband and children—I have had nothing."

II

Near the end of the first year of Lee's presidency there suddenly arose a situation different from any other. In these troubled postwar months, horse-stealing had become common, and a recently enacted law gave Virginia juries the choice of sentencing a convicted horse thief to death or to a minimum of eighteen years in prison. The small Federal garrison in Lexington had been moved to Staunton, nearly forty miles to the north; to combat the subsequent increase in crime, Lexington had only a magistrate-mayor, a sheriff, known as the town marshal, and a jailer.

A man named Jonathan Hughes had become particularly skillful at stealing horses in the vicinity of Lexington. People knew who he was and what he did, but they could not catch him. On a May afternoon, the word suddenly spread that Hughes had been apprehended and was in the Lexington jail. Farmers, some of whom had lost valuable horses to Hughes and intended that he should never steal another, mounted and rode into town. Soon an angry crowd was in the courthouse yard, surrounding the jail. Men began to talk of pulling Hughes out of his cell and hanging him from a nearby tree. Voices grew loud and uncontrolled; men shook their fists at the barred windows. The town marshal was nowhere to be seen.

The word flashed through town and across the college campus — there was going to be a lynching any minute. A student named Charles Graves was one of those who ran to the courthouse to see what was happening. "At the top of the jail steps," he reported, "in front of the locked door, stood the old jailor, Thomas L. Perry, holding the jail keys high above his head, and facing, with grim and resolute aspect, the would-be lynchers who surrounded him. For some reason, perhaps respect to the old man's gray hairs, the men next to him had forborne to seize him and snatch from him the jail keys, as they could easily have done." Events were building to the moment when they would take those keys, open the jail door, and pull their man out and kill him.

Then the student turned and saw Lee. He was "moving quietly about the crowd, addressing a few words to each group as he passed, begging them to let the law take its course." Many of the men were his veterans. Lee continued to move through the mob. Men stopped shouting and shaking their fists. Silence fell.

"The end was there," the student said. "Those stern Scotch-Irishmen, whose tenacity of purpose is proverbial, remounted their horses and rode out of town. They could not do a deed of lawless violence in the presence of 'Marse Robert.' " The horse thief was duly tried and sentenced to eighteen years in prison.

III

At the end of June, during the week of Commencement Exercises, Lee sat down with the trustees and reviewed this first academic year of his presidency. With a sense of wonder, they looked at the money now at their disposal. Cyrus McCormick had sent five thousand dollars to add to his initial ten thousand. Warren Newcomb of New York, whose widow was to establish Sophie Newcomb College at Tulane, had given ten thousand dollars to endow ten scholarships. One of the college's fund-raisers, a traveling clergyman who had been admonished not to say that contributions were for Lee's salary but who constantly referred to "General Lee's College," had raised $45,280 in cash and subscriptions. Two other fund-raisers had brought in a total of twenty-seven thousand dollars. Including tuition fees, Washington College had received more than a hundred thousand dollars in the ten months since the trustees had borrowed fifty dollars so that Judge Brockenbrough could make the trip to offer Lee the presidency.

The ambitious program evolved by Lee and the trustees and faculty now went into action. The college was reorganized into ten departments, each designated as an independent school, although latter-day students would recognize them more readily as ten different "majors." Professors could now be hired; the faculty for the coming autumn would number fifteen, as compared with four at the close of the war. A local law school run independently by Judge Brockenbrough would be brought into a loose initial affiliation with the college. The preparatory department, which during the war had kept the school going by educating students under military age, would be continued, partly for younger boys from areas where schools were still closed, but also to assist Confederate veterans whose secondary school educations had been interrupted and who were not ready for the full college curriculum.

All this — students, donations, new curriculum, ability to hire new professors — had been attracted or inspired by Lee during his ten months at Washington College. His touch was felt in several recommendations that the trustees now approved. A new chapel, Lee's pet project, was to be built. There was to be a program for improving and beautifying the campus. A superintendent of buildings and grounds would be hired. A woodyard was to be set aside, and wood bought cheaply during the summer to heat the students' rooms the following winter. That was Lee the commander, thinking ahead for the welfare of his troops.

The trustees paid tribute to Lee as best they could. They decided to find someone to take on the position of "clerk to the faculty"; his principal task, unknown to Lee, was to lift some of his staggering load of paperwork. Lee's salary was doubled, to three thousand dollars a year.

The final item involving Lee was a resolution that "a mansion" be built for him and his family, a new and larger President's House, construction to begin when funds were deemed sufficient. The significance of this was not only the compliment to Lee and the desire that he and his family should have a more spacious and comfortable house; it meant that Lee, who had accepted the presidency with many doubts about his suitability for the job and a near-certainty that he would rather do something else, was going to stay, for a time at least.

The most important thing was not dollars or the bricks and mortar or even the additional professors that the college could buy or hire. It was the high morale and strength of purpose felt by most of the students and all the faculty. Setting forth their sentiments concerning not only reorganization but academic standards, the faculty, in a memorandum outlining the new curriculum, spoke of a determination to bring Washington College "to a level with the best institutions in the country."

By the end of his first year as an educator, Lee presented an interesting picture of a soldier turned civilian. In his bare, whitewashed bedroom, next to Mary's much more elaborate room, he slept on his old camp bed. His service revolver hung from a corner of that bed. In an umbrella stand in the corner was a fabulous collection of swords: two that had been presented by the Continental Congress to George Washington and had been handed down in the Custis family, one that had belonged to Lee's father, and two of Lee's — the one, presented to him by the Confederate Congress, that was known as "the Sword of the Confederacy," and the one he had worn when he surrendered to Grant at Appomattox. The line between what a former professional officer would and would not do was in some instances visible only to Lee: he had no hesitation about being seen with a market basket on his arm, shopping for groceries, but he would not use an umbrella in even the heaviest rain.

The students and townspeople were learning to make no assumptions about what Lee might do or say. A student, walking through a pelting rain, suddenly found himself face to face with Lee, who, with a grey cape about his shoulders and rain dripping from the wide brim of his campaign hat, was the very picture of silver-bearded military dignity. The boy halted at something approximating the position of attention, and found that Lee was asking after the health of the several young ladies for whom he had signed photographs of himself as a favor to this boy, whose correspondence with the girls at home had greatly profited thereby. The student answered that they were all well and was starting to say something else when the commander of the Army of Northern Virginia said, "This is a good day for ducks. Good-by," and was gone.

Lee never stretched for wit, but occasionally he found a pun irresistible. A Miss Long, one of his daughters' friends, was staying at the Lees' for a visit. She was very petite, and she had an ardent suitor, a Lexington gentleman who had fallen in love with her and was calling at the house several times a day, with the most serious intentions. When a lady remarked on this man's obvious devotion to the small and pretty Miss Long, Lee said, "Yes, he is different from most men; he wants but little here below, but he wants that little Long."

On political matters, too, people learned not to anticipate his reactions. Just days before he handed their diplomas to the first seniors to graduate under his administration, he wrote to a man in Richmond who was soliciting funds for a monument to be erected in honor of Stonewall Jackson. Lee told him that his students and local residents were too poor to be asked to donate, much as they honored Jackson's memory, and went on to oppose the plan itself, saying, "I do not think it is feasible at this time." Although Lee believed that the erection of Confederate monuments would keep alive the wartime passions that he was trying to eradicate, the sight of Northern soldiers in Southern streets bothered him as much as it did any Confederate. Walking through downtown Lexington, Lee saw a student stagger out of one of the town's saloons, and burst out to his companion, "I wish these military gentlemen, while they are doing so many things that they have no right to do, would close up all these grog-shops that are luring our young men to destruction."

Still, conciliation was his creed. Lee knew that the war was over and that everything depended on a new attitude for a new day. He was taken to call on a lady who lived north of Lexington, and she promptly showed him the remains of a tree in her yard. All its limbs had been shot off by Federal artillery fire during Hunter's raid, and its trunk torn by cannonballs. The woman looked at him expectantly as she showed him this memento of what she and her property had endured. Here was a man who would sympathize.

Lee finally spoke. "Cut it down, my dear Madam, and forget it."

Chapter 18

JUNE 30 was the Lees' thirty-fifth wedding anniversary. On that rainy night in 1831, six bridesmaids and six groomsmen, five of them military officers wearing dress uniforms, had escorted Mary Anna Randolph Custis and Lieutenant Robert Edward Lee into the large drawing room at Arlington, where family and friends were assembled to hear their vows. Lee remembered the tall, cadaverous minister intoning the ceremony "as if he had been reading my Death warrant, and there was a tremulousness in the hand I held that made me anxious for him to end."

The bride was a plain-featured girl who was aglow with love — a graceful and energetic young woman, singularly well-read and well-educated, who loved to dig in her garden on hands and knees, and who enjoyed riding her mare across the pastures and through the forests of Arlington. Anyone looking around the brilliant candlelit rooms of Arlington that night, seeing the great-granddaughter of Martha Washington marry a United States Army officer whose father had been one of George Washington's Continental Army officers, could not have conceived of a day when the groom would be indicted for treason and the bride's house would be confiscated by the government of the United States.

On that night the groom was twenty-four and the bride was twenty-two. Wherever future years took him, Lee never forgot to write Mary on that date. From the terrible siege of Petersburg he wrote, "Do you remember what a happy day thirty-three years ago this was? How many hopes and pleasures it gave birth to!"

Their marriage had possessed a character entirely its own. Lee had married Arlington as well as Mary, and in the first years of their married life she frequently preferred long visits at home with her mother and father to being with Lee at his dull military post. After she had taken their first child, Custis, then little more than a year old, off for one of these visits, Lee wrote her from Fort Monroe:

> My sweet little Boy what would I give to See him! The house is a perfect desert without him and his Mother and there is no comfort in it . . . I am waking all night to hear his sweet little voice and if in the morning I could only feel his little arms around my neck and his dear little heart fluttering against my breast, I should be too happy. The want of so much that I have been accustomed to drives me from my bed sometimes before day.

That letter he signed: ". . . keep for yourself and little boy a thousand Kisses from

Yours truly and forever

R E Lee

Although Mary somewhat came to heel and accompanied him when he was stationed at St. Louis, in New York, in Baltimore, and at West Point, her passionate attachment to Arlington, and the feeling of this only child for her adoring and indulgent parents, was always present. Lee came to share much of this feeling. He was truly stricken when his in-laws died, and Arlington was more of a home to him than any other place in his life.

It was one thing to exchange vows in a bright and spacious drawing room, and another to discover each other. Lee might be known as "the handsomest man in the Army," with a robust body, exceptional intelligence, and a kind, determined nature, but he found himself married to a woman who was a highly developed individual with great strengths of her own. While tending to her eight-month-old son Custis at Fort Monroe, she wrote to her mother, who was about to visit them, "Will you bring down a Latin dictionary, as I brought a Greek one by mistake." Mary never suffered fools gladly; in 1833 she found the parties among the officers and their wives at Fort Monroe "rather stupid," and in 1860 she found the company at a hotel in Canada "intolerably stupid." She could read French with ease. In St. Louis, while her little sons were running around imitating steamboat whistles and flailing their arms as paddle wheels, she busied herself reading such

English poets as Coleridge, Shelley, Wordsworth, and "Goldsmith's Life & poems."

In regard to slavery and gradual emancipation, Lee learned many of his attitudes from Mary. Although fully alive to the codes of his class, Lee's practical experience with the ownership of land, with the difficulties of farming, and with slaves, all came through life at Arlington and the other Custis farms. Before the war, Lee had sent to Liberia those freed Custis slaves who wished to go there, but it was Mary who had, long before that, been contributing to the agency that arranged this — the American Colonization Society, a nondenominational group supported by donors from both North and South. In her days at Fort Monroe she took great pains at Sunday school with "my black class of 6, 3 of whom read quite well." She taught her household servants at Arlington to read, although it was technically against the law to do so in Virginia; to a young relative who had inherited some slaves, she wrote in 1846, "Let no motive of worldly interest induce you to act an unkind or ungenerous part towards them. I well know what a trial they are, but think we are little disposed to make allowances for their peculiar ignorance and debased condition."

By the time of their thirty-fifth anniversary, what had happened over the years to those "many hopes and pleasures"? How had bride and groom evolved, as man toward woman and woman toward man? Mary Lee was in love with her husband; after Lee's death she would write of the days when she anxiously awaited his letters at the time she was hoping he would propose to her.

On Lee's part, despite a letter signed "a thousand Kisses," there was no indication of emotional turbulence, of falling in love, of being in love. At first glance, it would seem that the stage was set for a repetition of the marriage of Light-Horse Harry to Lee's mother; the dashing man to the plain, trusting woman who learned soon enough that there were successful rivals for her husband's heart and arms. From the birth of their daughter Mary in 1835, four years after their wedding, Mary Lee began a slow decline into invalidism. Lee had sentimental crushes on a number of young women: the "handsomest man in the Army" was getting on; two years before the war, at the age of fifty-two, he was writing his nineteen-year-old cousin Annette Carter about a wedding that he could not attend, where she would be one of the bridesmaids. "I shall want so much to see you tonight my beautiful Annette, for I know how sweet you will look, and of all those that will see you, none will appreciate the happiness as much as I would . . . I wish very much I could go down today, I do not think I would take up much space, or be much in the way, but your cousin M—— won't let me go — "

No one praised Mary for her beauty. She was plain, and not interested in her appearance. One account makes clear the difference in this couple's looks.

> While a beautiful Virginia girl, stopping at a summer resort in the early fifties, was going with her father to their rooms, they met on the stairs a man so gloriously handsome that the girl fairly held her breath, and pressed her father's arm.
>
> "Who is he?" she whispered. "Isn't he splendid?"
>
> "That is Captain Lee," said Mr. R. "He is a very good man, as well as a very handsome one."
>
> As they walked on through the upper hall a group attracted them. A dark-eyed lady was sitting in a rocking chair; she wore a calico dress, low shoes and blue cotton stockings, which most probably she had knit for herself . . . Around her several little children were playing.
>
> "That is Mrs. Lee," said Mr. R.
>
> "She is not dressed as well as her husband," the girl said to her father.

Take such a man, take such a wife, add her increasing invalidism, and then send him two thousand miles away to a Texas frontier that he once called "a desert of dullness." What might happen when an attractive woman smiled upon him?

This is what happened, as Lee recounted it. There was a young widow in San Antonio.

> I was invited to her house to a musical party, but declined. About a week afterwards I thought it incumbent on me to return the compliment by a call. I found the house and made myself as agreeable as I could for about 5 minutes, and when I rose to depart she took me out in her garden to see her corn and potatoes by *starlight*. But she had waked the wrong passenger. I told her I had no knowledge of horticulture, and took no interest in agriculture in Texas. I have not seen her since.

And to whom did Lee write this? To Mary. She understood his need to look upon the youthful beauty she could not provide, and his pleasure in the gallant banter that was a part of Southern manners. Soon after his death she wrote, "No one enjoyed the society of ladies more than himself. It seemed the greatest recreation in his toilsome life."

Chapter 19

O N SEPTEMBER 13, the second year of Lee's presidency began when more than three hundred students, twice the number present the past June, appeared to begin the new session. More came during the next weeks. In these warm days, there was a new sight on campus; Lee would ride Traveller to the edge of a baseball field to watch the students play this game of Northern origin, which had come to the South since the war. In this era, pitching had little finesse, and batters hit almost everything that came near the plate. This, combined with the fact that the fielders had no gloves, produced such scores as 34 to 19, and 66 to 22.

In his office, Lee greeted a twenty-four-year-old Confederate veteran who was to make himself singularly useful. This was Edward Clifford Gordon, who had been educated at the University of Virginia, had served as a first lieutenant of artillery, and was trying to make some money to further his studies for the Presbyterian ministry. He had been hired to serve both as the superintendent of buildings and grounds that Lee had requested and as secretary of faculty, the title under which he was to provide the clerical assistance for Lee that the faculty wished him to have. At various times Gordon would also act as the school's treasurer, dormitory and examination supervisor, and part-time librarian. In his little spare time, he took mathematics courses. Gordon was everything Lee would approve of in an assistant: a highly intelligent Confederate veteran who wished to enter the Christian ministry and was prepared to work hard at every task set before him.

Lee's first instructions to Gordon were pure Regular Army: he was to go to the man "who is now in charge of the property of the college used in repairing the buildings and improving the grounds. Get from him a complete list of all the property in his hands, verify it, then give him a receipt for it, after which you will be responsible for it."

That was the beginning of a relationship that brought Gordon into daily contact with Lee. Fortunately for both of them, and for those who eventually would read Gordon's description of his experiences with Lee, he was not in awe of his former commander, although he came to admire him even more than he had when they were both soldiers. There were surprises for Gordon, who had expected to encounter a consistent military mentality. Asking Lee about the arrangement in which he wished new trees planted on the front campus, he got this answer: "Not in rows; Nature never plants trees in rows." As for a fence that had to be put up to keep out some cows: "A fence is a blot on any lawn. We must have a fence; but select a color which will render the fence as inconspicuous as possible: one that will harmonize with the surrounding colors." This nonmilitary approach touched other things; the new chapel under construction was Lee's favorite project, but in this second year of his presidency he decreed that attendance at the college's morning prayer services was no longer compulsory. When two new students asked him for a copy of the college's regulations, Lee told them that there were no written rules — everyone was expected to act like a gentleman.

In his work around the campus, Gordon soon understood what it was to be in the company of a man who had spent most of his military service in the Engineers. "He could look at a mass of mortar and at once detect whether it had too much or too little lime in it. If a stepstone was half an inch out of line he noticed it." Another quality impressed Gordon even more: "There was something uncanny about his ability to read other men's thoughts." Several Federal generals would have agreed.

The previous autumn, Lee had been forced to catch up to poor student grades or behavior from behind, like a cowboy thundering up behind a steer with a lasso. This year, he had his system perfected and waiting. On the basis of classroom recitations and written tests, every student received a grade every week in every course. Copies of these grades were duly transmitted to the president's office. At his weekly faculty meetings Lee would bring up the name of any student whose performance concerned him. What he learned at the meeting and what he knew from his own initial interview with each student gave Lee the knowledge and opportunity to move quickly when he thought a young man was in trouble or heading for it. "An invitation to visit General Lee in his office was the most dreaded event in a student's life," said one who knew.

Increasingly, the students came to realize that the president had a greater involvement with them than just knowing their names, grades, and whether they had engaged in any sort of unacceptable behavior. A student received word, several days after it happened, that his mother had died at home in Kentucky. It was too late to get to her funeral. The boy asked his roommate to go to the president's office and explain that he was going to stay in his room and not attend classes for two or three days.

Writing fifty-six years later, he recalled:

> At the end of the month when my report came out there was not a single absent mark against me. This can only be accounted for by General Lee's going to each professor to whom I recited and telling him. To me this is a remarkable illustration of his kindness to and care for the boys entrusted to him. If I had no other reason, I would love him for that yet.

At his desk, Lee read every kind of letter. Sir John Dalberg Acton, the English historian whom Matthew Arnold described as the most influential of Gladstone's advisers, wrote seeking Lee's views on American postwar constitutional questions and the South's political future. He pledged that a new political magazine run by Gladstone's Liberal followers "shall follow the course which you prescribe." Answering this, Lee assured Acton that the south accepted the de facto results of the war and "the extinction of slavery," but that he was concerned that an overly powerful Federal government would prove to be a threat to "the rights and authority reserved in the states and to the people," and would result in a nation that was "sure to be aggressive abroad and despotic at home." Lee believed in "the right of each state to prescribe for itself the qualification of suffrage," and pointed out that if the Union was "inviolable and perpetual" and it was wrong for a state to secede, then it was equally wrong to prevent a state from resuming its full role and having representation in Washington. Now that slavery had been ended both by the war and the Thirteenth Amendment, Lee hoped that the Constitution "may be handed down to succeeding generations in the form we received it from our forefathers."

Lee's reply to the future Lord Acton was statesmanlike, but the significance of this exchange was that Acton had chosen to ask these questions of Lee. To ascertain the views of the South, Acton had written not to Alexander H. Stephens, the Vice-President of the Confederacy, nor to any of its other civilian officials, but to Lee, a general who had never held elected office. Acton was specific about it; to hear the voice of the South, he told Lee in his letter, he had decided to "venture at once to proceed to Headquarters."

As for the American political situation, things were quiet in Lexington, but during the past summer there had been race riots in Memphis and New Orleans that were, in effect, massacres of blacks by whites. The Ku Klux Klan had been formed the previous spring, and its white-hooded nightriders were spreading through the South. In this autumn of 1866, the nation was engaging in an important congressional election that was turning into a Northern referendum on the course to be pursued in the treatment of the South. President Johnson was trying to sell the nation his policy. As part of it, the former Confederate states could be readmitted to the Union without granting the blacks the vote. The Republican candidates, moving increasingly toward the Radical position, were insisting that the Southern states should not be allowed back into the Union unless they adopted the Fourteenth Amendment, which provided for reduced representation in Congress if the blacks were denied the vote.

Lee was for Johnson's policy, but above all he counseled a calm, law-abiding acceptance of reality. To Mrs. Jefferson Davis, in declining her request that he answer an attack upon her imprisoned husband, he wrote, "I have thought from the time of the cessation of hostilities, that silence and patience on the part of the South was the true course, and I think so still." To General Jubal Early, who wrote from Mexico City, "I hate a Yankee this day worse than I have ever done & my hatred is increasing every day," Lee replied: "We shall have to be patient, and suffer for a while at least; and all controversy, I think, will only serve to prolong angry and bitter feelings, and postpone the period when reason and charity may resume their sway."

The South was listening to Lee. Some whites had turned to violence, but an infinitely greater number were taking the path he constantly recommended. From Vicksburg, he heard from Brigadier General Nathaniel H. Harris, who had led Lee's brave Mississippi infantrymen through battle after battle, and had marched at their head as the survivors surrendered at Appomattox. He wrote: "Your great and wise example of retirement and peace, obedience to government and law we are all pursuing and following . . . All your old men here are peacefully at work trying to build up their shattered fortunes, and the Country, its peace and prosperity." More and more Southerners were honoring him not for what he had been in war, but for what he was in peace. The two editors of South Carolina's *Charleston Gazette* wrote Lee, offering free advertising space for Washington College in their newspaper, and one added: "The writer has an only son, and that son bears your name; but it was not in the day of your glory and power he was christened — he was born and baptized six months after your dark defeat."

II

At the beginning of December an apparent murder attempt occurred in one of the college dormitories. Early one snowy morning, just after he had placed an additional stick of firewood in his potbellied stove, an explosive charge went off in the room of Edward S. Joynes, professor of modern languages. The stove blew into a hundred hot metal fragments, every one of which miraculously missed Joynes, and set the college building afire. The blaze was soon out, but as a freshman said with a degree of understatement, "Of course it created something of a sensation." Professor Joynes had no doubt that an undergraduate had attempted to kill him by putting an explosive-filled log on the pile in his room, knowing that sooner or later he would slip it into his stove.

Lee did not know what to think. At chapel service that morning he engaged in some understatement of his own: "He then said he would be glad to have any one who knew about the explosion call at his office during the forenoon."

At eleven A.M. two shaken freshmen appeared, and Lee told them to wait outside his office. He was talking with Garnet Wolseley, a brilliant young British officer who had been with Lee's army as an observer in 1862; now on his way to an assignment in Canada, he had come to Lexington to see again the man he considered the finest soldier of the era. While the freshmen waited outside the half-open door, they heard Lee say that Nathan Bedford Forrest, the Confederate cavalry general from Tennessee, was the greatest genius to have emerged during the war. "He accomplished more with fewer troops than any other officer on either side." This electrified the two boys, who were from Tennessee.

The future commander of the British Army left, and Lee bade the two frightened boys be seated. One of them, Jonathan Graham, explained that someone had been stealing wood from the room where he and three other students studied. In order to find the culprit, Graham had bored a hole into a stick of firewood, filled it with gunpowder, and sealed it with clay. Then he replaced it on the pile of firewood, warning his study mates "under no circumstances to put that particular stick in our stove." Graham had thought that when the culprit, probably another student, put the loaded piece of firewood into his stove, wherever in the building it was, there would be a loud pop and a cloud of powder smoke — just enough to detect the offender, but not enough to do any damage.

What Graham had not known was that a janitor, charged with the responsibility for keeping sufficient wood in the professors' rooms, had been taking some that was already in the students' rooms rather than make a trip through the snow to a woodpile more than two hundred feet away. That was how the lethal log had come to Professor Joynes's room, and the rest was history.

When the unhappy student finished, Lee laughed. "Well, Mister Graham, your plan to find out who was taking your wood was a good one, but your powder charge was too heavy. The next time use less powder." The matter was closed.

☆   ☆   ☆

The year before, at Christmas of 1865, the students had been given a week's vacation. This year, Lee decided to follow the example of the University of Virginia, which was making only Christmas Day a holiday. Disappointed and indignant, the students petitioned the faculty to have the week's vacation restored, but the request was not granted.

Then came a confrontation. The students held a meeting and passed around a paper; those who signed pledged themselves not to attend any lectures from Christmas through New Year's Day. This was placed on the bulletin board; looking at the sixty-nine signatures already on it, some of the faculty talked of giving in to the students' demand.

Enter Robert E. Lee. He said in the hearing of a knot of students, "Every man that signs that paper will be summarily dismissed. If all sign it, I shall lock up the college and put the keys in my pocket."

One boy who had not signed, and was boarding with a family out in the country, told his roommate what the general had said. The roommate ran a mile and a half through the snow to scratch his name off the list; when he arrived, panting, at the bulletin board he found that other students had beaten him to it and had destroyed the petition and the list of names. Another student said, "The attendance at lectures that Christmas was unusually large."

Chapter 20

WITH THE YEAR 1867, all the events that white Southerners had been fearing began to unfold. On January 7, the Congress passed a resolution directing the House Judiciary Committee to inquire into President Johnson's conduct of office to see whether he could be tried for "high crimes and misdemeanors." While it was true that Johnson had been abrasive, inconsistent, and ill-advised, his great offense was that his policy toward the South was not the one the Radicals wished to impose.

On March 2 came a thunderous echo of the deliberations begun the year before by the Joint Committee on Reconstruction, at whose hearings Lee had testified. Spurred by the refusal of Southern legislatures to ratify the Fourteenth Amendment, with its provisions protecting blacks and restricting the rights of former Confederates to hold office, the Congress passed the first of four bills known as the Reconstruction Acts. "Whereas, no legal state governments exist . . . in the rebel states . . . said rebel States shall be divided into five military districts." On March 13, Virginia ceased officially to be a state, and became Military District Number One. Any civil government that did exist in the state was deemed to be purely provisional in nature, existing at the sufferance of Washington. The Congress declared that it had the right to abolish or change any aspect of local government throughout the South, at any time and without previous notice. With the exception of Tennessee, which had been brought back into the Union under special circumstances near the end of the war, the South was now formally and unequivocally a zone of military occupation, with no other status in the eyes of the Federal government. The lock was on.

Having finally made a reality of the "conquered provinces" view of the South, the Congress restated the price for readmission to the Union. Once again it combined political ostracism of Confederates and voting rights for the blacks. Under close Federal supervision, with blacks voting and many Confederates excluded, any former Confederate state could elect delegates to a state constitutional convention, as long as it included no Confederate officers or officials among those delegates. Then, if the convention adopted the Fourteenth Amendment and presented to the Congress a state constitution modeled on the United States Constitution, the Congress would let any such state back into the Union.

From the Northern point of view, this seemed a reasonable compromise between the South having representation in Congress, and continuing to have no representation. For the South, it was the final bad dream. The vote would confer on the blacks a status and power that Southern whites were unwilling for them to have and did not believe they could handle. With the disfranchising of so many Confederates — initially one out of every four white men was barred from voting or holding office — there would be more black voters than white in five Southern states. The Federally supervised state legislatures were certain to be coalitions of blacks and of whites whose essential qualification was that they had not fought for the Confederacy or held office under it. Opportunistic Northern whites would soon flock south; the real carpetbagger era was opening. Northerners would be elected to Southern legislatures by black voting majorities. Soon, the Federally appointed governor of Virginia would be a New Yorker.

For the next century, there would be differing views on how inefficient and corrupt these new state governments were or were not, and how much good for the blacks they did or did not accomplish, but one thing was instantly clear. The overwhelming majority of the eight million whites in the South felt no identification with the entire process and thought that it was being rammed down their throats with bayonets.

Mary Lee was beside herself with rage at all this. "It is bad enough to be the victims of tyranny," she wrote, "but when it is wielded by such cowards and base men ... it is indeed intolerable. The country that allows such scum to rule them must be fast going to destruction."

Another letter complained, "They still desire to grind to dust & wish to effect this purpose by working on the feelings of the low & ignorant negroes many of whom do not even comprehend what *a vote* means. My indignation cannot be controlled, and I wonder our people, helpless and disarmed as they are can bear it. Oh God how long?"

Ninety yards from where Mary sat writing this, Lee was at his desk, immediately coming to grips with the new political reality. "I look upon the Southern people as acting under compulsion," he wrote General Dabney H. Maury in New Orleans, but added that they should not leave the political arena. To Judge Robert Ould in Richmond he wrote, "I think all persons entitled to vote should attend the polls and endeavour to elect the best possible men to represent them in the convention, to whose decision every one should submit." It was what he had said on the road from Appomattox to Richmond, and he would say it again and again. Get back into the political process any way that you can. And with it was always this corollary, repeated now to Judge Ould: "The preservation of harmony and kind feelings is of the utmost importance."

II

Nine days after Virginia was stripped of its statehood, some Washington College students heard that white Northern speakers were going to make speeches to the blacks of Lexington that night. Five students, three from Texas, one from Georgia, and one from Alabama, angrily headed into the evening, not certain of what they were going to do. The boy from Alabama took along a pistol.

Coming to the schoolhouse in which the Freedman's Bureau conducted classes for blacks, the boy from Alabama went up to a window to see if anyone was inside. Suddenly, a black man stepped out of the shadows to intercept him. The startled boy drew his pistol and started hitting the black man with it. The other students pulled them apart and rushed the boy from Alabama into the night, but in a few minutes all were apprehended, except for the young man with the gun, who vanished.

A few more minutes, and the word was all over campus that fellow students had been in a fight with a black man at a meeting — Freedman's Bureau, white Northern agitators, damn Yankees — and had been thrown in jail. There were close to four hundred students now in the college, and most charged out of their rooms, determined to rescue their college mates. It looked as if there was about to be an angry march to the jail, and a scene similar to that when the horse thief had been imprisoned, except that this time Lee was at home, with no idea that anything was happening. The students were going to storm the jail and free their comrades.

Suddenly a student appeared as Lee had, but this was no ordinary student. He was Givens B. Strickler, the former captain of the Liberty Hall Volunteers who had led an attack that carried into the Union lines at Gettysburg, where he had been captured. "Steady men!" he was saying as he had heard it said, and had said it to others, on a score of battlefields. "Steady men! Steady men!" As each group stopped shouting to look at him, he added, "Remember General Lee! No violence! Remember General Lee. Let the law take its course. You must do what General Lee would wish."

The excited crowd dispersed. The four jailed students were tried by the mayor and fined for disturbing the peace. When they were released, they were asked to come to Lee's office. As they entered, they saw that the student from Alabama who had escaped detection was also there, voluntarily coming forward. This youth, who had carried the pistol and struck the black man, explained what had happened and said that the fault was entirely his. Lee nodded and instantly expelled him. The others he formally reprimanded and put on probation. By the time an official of the Freedman's Bureau wrote Lee a letter of complaint and inquiry, the offender was back in Alabama, and Lee's explanation of the actions he had taken satisfied the Freedman's Bureau. Lee understood better than anyone that this was now a situation in which one wrongful, passionate pull of a trigger could close Washington College, perhaps permanently.

Two years after Appomattox, Lee's attitudes were winning him friends in many places. In Poughkeepsie, New York, a "Lee Association" was formed at the Eastman Business College — a group of young Northern admirers. Lee wrote, accepting their offer of honorary membership. The *Daily Sentinel* of Evansville, Indiana, came out with an editorial urging the Democratic Party to nominate Lee for President of the United States in the 1868 elections. Jefferson Davis was released from prison; among the Northerners present in Richmond to sign his bail bond was Horace Greeley, an ardent Union man but one more Northerner who thought that enough was enough. Lee wrote to Davis, "Your release has lifted a load from my heart which I have not words to tell," but even though the former Confederate President was now out on bail and available to his former constituents while he awaited trial, it was to Lee that the South continued writing.

To Rob, who, like Rooney, was working hard on his Pamunkey farm, he wrote words about agriculture that had wider meaning: "You will gain by cultivating less and cultivating that well." Lee was cultivating one corner of a devastated land, one college in one town, but his thoughts ranged wide. A student from Lexington who lived at home with his family had broken his leg, and Lee called on him a number of times in the spring evenings to see how he was mending. The boy's mother recalled:

> He would sit and talk in the twilight . . .
> Once, I remember he sat still for sometime by the window and his face looked so sad. He spoke of the Southern people, of their losses, privations, and sufferings, and also of our vain struggle. "I cannot sleep," he said, "for thinking of it, and often I feel so weighted down with sorrow that I have to get up in the night and go out and walk till I thoroughly weary myself before I can sleep." That was the only melancholy sentence I ever heard him utter, and the only time I ever saw that heartbroken look on his face.

In the late spring of 1867, Lee found person after person railing against the Reconstruction Acts, against the Republican Party, against Washington, against the damn Yankees. To a Confederate widow who was expressing hatred for the North, he said: "Madam, do not train up your children in hostility to the government of the United States. Remember, we are all one country now. Dismiss from your mind all sectional feeling, and bring them up to be Americans."

III

On a starlit May evening shortly before final examinations began, two freshmen walked up Lexington's Main Street, talking intently, and sat on the doorstep of a merchant named William White to continue their earnest conversation.

The younger of the two was Jo Lane Stern, a great favorite of the Lees. On one occasion when Lee was out of town, Daughter told Stern that he could ride Traveller if he would go out to a friend's farm and bring back some celery to be used in the salad at the Episcopal church fair. It is doubtful that Lee would have approved of anyone else riding his horse, even for a worthy cause, but Stern had the distinction of being the only Washington College student to mount Traveller. Three years before this May, when Stern was fifteen, a Confederate officer had asked him to carry a message through an area just north of Richmond in which Sheridan's cavalry was operating. On the eve of the Battle of Yellow Tavern, Stern strolled past Federal patrols, carrying the message in his pocket; a fifteen-year-old boy ambling along a road was not the kind of Confederate courier they expected.

The older of the two freshmen was a veteran named Samuel Zenas Ammen, a descendant of Swiss-Germans who had settled in neighboring Botetourt County. He had served in both the Confederate Army and Navy and, near the end of the war, as a member of a mounted guerrilla unit operating along the West Virginia border. Ammen was to gain a reputation as the "most intellectual collegian" in the school; in time he would become the editor of the *Baltimore Sun.*

Ammen and Stern were discussing the tiny, struggling fraternity to which they belonged. Four Washington College students had founded Kappa Alpha in December of 1865; seventeen months later, there were only twelve members in good standing, and they did not even have a room of their own in which they could regularly meet. Of the twelve members, Ammen and Stern were the most interested in what they called "the Lodge," but even they were profoundly discouraged. On that doorstep on quiet Main Street, Ammen said, "The question we discussed was 'Shall we let the Lodge die?' We sat long considering the matter ... whether to succumb to our discouragements, or fight on.

Had we decided on K A's death, it had died. But we decided to keep up the fight, and from that time on our prospects improved."

Ammen had a vision of something different from the other fraternities that existed at Washington College and elsewhere. Like all his fellow students, he was intensely aware of Lee: "We likened him to Agamemnon, and we were his Achaioi, battling on the windy plains of Troy. Spiritually, then, he thoroughly dominated us." To Ammen and those who would join him in increasing numbers, Lee represented an ideal — "the chivalrous warrior of Christ, the Knight who loved God and country, honours and protects pure womanhood, practices courtesy and magnanimity of spirit, and prefers self-respect to ill-gotten wealth."

These two young men sitting on a doorstep in Lexington on a night in this postwar era were thinking toward a Southern equivalent of what was once said of Confucius: "He saved the blueprints of Chinese civilization." They wanted to preserve what they saw as being best in their nearly destroyed homeland, and they believed that the surest way to do it was to become spiritual followers of Lee. "Something might thus be saved," Ammen wrote, "from the wreck of material interests and political rights caused by the war."

Adopting the terms and rituals of chivalry, this handful of young men in Lexington became the Kappa Alpha Order. Alone among American fraternities, Kappa Alpha would dedicate itself to emulation of the character of an individual, Lee. Their fellowship would grow beyond the imagining of two young friends who "decided to keep up the fight" on an evening in 1867; one hundred and thirteen years later Kappa Alpha would be a national fraternity with more than seventy thousand living members, and chapters at one hundred and fifteen colleges and universities throughout the United States.

IV

As the students finished their final examinations in June, Lee and the trustees reviewed the second year of his administration. Not only had four hundred students been in residence, but some were from outside the South — Massachusetts, New Jersey, Pennsylvania, Kansas, even California were represented. The fund-raisers had again done well. The present faculty of fifteen would increase to twenty-two during the coming autumn, but sixty students would not be coming back — ten for disciplinary reasons, and fifty who had been "permitted to withdraw" for causes ranging from financial to academic.

As Lee walked home from the meeting, he passed by other results of his work. Under the supervision of his able young assistant, E. C. Gordon, new lawns, new trees, new walks under the trees had all come into place. The chapel was going up, and a gymnasium was under construction. The halls housing the two debating societies, the Graham and the Washington, had been enlarged. On other existing buildings, there were new roofs, new windows, fresh paint. In a few days, parents would be coming from all over the South to attend their sons' graduation; what they would see around them bore scant resemblance to the war-wrecked school Lee had taken over twenty-two months before.

Lee had changed the college, but the college was also changing him. Because he was worried about his health, he spoke in a letter to Rooney of resigning in another year and retiring "east of the mountains," but Rob knew that his father had "determined to devote himself entirely to the interest and improvement of that institution. From this resolution he never wavered."

Lee had discovered the charms of liberal education and the fact that there could be discipline without regimentation. Twenty-six months after Appomattox, the soldier of thirty-nine years' service was telling the faculty, "Make no needless rules." The essence of the future Honor Code of Washington and Lee University was present in these words in Washington College's catalogue for the coming academic year: "The discipline has been placed upon that basis on which it is believed experience has shown it can be most safely trusted — upon the honour and self-respect of the students themselves." Lee was extending his feelings about personal freedom in several directions. He was pushing as hard as any educator in the nation for an elective system and an expansion of that elective system. Whenever the students and faculty of V.M.I. and Washington College marched in a joint procession, to the sound of a drum, Lee made a point of marching out of step. To Assistant Professor Milton W. Humphreys, whom Lee had scolded, when he was an undergraduate, for saying that he considered his service in the Confederate Army as time lost, he now said, "The great mistake of my life was taking a military education."

V

Lee was sitting on the platform during the Commencement Exercises for the Class of 1867 when he saw a friend coming toward him out of the audience. This was a little boy, five years old, named Carter Jones. He was the son of Lexington's Baptist minister, and on the mornings when his father took his turn conducting the weekday chapel service, Carter would climb onto the bench where Lee was sitting amongst the students, and nestle beside him during the brief readings and prayers.

Today was different, but not to Carter. Seeing his friend on a platform instead of in the crowd, he escaped from his parents and climbed up on the stage. Lee was sitting in a chair, so the boy settled down at his feet, leaning his head against the knees of his grey-clad friend. A speaker was going on and on, and in a few minutes Carter was asleep.

This graduation ceremony called for Lee to stand as he congratulated the winners of prizes and handed their diplomas to the graduates. Rather than disturb his friend, Lee did this seated, and Carter slept through it all.

Chapter 21

T HE STUDENTS quickly dispersed for summer vacation. The previous summer Lee had sent Mary and his daughters to the nearby Rockbridge Baths resort while he remained in Lexington, catching up on his correspondence and starting his work as editor for the new edition of his father's Revolutionary War memoirs. This year he decided to take his first real vacation since the war.

The first part was an expedition with Mildred to the Peaks of Otter, a mountain thirty miles to the south that offered particularly beautiful views. Lee rode Traveller, and Mildred was on Lucy Long, a second-string war horse of Lee's that had been lost at the war's end and only recently recovered. All the clothes they would need for this five-day trip were in their saddlebags.

"We started at daybreak one perfect June day," Mildred said. Her father was "in the gayest humour, laughing and joking with me," and Traveller "seemed to sympathise with his master, his springy step, high head, and bright eye clearly showing how happy he was and how much interest he took in this journey."

At noon they dismounted and ate a picnic lunch while sitting on thick grass under a wild-plum hedge; it was the first time that Lee had eaten under the open sky since the war.

After lunch, they rode on to the James River. There was no bridge here. The man who ran the little ferry was one of Lee's veterans; he took them across and refused to accept payment, despite Lee's efforts to have him do so. Lee and Mildred thanked him and led their horses ashore. Mildred's account continued:

Further on the road, as our horses were climbing a steep rocky ascent, we met some little children, with very dirty faces, playing on the roadside. He spoke to them in his gentle, playful way, alluding to their faces and the desirability of using a little water. They stared at us with open-mouthed astonishment, and then scampered off up the hill; a few minutes later, in rounding this hill, we passed a little cabin, when out they all ran with clean faces, fresh aprons, and their hair nicely brushed, one little girl exclaiming, "We know you are General Lee! We have got your picture!"

The next morning, having spent the night at a small inn at the foot of the mountain, Lee and his daughter set off for the higher slopes on horseback, accompanied by the proprietor. They managed to get their horses to a point nearer the peak known as Sharp Top than anyone had previously ridden; then, tying their mounts to trees, they climbed the rest of the way on foot.

"When the top was reached," Mildred said, "we sat for a long time on a great rock, gazing down at the glorious prospect beneath. Papa spoke but a few words, and seemed very sad."

The plan was to ride south from here, visiting friends and returning to Lexington by a different route. That afternoon a thunderstorm overtook them.

We galloped back to a log cabin we had just passed. Papa lifted me off Lucy and, dripping with water, I rushed in, while he led the horse under an adjacent shed. The woman of the house looked dark and glum on seeing the pools of water forming from my dress on her freshly scoured floor, and when papa came in with his muddy boots on her expression was more forbidding and gloomy. He asked her permission to wait there until the shower was over, and praised her nice white floor, regretting that we had marred its beauty.

Lee's manner somewhat softened the woman; she asked them into the cabin's best room, which had on its walls colored prints of Lee, Stonewall Jackson, Jefferson Davis, and General Joseph E. Johnston.

When the shower ceased and papa went out for the horses, I told her who he was. Poor woman! She seemed stunned, and kept on saying: "What will Joe say? What will Joe say?" Joe was her husband, and had been . . . a soldier in the "Army of Northern Virginia."

That evening they arrived at the house of friends in what is now the town of Bedford. When Mildred appeared for dinner in a crinoline hoop skirt, her father could not imagine how this dress had made the journey, and was much amused when Mildred explained that it was possible to squeeze the hoops into saddlebags without breaking them. Two mornings later they rode on to the prosperous farm of Captain Pascal Buford, with whom Mary Lee, Daughter, and Agnes had spent a visit during 1863. In writing ahead to Captain Buford, Lee had said that he was bringing his "little girl," and Buford was expecting Mildred to be a child.

"Why, General," this robust old farmer in shirt sleeves said as he threw his arms open in greeting them, "you called her your 'little girl,' and she is a real chunk of a gal!"

Supper was an experience: "his table fairly groaned with good things."

Before he went to bed, Lee asked his host what time he wanted them to appear for breakfast.

With no idea that it might be considered funny, the captain replied, "Well, General, as you have been riding hard, and as you are company, we will not have breakfast tomorrow before sun-up." This meant that he expected them to be at the table at five A.M., and they were.

II

Back in Lexington after this very satisfactory trip — Captain Buford soon sent along a Jersey cow so that the Lees could have a milk supply right in their yard — Lee began planning a longer vacation for the entire family.

By the summer of 1867, two years after the war, a number of Southerners who could again afford it resumed their prewar practice of spending time at the famous hot-springs resorts of the South. It had been one of the great Southern social customs. While engaged in for pleasure, to escape the summer heat of New Orleans or Charleston or Baltimore by sojourning in the mountains of Virginia, North Carolina, or Tennessee, these yearly migrations had a subtle effect in unifying the

South. Families from places as disparate as Texas and Florida — and their eligible sons and daughters — would generally divide their time among two or more of these resorts. The men would talk politics; their wives would become friends; their children sometimes married each other. Many who had graced those prewar summers were dead, and many more were too poor to come again, but those who could now did. It was said of one war-impoverished Virginia belle that she set off for her former haunts with "one black silk dress and her grit."

The Lees had occasionally gone to some of the best-known springs before the war, and now Lee was seriously interested in any relief that their thermal baths might afford Mary. The family decided to go to what was perhaps the most famous of these resorts, the White Sulphur Springs, later known as the Greenbrier. One of its historians called it "practically the clearing house of the South"; before the war many political meetings had been held there, and many large financial ventures were planned by partners from different parts of the South who met there for discussions. Fifty miles west of Lexington, the hotel and its hot springs had formerly been in Virginia, but the war had changed that, along with so much else. In 1862 the western counties of Virginia had seceded from the secession, and the State of West Virginia, in which the White Sulphur was located, was born. Traveller would be returning to his birthplace, Greenbrier County.

They set off in July, making the trip in easy stages. Lee rode Traveller, accompanied by Professor White, the young former Confederate captain who had taken Lee to stay at his father-in-law's house his first night in Lexington. At the end of their day's ride they would rendezvous at a wayside inn with the rest of the party, who were traveling by a combination of carriages and stagecoaches and, where it was available, railway. Others in the group were Mary, their daughter Agnes, and their friend Mary Pendleton, a daughter of Lee's former general who was Lexington's Episcopal clergyman. Custis was traveling with them, carrying his mother on and off the different forms of transportation and placing her in her rolling chair at the stopping places.

At a roadside tavern where all the Lee party was stopping for midday dinner, a stagecoach from Covington pulled up, and a group of girls from Maryland, and their chaperones, climbed down from their uncomfortable seats. One of them was a young beauty named Christiana Bond. Like her companions, she was on her way to the White Sulphur and had no idea who was inside the little two-story tavern beside the road. Inside, she found out.

> . . . we were aware of some one standing at the turn of the steep stairway above us. Looking up, at the sound of a rich, beautifully modulated voice, we knew that we were in the presence of General Robert E. Lee, the hero of our dreams.
>
> The man who stood before us, the embodiment of a Lost Cause, was the realized King Arthur. The soul that looked out of his eyes was as honest and fearless as when it first looked on life. One saw the character, as clear as crystal, without complications or seals, and the heart, as tender as that of ideal womanhood. The years which have passed since that time have dimmed many enthusiasms and destroyed many illusions, but have caused no blush at the memory of the swift thrill of recognition and reverence which ran like an electric flash through one's whole body.
>
> General Lee stood above us on the stairway, clad in Confederate grey, his wide, soft hat in his hand, which still wore his riding gauntlet. He looked very tall and majestic standing there, beaming down upon us with his kindly, humorous smile and the wonderful beauty of his dark eyes. When we recovered our wits we found a courteous invitation was being extended to refresh ourselves in the rooms which had been reserved for Mrs. Lee's party.

That was the beginning of one more friendship between Lee and a young woman — innocent, needed by him, treasured by her.

III

The White Sulphur centered on an immense hotel building, white wood with large columns and wide-roofed porches that ran its length. Across stretches of lawn shaded by handsome old trees were rows of small whitewashed cottages, some yellow and some white. The Lee party was established in a cottage in Baltimore Row — a pleasant, modest structure with vines climbing around a roofed front porch. Mary Lee took her meals there.

The hotel's high-ceilinged rooms were filled with the news that Lee had arrived. That summer a tense social situation existed. Northerners, some of them army officers and their families, had come there on vacation, and were being left to themselves by the Southerners, who made up a large majority. On the first evening that Lee and his party were to appear in the huge dining room, some of the Southern hotel guests held hasty and inconclusive discussions about what they should do to acknowledge that Lee was about to dine in their midst. They were determined that, whatever the Northerners might do, some sign of respect must be paid to Lee, but when the dinner gong rang on the long verandah, nothing had been decided.

The Southerners need not have worried. When Lee entered the enormous room in his grey frock coat, Miss Mary Pendleton on his arm and Agnes following with Captain White and Custis, every one of the five hundred guests spontaneously rose and stood silent until they were seated.

In the evenings at the White Sulphur, there was a custom known as "the Treadmill." This was a great promenade. The guests walked up and down the long uncarpeted parlor in lines of three or four, stopping to chat and to make introductions. This was followed by a dance in the dining room, which was nightly converted to a ballroom by the removal of many of its tables. The Northerners had stayed out of this, even the prettiest Northern girls remaining seated on the sofas along the walls.

Lee sized up this situation, and one evening soon after his arrival had an opportunity to do something about it. Even though they were now in West Virginia, many of the Southerners felt particular bitterness toward those West Virginians who had broken away from Virginia and fought the South. They reasoned that a man from Massachusetts did not know any better, but there was no excuse for one of these former Virginians.

There was a West Virginia girl at the hotel who was, a former Confederate major said, "very beautiful and very attractive and more handsomely dressed than any woman at the Springs." The major had a less enthusiastic view of the girl's father: "The man had been a Union man during the war and had remained at home and made a fortune, while the men in the South had gone into the army and lost all they had."

The Southern men at the hotel would have been happy to forgive the splendid daughter her father's political sins. "But the women would have none of her," the major said, and their menfolk dared not risk their wrath. She became "very lonely."

One evening, when the Treadmill before the dance was in progress, this lovely girl was sitting in one of the parlors some distance away, reading. While some of the Northern girls sat near the Treadmill and later watched the dance, even though they were not asked to join in, this beauty felt more comfortable in being entirely away from the music.

She became aware that a brilliantly shined pair of black shoes had stopped before her. Looking up from her book, her eyes met those of General Robert E. Lee. He smiled, bowed, and asked for the honor of her company in the Treadmill. The young woman murmured something, put down her book, and took Lee's proffered arm.

The major knew a happy ending when he saw one: "When the promenade was over and General Lee led the girl to a seat, there was a general rush for introductions, and from that time on the girl not only had all the partners she wanted but actually became the belle of the season."

IV

The mornings of his vacation Lee kept to himself, riding Traveller through the beautiful surrounding hills. Returning his horse to the stables, he would walk about the resort's spacious grounds. Soon he found that two Englishmen who were touring the United States had heard that Lee was at the White Sulphur and had hastily come there to meet and spend time with him. In the noon hour, while some other guests were either immersed in the sulphur baths or drinking the hot mineral water, they would catch up to him in his walk and accompany him.

A young woman who knew the general asked him if this intrusion did not annoy him.

"Yes," Lee said, "they trouble me a little, but I think I get even with them. When they join me in my walks, I always take them down to the Springs and make them drink the water. They are too polite to refuse, when I hand them the glasses, and I fill them up with that nauseous water, and thus have my revenge."

At two o'clock, Lee would sit down to midday dinner in the large dining room. At his table was a new acquaintance, W. W. Corcoran, a millionaire banker from Washington who was to give the nation the Corcoran Gallery of Art, derived from his personal collection. He was sixty-nine; at the age of fifty-six he had retired from his eminently successful career as a banker and had begun a new career of giving away the money he had made. He had founded the Louise Home for Women in Washington, and his philanthropies embraced religious and educational institutions. Washington College was soon added to the list; in all, Corcoran would give the school thirty thousand dollars.

The late afternoon hours Lee spent with Mary, sitting on the porch of their cottage, often chatting with friends they had not seen for years. Even here, the public would intrude. Preceded only by the briefest introduction performed by companions who were passing the cottage, one man advanced up the steps to the porch where the Lees were sitting with friends. "Do I behold," this man said, "the honored roof that shelters the head of him before whose name the luster of Napoleon's pales into a shadow? Do I see the walls within which sits the most adored of men?" The self-styled orator had gained the porch; he turned to Mary. "Dare I tread the floor which she who is a scion of the patriotic house of the revered Washington condescends to hallow with her presence?"

Lee was speechless. The man was continuing, "Is this the portico that trails its vines over the noble pair — " when Mary smiled at him and cut in with, "Yes, this is our cabin; will you take a seat upon the bench?"

☆　☆　☆

In the evenings, during the dance, Lee sat at its edges, surrounded by a coterie of adoring Southern girls. This suited him perfectly; not only did he enjoy their lively company, but it protected him from Southern men who wanted to talk about the war or postwar politics. As for the younger men, some of whom had empty sleeves as evidence that they had been on the same battlefields with Lee, they were satisfied simply to approach his group long enough to ask one of the young ladies to dance.

On occasion Lee would sally forth from his defensive position to draw into the social mainstream those he felt were being neglected. One evening in the ballroom before the dance began, Lee was already sitting surrounded by his court of belles. Christiana Bond said that he looked far across the room, where "a group of recent arrivals sat somewhat apart, with the air of mere lookers-on. They were from a Northern State and the name was one celebrated in the annals of the war." It was the party of Andrew Gregg Curtin, the wartime governor of Pennsylvania and a man who had been one of Lincoln's closest advisers. Curtin's creation of the "Pennsylvania Reserves" and his efficient and energetic mobilizing, equipping, and supplying of his state's abundant manpower had played no small part in the Confederacy's defeat.

Lee asked if any of his young friends had made the Curtin group's acquaintance. They shook their heads; what they meant was "Certainly not!" Lee pointed out to Christiana and the others that "we were on our own soil and owed a sacred duty of hospitality." The girls busied themselves with their fans.

Lee stood. "I have tried in vain," he said, dropping his cheerful manner, "to find any lady who has made acquaintance with the party, and is able to present me. I shall now introduce myself, and shall be glad to present any of you who will accompany me."

These girls thought, at least, that they would be willing to die for General Lee, but as he stood waiting, there were no volunteers to cross the ballroom and be introduced to the Pennsylvanians. Finally Christiana rose and stood beside him. "I will go, General Lee, under your orders."

"Not under my orders," Lee said gently, "but it will gratify me deeply to have your assistance."

As the young girl and the general crossed the ballroom, he stopped at its center, under a chandelier on which many candles were burning. Fifty-eight years later Christiana remembered exactly what he said to her: "He told of the grief with which he found a spirit of unreasoning resentment and bitterness in the young people of the South, of the sinfulness of hatred and social revenge, of the duty of kindness, helpfulness and consideration for others."

Christiana impulsively replied, "But, General Lee, did you never feel
resentment towards the North?"

Standing in the colors thrown by the candlelight through the crystal
pendants of the chandelier, Lee told her that he was neither bitter nor
resentful. "When you go home," he added, "I want you to take a message to your young friends. Tell them from me that it is unworthy of
them as women, and especially as Christian women, to cherish feelings
of resentment against the North. Tell them that it grieves me inexpress-
ibly to know that such a state of things exists, and that I implore them
to do their part to heal our country's wounds."

They walked on across the ballroom toward the Pennsylvanians,
who rose to welcome them as they came.

V

During his vacation, Lee had some promising news. Although he was
possessive of his daughters, he truly wanted his sons to marry, and had
been heartbroken when Rooney's wife died. Now Rooney wrote his
mother from his farm on the Pamunkey that he was in love with Mary
Tabb Bolling, a girl from Petersburg, and hoped that she would marry
him.

Lee was delighted. During the long and terrible siege of Petersburg,
he had sometimes gone to the Bollings' house to share what little they
had to eat, and had admired the tall young girl, now nineteen, who
might become the bride of his six-foot-three son Rooney, who was
thirty. "I saw the lady when I was in Petersburg," he wrote Rob, "and
was much pleased with her."

☆   ☆   ☆

In the August 10 edition of the *White Sulphur Echo* — the motto of the
spa's newspaper was "We Purge the Truth of Its Impurities" — there
were two advertisements, one above the other, that were symbolic. One
was for Washington College, and had been placed there by Lee. The

one that happened to appear directly beneath it was from the Brazil Emigration Agency, advertising here as elsewhere in the South: "The Government of Brazil will advance passage, provisions for six months, the first seeds and implements, 150 acres of land, with a provisional home, to emigrants." There had been severe crop failures in parts of the South during the summer. Some areas had virtually recovered from the war, but others were still suffering.

Through all that he read and heard, Lee hewed to a line that was clear to him, if not to others. A rumor swept the hotel that General and Mrs. Grant had made a reservation and would arrive in a few days. One of Lee's circle of belles, tired of being told by him that she should be friendly to every Northerner in sight, turned to him and said, "Well, General Lee, they say General Grant is coming here next week; what will you do then?"

Christiana Bond said that "some of us would gladly have slain her on the spot," but Lee was already answering, an "earnest, far-away look" in his eyes.

"If General Grant comes I shall welcome him to my home, show him all the courtesy that is due from one gentleman to another, and try to do everything in my power to make his stay here agreeable."

Grant did not come, but Lee's example was beginning to penetrate even the hardest young Confederate hearts. Christiana said that "we saw, moreover, his absolute loyalty to the allegiance he had sworn when he laid down his arms. His whole soul was engaged in the work of reconstruction, and he lost no opportunity to promote it socially."

Chapter 22

AT JUST THE TIME that the Lees were to move on to another resort
known as the Old Sweet, he became sick. It appeared to be a bad
cold with rheumatic complications. In a few days he recovered suffi-
ciently to ride Traveller at a slow pace to join his family at the Old
Sweet. Here, however, he was in bed for two weeks, and wrote the authorities at the college that they must finish their preparations for the
autumn session without his assistance. Eventually, stopping each day
after a short ride, he managed to get himself and Traveller back to
Lexington on September 17.

Here there was news to cheer a sick man. Rooney and Tabb were
engaged. The wedding was to be in Petersburg at the end of November. The nation might be embroiled in important events — congressional elections nearly as important as those the year before, and the
impending collision between President Johnson and the Congress that
would bring about his impeachment trial — but in the Lee house all
the talk was of Rooney's wedding. Mary Lee was too infirm to make
the trip, and Agnes decided to stay home with her. Mildred was practically there already, wild with excitement at being a bridesmaid.
Custis would go down from Lexington, and Rob would come up to
Petersburg from his farm.

Lee was happy with Rooney's choice of a bride, but he did not want
to see Petersburg again. Of all the suffering he had seen Southern civilians endure in the war, the harshest had been in that city's bloody ten-
month siege; with its end had come the final swift collapse. The people
of Petersburg had backed him to the end, befriending him in every way
during the siege, inviting him to dine and sending food to his tent; his

worst memory was of the night he had had to march away from them and their wrecked city, leaving them to the oncoming Federals. For Lee, Petersburg was still that place of exploding shells and hungry children; he could think of it and its gallant population in no other way.

He wrote Rooney that his health was better, but that he felt he would really see little of the bride or the groom in the midst of a busy wedding and reception; wouldn't it make more sense for them to come up to Lexington right after the wedding for a nice visit with all the family there?

Rooney's response was to travel to Lexington as soon as he received his father's letter, and depart with Lee's promise to attend. He also had with him his father's measurements for a black broadcloth suit that was to be made at a tailor's in Richmond — Lee's first new suit since the war. Soon Lee received a letter from one of his former generals, William Mahone, asking him to stay at his house in Petersburg during Rooney and Tabb's wedding.

To open a letter from Mahone was to hear the guns firing again. "He was the sauciest-looking little manikin imaginable," a Confederate wrote of Mahone. "His person and attire were simply unique: he was not over five feet seven inches tall, and was as attenuated as an Italian greyhound . . . his nose was straight, prominent, and aggressive . . . he wore a large sombrero hat, without plume, cocked on one side . . . boots as small as a woman's . . . no sword, but . . . in his hand he carried a slender wand of a stick." Mahone's star rose throughout the war; the little Irishman got better as things got worse. In the middle of the disaster at Sayler's Creek, just days before Appomattox, Lee saw thousands of his demoralized men fleeing past him in such disorganized fashion that he cried out, "My God! Has the army been dissolved?" It was Mahone, at the head of his steadfast division, who answered quietly, "No, General. Here are troops ready to do their duty."

To be in Mahone's company would be to relive it all, but Lee wrote and said that he would be delighted to stay at his house.

II

Custis accompanied his father to Richmond. Both of them had been summoned to appear, two days before Rooney's wedding, at the Federal Circuit Court. They were to hold themselves ready for possible questioning as witnesses in the pending trial of Jefferson Davis, now free on bail. Then they could go on to Petersburg and Rooney's wedding.

On the evening of November 25, the day before he was to appear in court, Lee went to a party in Richmond and saw Jefferson Davis for the first time since the war. The next day he wrote Mary that Davis looked "astonishingly well, and is quite cheerful. He inquired particularly after you all." It was a strange meeting, the former President chatting with the former military chief of a separate Southern nation that had existed for just four years. They were in Richmond, capital of that Confederacy and of Virginia, a city now considered not to be the capital of anything, but only the headquarters of Federal Military District Number One.

After a day's delay, on the afternoon of November 27, Lee was sworn as a witness in the grand jury proceedings preliminary to a possible trial of Jefferson Davis. Lee did not know all the facts, but the Federal government was taking an ambivalent attitude toward Davis, just as it had toward him, although for different reasons. Davis refused to ask for a pardon; he wanted a trial, which he thought would find him innocent of treason. Even before Davis was released on bail, Chief Justice Salmon P. Chase of the United States Supreme Court had pointed out to the attorney general that a state's right to secede had never been decided in the courts, and that to try Jefferson Davis for treason was to ensure that precisely that question would be brought before the Supreme Court and the nation. There was a possibility that the Supreme Court might be forced to rule that the North had violated the law by marching into the South. Secession was dead because it had been slain on the battlefield; why not leave it there?

Caught between a desire to punish Davis further and a fear that excellent defense lawyers might thereby have the opportunity to appear before the nation's highest court to argue, even now, the right of a state to leave the Union, the government prosecutors kept shifting their ground. Conveniently losing the record of their earlier indictment of Davis for treason, they revised the charges against him to read as if what had happened between 1861 and 1865 had been a massive disturbance of the peace within an existing entity, rather than a war against the Union waged by a confederation of seceding states. They hoped that this would somehow avoid the secession issue.

It was in connection with this revised indictment that Lee had been summoned to answer questions in front of the Federal grand jury that might be asked to recommend that Davis finally be brought to trial. There was an element of threat and coercion in the treatment of Lee and the other witnesses. Lee was well aware that the government could at any time reopen its treason case against him; further, he was a presumptive conspirator in this case. The implication was that if Lee would turn state's evidence and agree with the prosecution's contention that Davis was the man ultimately responsible for all Confederate military actions, Lee would have nothing further to fear from Washington. As soon as Lee was on the witness stand, the Federal attorney began a line of questioning meant to establish the idea that Lee was just a military man who had no choice but to carry out the orders given by a civilian chief executive.

Lee saw the plan; initially he fell back. He could not deny that Davis was commander-in-chief of the Confederate Army; the Confederate Constitution provided for that, just as Lincoln had been the Union commander-in-chief. It also could not be denied that Lee and the other Confederate generals had followed the orders given by Davis.

That was as far as the Federal attorney could take him; Lee dug in his heels. "I am responsible for what I did," he told the grand jury, "and I cannot now recall any important movement I made which I would not have made had I acted entirely on my own responsibility."

After two hours devoted to a simple recital of the movements made by the Confederate forces under his field command — facts known to everyone, but which were now to be put in the record as evidence of treasonous military activity — Lee was excused.

III

The next afternoon, Lee and Custis boarded a private railroad car for the wedding guests that had been attached to the regular train going the twenty-two miles from Richmond to Petersburg. It was a short trip for the cheerful and excited young men and women who were all around him, but Lee was silent as the train passed the little stations that had been the scene of terrible battles. He was bracing himself for Petersburg and beggars among the ruins.

The train rolled into a city that had been rebuilt. Gleaming draft horses pulled wagons laden with goods. Well-dressed people walked the streets. At the station, thousands were waiting for Lee. As he stepped onto the platform, a band thundered into "Dixie," and the crowd went wild.

Little General Mahone came forward, as composed among this roaring throng as on the day he had said, "Here are troops ready to do their duty." Since the war, he had become the leading railroad entrepreneur in Virginia. Outside the station was Mahone's carriage, drawn by four white horses. Men in the crowd wanted to take the horses out of their traces and pull the carriage themselves. Only when Lee said that if men were going to pull the carriage, he would have to pull it too, did they draw back and let them drive off amid the frenzied cheering.

At Mahone's house, a midafternoon dinner was waiting. Another Confederate officer who had been invited had an eye for the amusing scene that followed.

> General Mahone drew his chair back, and was in the act of sitting down, when Mrs. Mahone, with a woman's quick intuition, noting that General Lee was reverently standing, said: "Mr. Mahone, perhaps the General is accustomed to saying grace."
> At that General Mahone, who was about half way down in his seat, stopped in mid-air, and turning his face up towards General Lee, gave him one of the most puzzled and comical looks that I ever saw on a human countenance. But he said nothing; which General Lee, appreciating, quietly remarked to Mrs. Mahone: "Well, Madam, at home I usually do so," the meantime proceeding to sit down, as nobody had yet asked him to officiate. In those days the

saying of grace was not part of General Mahone's table ritual. He could charge a battery, or retake a "crater," but to ask a man to lead in prayer was beyond the limit of his courage.

☆　☆　☆

After Lee had called on Tabb, presenting her with a string of pearls, he went to see old friends, the Banisters. As with the Bollings, to whom he was now to be related by marriage, he had shared many a spartan Sunday dinner with them during the siege. He found this household in happy excitement; their daughter Mollie was to be one of her cousin Tabb's ten bridesmaids at the wedding this evening. Lee saw again another survivor of the siege; young Anne Banister had been thirteen when the shells were flying through these skies. Now she was sixteen, and tonight she would wear her first long party dress. Lee told her that he wanted to have the honor of taking her in to supper at the reception after the wedding.

"I was so happy," the girl said as she recalled being singled out this way, "I literally danced around him in my delight."

The next morning Lee came downstairs at General Mahone's before breakfast to write his wife a letter.

My Dear Mary:

Our son was married last night and shone in his happiness. The bride looked lovely and was, in every way, captivating. The church was crowded to its utmost capacity, and the streets thronged.

The streets had indeed been thronged, the first spectators lining the sidewalks three hours before the wedding, and they had not come to see the bride. The father of the groom had arrived in General Mahone's open carriage drawn by four white horses, and he was wearing his new black broadcloth suit — the first time since the war that he had appeared in anything except Confederate grey.

Lee tried to describe a bit more of the wedding and reception, but, other than mentioning the names of some of the guests, the best he could do was a description of Mildred as bridesmaid: "Mildred was all life, in white and curls." He was not a social reporter: "Everything went off well, and I will enter into details when I see you."

Chapter 23

"THE MOUNTAINS AND HILLS are covered with a thick mantle of snow," Lee wrote Mary's cousin Markie Williams on New Year's Day of 1868, "and present this morning a mild representation of Alaska."

This year, opening in winter silence in Lexington, was to bring the nation the unprecedented convulsion of President Johnson's impeachment trial. The troubled process of readmitting former Confederate states to the Union continued; by year's end, only Virginia, Texas, and Mississippi would still be zones of military occupation. In the first presidential election since Appomattox, the Republicans would rely on the newly enfranchised blacks of the South to give them the margin of victory; before the year was out, Ulysses S. Grant, who had become embroiled in one of the crises that precipitated the impeachment trial, would be elected President of the United States.

In Lexington, explosive events were to threaten the life of Washington College. Lee would come to national attention several times during 1868, both as the subject of bitter Northern attacks and astonishing Northern tributes.

As the year began, Lee was untouched by the impending political battles. In his office, he finished editing his father's Revolutionary War memoirs, adding the prefatory biographical sketch of Light-Horse Harry that the publisher, C. B. Richardson, had been confident would guarantee a large sale because it was from Lee's pen. Neither Lee nor Richardson could know how heatedly the name of Lee would be attacked and defended in the coming months; when Richardson saw that the recent war was being fought all over again during the presidential campaign, he delayed publication for close to two years.

Despite his varied paperwork and usual heavy correspondence, Lee was working hard and successfully on the development of the college. The new chapel, made of brick and native limestone, was almost finished. A new dining hall would soon open; Lee proudly described it as "capable of comfortably accommodating 175 persons." The library, an empty-shelved wreck three years before, now had five thousand books. A planetarium was bought for the astronomy students; when it had first been offered to Lee in October of 1865, he had made the terse notation "No money" on the letter from its inventor. There were four hundred and eleven students in the college, ten times the number present at the war's end, and three times as many as enrolled during Lee's first year as president. A small but growing number were from outside the South.

Lee's commitment to his postwar career continued to deepen. When one of his generals, Richard S. Ewell, sent the college five hundred dollars with the stipulation that it be used to increase Lee's salary, Lee wrote Ewell asking that he allow the gift to be used instead for the school's general endowment, and added, "For my own part I much enjoy the charms of civil life, and find too late that I have wasted the best years of my existence."

Excellent job offers kept coming to Lee; his son Rob described one as "an offer that he should be at the head of a large house to represent southern commerce, that he should reside in New York, and have placed at his disposal an immense sum of money." In declining this, Lee wrote something close to a summation:

> I am grateful, but I have a self-imposed task which I must accomplish. I have led the young men of the South in battle; I have seen many of them die on the field; I shall devote my remaining energies to training young men to do their duty in life.

As for those "remaining energies," Lee was working as much as ever, but his arteries were hardening. One of his former officers, Lieutenant James B. Craighill, now saw him for the first time since the war and said, "He looked twenty years older than he seemed to be as I remembered him in Richmond. His hair and beard were very gray, almost white in fact, and he had taken on so much flesh that he had become quite portly. But with added years had come added majesty."

Lee was prepared for death; indeed, he expected it to come at any time. In his New Year's letter to Markie, he spoke of "those eternal shores to which I am fast hastening," and in urging his new daughter-in-law Tabb to visit them in Lexington he said, "You must not postpone your visit too long, or you may not find us here."

None of this changed his approach to daily tasks. If death came, in peace as it nearly had in war, it would find him doing exactly what he thought he ought to be doing. All that he was planning at his desk and discussing with the faculty and trustees was costing money and would require even more of it, and he was pleased to see a new and particularly promising source of money on the horizon. A fund-raising meeting for Washington College was to be held in New York City at the beginning of March. Scores of prominent New Yorkers were to attend; a crowd of five hundred potential contributors was expected. It was a Northern tribute to Lee's conduct since the war and a statement of support for Southern education in this difficult time. The fact that such a meeting could be held in the city where a crowd had shouted "Hang Lee!" three years before showed that an increasing number of Northerners were in a magnanimous mood and were willing to believe that the leading enemy general of 1865 could be an important friend in 1868. The master of ceremonies and principal speaker was to be Henry Ward Beecher, the nation's best-known and best-paid preacher, who had been one of the first Northerners to perceive and to hail Lee's conciliatory postwar actions and attitudes. Washington College needed Henry Ward Beecher far more than he needed it, and his support symbolized the good fortune that now seemed to attend the school into which Robert E. Lee daily placed so much effort and hope.

All the good intentions of the friends of Washington College were about to be blasted by an incident of seemingly limited importance. A fracas in Lexington was to give Washington College and its leader a bad press as far away as Boston and Chicago.

On the afternoon of February 4, a Union Army veteran named E. C. Johnston went skating on the long stretch of ice above the dam on the North River. It was a cheerful, peaceful scene of children shouting and young men skating up beside girls whose faces were flushed from the cold, but Johnston's appearance on the ice changed things. He was thought of as a particularly meddling Yankee, who taught in an

American Missionary Association school for blacks and ran a store that was considered to be a carpetbagger intrusion into the local economy. Johnston was well aware of all this hostility; although no one had physically attacked him in his more than two years in Lexington, he carried a concealed pistol, and had it with him even for this outing on the ice.

As soon as he got onto the ice, all the nearby skaters deliberately turned their backs on him. Johnston skated down the river for more than a mile, alone. Turning a bend, he found a new crowd of skaters, including town boys and Washington College students. These greeted him with catcalls when he passed. As he came back the way he had come, several youths skated toward him, shouting, and a twelve-year-old boy came up to him and yelled into his face, "You son of a bitch!"

Johnston grabbed the boy with one hand, drew his pistol with the other, and told the terrified lad that he would shoot him if he used those words again. As Johnston let the boy go and skated off, the entire crowd surrounded him, cursing and shouting "Hang him!" He was told to leave town and was warned that if he said anything to the authorities about these threats, men would come to his store and lynch him. Johnston scrambled up the riverbank, pelted with chunks of ice and stones that caused some bumps and bruises. That night a group of men appeared in front of his store, pounded on the door, banged the shutters, cursed, and eventually went on their way.

The next day, Johnston started complaining to the authorities. Within a few days, a major general of the occupation forces was in Lee's office, armed with the names of three students who were alleged to have been involved. After the general left, Lee called them in; two admitted to being in the altercation and were told by Lee that they would be leaving school, and the third, who had been present but took no part, asked permission to withdraw from the college and was granted it. The major general sent a report to the adjutant general's office in Washington, closing the case and adding, "Mr. Johnston is partly to blame himself, as he threatened to shoot one of the small boys when they first set on him."

Johnston soon packed up the stock of his store and left for Covington, Virginia, claiming that word had been sent him that he and his store were to be the destination of a riotous nighttime student march. As far as he and his friends in Lexington and elsewhere were concerned, he had received no justice in Lexington and insufficient protection from the United States Army. They intended to complain about all this and to criticize the students of Washington College and its president. They were going to write letters, and their timing was remarkable.

II

 Eight days after the major general's report was written about the incident on the ice, and two weeks before the scheduled fund-raising meeting for Washington College in New York, Lee's name was suddenly the subject of a sharp dispute on the floor of the United States Senate. The abrupt exchange had nothing to do with recent events or with Washington College and, in fact, had little to do with what the Senate was debating. Nonetheless, at this moment when the House of Representatives was about to vote that the Senate bring the President to trial for "high crimes and misdemeanors," and every legislator was exercised about the underlying issues of Reconstruction and the political fate of blacks and whites in the South, it was not a good time for Lee to have his name mentioned in any manner.

 The Senate was arguing whether to seat Philip F. Thomas, the properly elected junior senator from Maryland. The Radicals did not dispute that he had been legally elected, but they were refusing to let him serve on the grounds that he had consorted with Confederates right to the outbreak of the war and that his son had served in the Confederate Army.

 The Radicals were to succeed in rejecting this senator, but in the course of the debate on his actions on the eve of war, examples were given of other men's behavior during those same April days of 1861. Senator Simon Cameron of Pennsylvania, who had then been Lincoln's secretary of war, rose to state what he believed to be the facts concerning Lee's conduct at that critical hour.

 When Lee was offered command of the Union Army, Cameron said, "it was accepted by him verbally, with the promise that he would go into Virginia and settle his business and then come back to take command. He never gave us an opportunity to arrest him; he deserted under false pretenses."

That was exactly the reverse of the truth: Lee had declined the offer when it was made by the government's go-between, who was not Senator Cameron. Though he had been secretary of war, Cameron had not been present on that occasion, nor had he been present when Lee had his final painful talk with the army's seventy-four-year-old commander, his friend and mentor Winfield Scott. "I suppose you will go with the rest," a staff officer in the corner heard Scott say to Lee, making it clear that Scott understood that the man he had called "America's very best soldier" was about to join the other Southerners who were resigning. Indeed, Scott understood Lee's intention so well that he urged Lee to resign quickly, and within forty-eight hours Lee did.

On the Senate floor, nearly seven years later, here was this matter-of-fact statement that Lee had lied and deserted, made by a man whose position at the time seemed to guarantee the accuracy of what he said. It was about to enter the nation's records as undisputed fact.

The senior senator from Maryland rose. He was Reverdy Johnson, no relation to the President but, like him, a Southerner who had remained loyal to the Union during the war. Now he found its Reconstruction policy harsh and impractical. As a Democrat, he was under almost constant fire from the large Republican majority in this chamber, and today, fighting a losing battle to get the Senate to accept the credentials of the junior senator from his state, the last thing he needed was an additional duel about a man whose name was anathema to the Radicals. Although he was a friend of Lee's, Senator Johnson did not know what had happened when Lee ceased being a colonel in one army and in a few days appeared as a general in an opposing one; at that time few people did know. Nonetheless, he was certain that Lee could never have lied, never have deserted, and he met the charge head on. With just one question, he extracted from Cameron the admission that he had not been present when Lee made his alleged promise to fight for the Union. Cameron went on to insist, however, that his information came "through a gentleman who had my confidence and in whom I relied entirely."

"That is another matter," said Johnson, who had cross-examined many a witness in his younger days as a lawyer. It was hearsay evidence, and Johnson emphasized this by saying of Lee's supposed pledge that he would lead the Union Army, "The statement was not made to the honorable member."

On the defensive, Cameron replied, "I have no doubt of its truth."

"That I am equally sure of," Johnson said, "but I doubt very much its truth. It is not in keeping with the character of Lee."

This word on Lee's behalf brought a derisive laugh from Senator John Conness of California, happily joined in by many others.

Johnson turned and faced the Republican side of the aisle. "Gentlemen may laugh, but I say to the honorable member from California, who engages in merriment, that General Lee is as honorable a man as any to be found in the State of California. He has offended; that I admit."

By the time Lee saw the transcript, the Senate was preparing for the trial of President Andrew Johnson. Nonetheless, Lee felt compelled not only to thank his senatorial defender, but also to put on paper for the only time his account of the matter. He identified the offer of command of the Union Army as coming from Francis Preston Blair, Sr., a Republican leader, the conversation being "at his invitation, and, as I understood, at the instance of President Lincoln."

Lee explained his decision simply. "After listening to his remarks, I declined the offer he made me, to take command of the army that was to be brought into the field; stating, as candidly and courteously as I could, that, though opposed to secession and deprecating war, I could take no part in an invasion of the Southern States."

Lee then mentioned his interview with Winfield Scott and his resignation, saying that he still "hoped peace would be preserved; that some way would have been found to save the country from the calamities of war." Thousands could have testified to what happened next: Virginia seceded; the North was clearly going to march on the South; Lee accepted command of Virginia's forces when he was asked to do so.

If Lee thought that with this letter he had cleared his name from public criticism and could look forward to a quiet spring with his family and students, he was mistaken.

Known as "the handsomest man in the Army," this was First Lieutenant Robert E. Lee of the Engineers at the age of thirty-one. This portrait was painted by William E. West in Baltimore in March of 1838, and was the first picture of any kind made of him. Lee graduated from West Point in 1829, was married in 1831, and at the time of this portrait was the father of three children. *(Washington and Lee University)*

RIGHT Painted by West at the same time as the portrait on the preceding page, Lee's wife, Mary Anna Randolph Custis Lee, was twenty-nine. The great-granddaughter of Martha Washington and sole heiress to thirteen thousand acres of Custis land, she was exceptionally well-read, and spoiled and headstrong. *(Washington and Lee University)*

BELOW By the close of the Civil War, Mrs. Lee had become an arthritic invalid who bitterly condemned the Federal government for its Reconstruction policies and for its confiscation of Arlington, her family home. This photograph was made in Lexington, Virginia, by Michael Miley, a Confederate veteran. *(University Library Archives, Miley Collection, Washington and Lee University)*

RIGHT General Ulysses S. Grant, in a picture made by the noted photographer Mathew Brady in 1864. The surrender terms Grant offered in April of 1865 impressed Lee as being extremely generous and honorable. From the day of his surrender until his death in 1870, Lee never allowed an unkind word about Grant to be spoken in his presence, and in 1869 he accepted President Grant's invitation to call on him at the White House. *(Library of Congress)*

ABOVE Union soldiers stand in front of the massive portico of Arlington House, the Custis mansion in which the Lees lived many of the years before the war. Standing on a bluff overlooking Washington from the Virginia side of the Potomac River, the house and its eleven hundred acres were seized by Federal forces in the first days of the war, and became Arlington National Cemetery. *(National Archives)*

A Northern artist named A. R. Waud had been following the Union armies, and quickly made this sketch when Lee rode away from the McLean House at Appomattox Court House, where he had just signed the surrender terms. It is the only record of the occasion made from life. Note the Union officer at left raising his hat to Lee as he passes by on his famous horse Traveller. *(Library of Congress)*

Lee on "the day but one" after he returned to his rented house in Richmond following his surrender at Appomattox Court House. Mathew Brady had been photographing the Union Army during the war; now he appeared and asked Lee to pose for him. "It is utterly impossible, Mister Brady," Lee answered. "How can I sit for a photograph with the eyes of the world upon me as they are today?" Brady asked a friend to intercede with Mrs. Lee, and soon Lee reappeared and said, "Very well, Mister Brady..." *(Library of Congress)*

The Lees' oldest son, Major General Custis Lee. A bachelor, on his father's death in 1870 he succeeded him as president of Washington College, then renamed Washington and Lee University, and served in that position until 1897. In 1883 the United States Supreme Court ruled that the wartime confiscation of Arlington had been illegal, and Custis, who had been the rightful heir to that estate, accepted the government's offer of $150,000 for the property. *(Collection of Mrs. Hunter deButts)*

Mary, the Lees' oldest daughter. Sharp-tongued, fond of the outdoors, she was noted for a fearlessness exemplified by her taking solitary walks through a countryside where robberies were known to occur. Like her sisters, she was intelligent and well-read; also like them, she never married. *(Collection of Mrs. Hunter deButts)*

The Lees' second son, Major General W. H. F. Lee, known to one and all as Rooney Lee. A kindly and popular man, given to running up debts while at Harvard, he was stricken by tragedies. His two children died in infancy, and his beloved young wife died while he was a wounded prisoner of war. After the war, during which Federal forces had burnt his house, he married happily and began a family whose descendants are alive today. *(Collection of Mrs. Hunter deButts)*

Captain Robert E. Lee, Jr., the Lees' youngest son. He started the war as a private in the Rockbridge Artillery, and on the battlefields of both Second Manassas and Antietam his father failed to recognize him because he was so covered with dirt, powder, and sweat. Like his brother Rooney, Rob farmed the remaining Custis lands after the war and started a family that carries on the line of Robert E. Lee. *(Collection of Mrs. Hunter deButts)*

Some of Lee's students. This is the first group picture of the Kappa Alpha Order, founded at Washington College in the autumn of 1865. From this handful of young men, all but one of them Confederate veterans, there grew a national fraternity dedicated to the emulation of Lee's character. At present there are more than seventy thousand living members. The student on the left of the front row was the Order's guiding spirit, Samuel Zenas Ammen, a veteran of both the Confederate Army and Navy and later editor of the *Baltimore Sun*. *(Kappa Alpha Order)*

The historic colonnade at Washington and Lee University in Lexington, Virginia. Except for the structure on the right, Lee would have seen all these buildings when he arrived in September of 1865 to become president of what was then Washington College. His first office can be identified by the open window on the second floor of the building on the left. *(Washington and Lee University)*

Lee's second and final office, in the basement of the chapel whose construction was one of his first priorities. It was here that he talked to students whose grades or behavior troubled him. One of them later wrote, "An invitation to visit General Lee in his office was the most dreaded event in a student's life." Everything in the room, including the papers on the table, has been left just as it was on the day he fell fatally ill. *(Sally Mann Photo, Washington and Lee University)*

The house on the campus where the Lees lived during most of his presidency, from late 1865 until June of 1869. Then they moved into the new President's House, a handsome larger structure built for them next door by the school's trustees. *(Washington and Lee University)*

Every day that he could, Lee went for a long ride on Traveller in the late afternoon. This lithograph is based on a photograph made by Michael Miley in 1866 at the Rockbridge Baths, eleven miles from Lexington. *(Michael Miley Collection, Washington and Lee University)*

Mildred, Lee's youngest daughter. Neither Lee nor his daughters were aware of how possessive he was, or of how much they acquiesced in that possessiveness. After his death, Mildred wrote, "To me he seems a Hero — and all other men small in comparison!" *(Collection of Mrs. Hunter deButts)*

Agnes, the prettiest of the Lee daughters. Breaking off her romance with Confederate Colonel Orton Williams, whom the war had turned into a hard-drinking and violent man, she was soon stunned by the news that he had been arrested within Union lines wearing a United States Army uniform, and hanged as a spy. A friend called it "a shock to Agnes from which she never recovered." *(Collection of Mrs. Hunter deButts)*

Taken in 1869 at the White Sulphur Springs resort in West Virginia now known as the Greenbrier, this is the only photograph, wartime or postwar, that shows Lee with a group of his generals. Lee is second from the left in the front row. His generals, all of them standing behind him, are, left to right: Brigadier General James Conner of South Carolina; Brigadier General Martin W. Gary of South Carolina; Major General J. Bankhead Magruder of Virginia; Brigadier General Robert D. Lilley of Virginia; General P. G. T. Beauregard of Louisiana; Brigadier General Alexander R. Lawton of Geor- gia; Brigadier General Henry A. Wise of Virginia; and Brig- adier General Joseph L. Brent of Maryland. The men in the front row are, left to right: Blacque Bey, Turkish minister to the United States; Lee; George Peabody of Massachusetts, the greatest philanthropist of his day and a contributor to Wash- ington College; W. W. Corcoran of Washington, D.C., another donor to Lee's school and the man who gave the nation the Corcoran Gallery of Art; and Judge James Lyons of Rich- mond, Virginia. (*Valentine Museum, Richmond, Virginia*)

The last painting from life of Lee was done by the colorful Swiss artist Frank Buchser, whose visit to Lexington in the autumn of 1869 is not mentioned in previous biographies. Buchser had hoped to have Lee dress in his Confederate uniform, but Lee declined to do so, saying, "I am a soldier no longer." Lee compromised by displaying on the table next to him the dress sword, sash, and coat he had worn when he surrendered to Grant at Appomattox, and a wartime hat and a pair of binoculars. This painting, the most original and interesting portrait of Lee, was sent to Switzerland and stayed there. (*Kunstmuseum Bern*)

One of the last photographs of Lee, probably made soon before the trip south for his health in the spring of 1870, a journey that turned into a series of large and wildly enthusiastic ovations. A comparison with the Brady portrait made just after Appomattox shows how dramatically Lee had aged in five years. During that time he did more than any other American to heal the bitterness between North and South. *(Michael Miley Collection, Washington and Lee University)*

This picture was taken during Lee's funeral at the college chapel that he had been so eager to build. The young men in grey are cadets from the neighboring Virginia Military Institute. Note the wide black ribbons of mourning on the building to the left. *(Michael Miley Collection, Washington and Lee University)*

The head of the statue of Lee lying in Confederate uniform above his tomb in the Lee Chapel at Washington and Lee University. It was carved by Edward Valentine, who, as a young sculptor, went to Lexington and did a bust of Lee from life. Each year thousands of visitors come to the chapel in which Lee worshipped daily with his students. *(Washington and Lee University)*

Chapter 24

NOW EVERYTHING HAPPENED. Since those who attended it were still unaware of the pistol-on-the-ice episode in Lexington, the New York fund-raising meeting for Washington College went splendidly. The school was praised; Henry Ward Beecher ringingly commended Lee to his moneyed audience as a man who was "pleading for mental bread for his students" and was trying to instill in them a love for the entire country. The campaign was off to a fine start in the nation's richest city. No collection was taken at the end of the meeting, the organizers feeling that the hundreds of potential large donors could best be approached by a further letter and by personal meetings in their offices.

Failing to pass the hat while they had the chance was a mistake, because New Yorkers were soon reading several blistering columns in the *New York Independent.* The newspaper was receiving complaints about the fund-raising from many old abolitionists who thought that a college headed by Lee was no fit destination for Northern dollars. Starting with the discredited accusation that Lee was responsible for the deaths of Union prisoners at Andersonville, the *Independent* told its readers: "We do not think that a man who broke his solemn oath of allegiance to the United States, who imbrued his hands in the blood of tens of thousands of his country's noblest men, for the purpose of perpetuating human slavery . . . is fitted to be a teacher of young men."

Then the *Independent,* harking back to an attack it had made on Lee soon after the war, came up with an imaginative variation of the recent slurs on him in the Senate: ". . . the last thing that Gen. Lee did, as an officer of the American Army, was to hold an interview with Gen. Scott at his request; and, when Gen. Scott, trusting to his loyalty, showed him his maps and drawings of the defences of Washington, he took them with him to Arlington, upon pretense that he wished to examine them more particularly and then, without returning them, went over to the rebel side!"

The newspaper then disinterred old and baseless stories that Lee had treated the slaves at Arlington "with atrocious cruelty," and moved to a new topic. In a story that confused V.M.I. with Washington College, it represented some cadets as saying that they wore grey uniforms because "we won't wear the d——d Yankee blue at Gen. Lee's school."

When the friends of Johnston of the ice-skating incident read this issue of the *Independent,* they knew that they had found their forum. One of them wrote a letter to the editor that began, "Residing in Lexington, and having seen more or less of the students and professors of Washington College daily since Lee ascended to the presidency of the institution, I feel it my duty to give the people a few facts, which will, I trust, show the philanthropists of the North the animus of the institution to which they are contributing." Then came an account in which everyone on the ice that day was a Washington College student. The twelve-year-old boy who cursed Johnston vanished from the story, and he pulled his pistol to save himself from a mob that, "without the least provocation," attacked him "only because he was a *hated* Yankee." Beneath this letter the *Independent* admonished its readers that money given to Washington College would be "worse than thrown away."

In the same issue the paper carried an article by the abolitionist William Lloyd Garrison, urging that no one contribute to Washington College. Unaware of, or unwilling to acknowledge, Lee's widely known conciliatory postwar attitudes, Garrison first characterized the South as being an area of "universal ignorance" that was "still wishing to rule in hell rather than serve in heaven." He went on to scorn Lee: "Who is . . . more obdurate than himself? *He* at the head of a patriotic institution, teaching loyalty to the Constitution, and the duty of maintaining that Union he so lately attempted to destroy! . . . Has Lucifer regained his position in Heaven? . . . If the South could reasonably hope to succeed in another rebellious uprising, and should make the attempt, who can show us any ground for believing that Gen. Lee would not again act as generalissimo of her forces?"

☆ ☆ ☆

That was only the beginning. The *New York Times* and the *New York Tribune* picked up the story, and the *Chicago Daily Tribune* called Washington College "a school run principally for the propagation of hatred to the Union." Even months later, the *Boston Evening Traveller* said that the job of the "arch traitor Lee" was to instruct his students in "more treason," and warned that Northern donations would be used for "paying traitors to teach their damnable treason to the flower of southern' youth." The *Independent* returned to the fray several times, once with a warning by a clergyman from Tennessee that money sent to Washington College would forge "implements for another and bloodier conflict" and sharpen "the knives wherewith to cut the throats of the givers." A Northern woman who had for a time taught a school for blacks in Lexington wrote, "Never did I walk the streets of Lexington without rudeness, in one form or another. Ladies glorified in compelling the Yankee woman, in her good nature, to step into the mud for their accommodation; the boys of the aristocratic school of the place hooted every time I passed them, and the students sneered and cursed alternately." She added that she had received threats that her school would be burned, and that "these same gentlemanly young men" had thrown brickbats at the school windows while she was teaching an evening class to black adults.

There was some truth in what the Northern woman wrote in her letter to the *Independent,* but the *Boston Evening Traveller* was demonstrably wrong on one count: as a college president, the paper said, Lee "is a perfect nonentity, except as to the drawing of his salary."

II

While this unfavorable publicity continued — the vital contributions from the North fell to a third of what they had been the previous year — a new crisis occurred in Lexington.

As with the ice-skating incident, the setting could not have been more peaceful. On the quiet evening of May 8, Mrs. John Brockenbrough, wife of the judge, was walking home with her son Francis, who was not quite old enough to attend the college. A group of black men were standing about the sidewalk in front of the Brockenbrough house. They "refused to give the pavement," as a student put it, forcing Mrs. Brockenbrough and her son to step into the gutter to get around them and to their front gate. Enraged, young Francis saw his mother to the door, came back down the walk, and attacked one of the blacks with a stick. The black drew a pistol and shot him in the chest.

The spring night became wild. At the same moment that the doctors were fighting to save Francis' life, one of his older brothers dashed into the room of a friend at the college "and said that his brother had been shot by a negro over in town. He asked me to dress and go out with them to catch the negro. He got a large crowd of students together and we went out in different directions around town. One party succeeded in getting him and they came very near lynching him."

They came very near indeed. The black, Caesar Griffin, would certainly have been hanging from a tree had it not been for one of those timely arrivals that had quelled earlier disturbances. This time the students had a rope around their intended victim's neck and had marched him to the courthouse square — the preferred place for lynchings, since it implied that justice had been done. Assistant Professor Harry Estill, a former Confederate captain, strode out of the night. The slender, black-bearded veteran ordered the students to turn their captive over to the jailer, and they did.

The shooting took place on a Friday night. On Sunday, with Francis still between life and death, the word began to be passed around the campus that should he die, some of the students intended to storm the jail and kill Caesar Griffin.

Rumor or genuine plan, word of it came to the lieutenant of the United States Twenty-ninth Infantry Regiment who was military commissioner for Lexington. He called on Lee, who judged it to be wild talk but moved swiftly nonetheless. Because it was a Sunday, the students were scattered all over the pleasant May landscape. Lee immediately communicated with Givens B. Strickler, the student who had left school at the end of his freshman year in 1861 to join and subsequently command the Liberty Hall Volunteers. Seven years later, he was at last a senior, soon to graduate. He was the president of the college's large

Y.M.C.A. group, which taught Sunday schools throughout the area and had a large meeting on Sunday evenings. Lee told Strickler to pass this message through the Y.M.C.A. network, and to have it read at the evening meeting, so that all students would be aware of it by nightfall: "I earnestly invoke the students to abstain from any violation of the law, and to unite in preserving quiet and order on this and every occasion."

For days, the situation in Lexington remained tense; several pistols were fired in the air. A company of the Twenty-ninth Infantry arrived to patrol the streets. Francis Brockenbrough recovered, and the calmed students prepared for their final examinations.

III

In mid-May, the drama of the impeachment trial in Washington moved toward its climax. Each day, President Johnson remained at his desk in the White House while his defense lawyers appeared on his behalf on the floor of the United States Senate. The prosecution was conducted by selected members of the House of Representatives. The judges were the fifty-four senators, of whom thirty-six had to vote "guilty" in order to remove Andrew Johnson from the presidency. Chief Justice Salmon P. Chase presided. The members of the House of Representatives, present as spectators, sat in chairs jammed along the back of the Senate chamber. Tickets to the Visitors' Gallery were the most sought-after pieces of paper in Washington; as if each day of the trial were a first night at the theater, the ladies vied in wearing the most fashionable dresses, and a shade that became known as Impeachment Blue was all the rage.

There was terrific after-hours lobbying among the senators to influence their votes. Lee's old adversary Ulysses S. Grant was among those working hard to oust President Johnson. Although the real case against the President was that he was thwarting the Republicans' Reconstruction program, the principal charge against him was that he had violated a questionable law known as the Tenure of Office Act. This

was a piece of legislation enacted by the Radicals for the chief purpose
of preventing Johnson from firing Secretary of War Edwin M. Stanton,
who was conspiring with Johnson's Radical foes while continuing to sit
in Johnson's innermost councils as a member of the Cabinet. In his efforts to precipitate a test of this law's constitutionality, President Johnson had asked Grant to continue serving as acting secretary of war after
he suspended Stanton from office. When the Senate refused to concur
in Stanton's removal, Grant stepped aside in a manner that Johnson
felt was a violation of the agreement between them. Johnson was out-
raged; Grant made excuses. In a barrage of public accusations and
counteraccusations between Grant and Johnson, Grant had fallen into
step with the Radicals and was on his way to the Republican nomination. Now, with his eye on the Republican convention in Chicago at
the end of the month, General Grant threw aside any pretense that he
was still an army officer who should stand aside from party politics. He
hated the President for the earlier acid exchange; Grant wanted Johnson out of the White House, now, and said so to every senator he could
find.

As for Lee, he had been summoned to Richmond to make an appearance in another trial, that of Jefferson Davis. When he arrived, he
found the proceedings again postponed.

All of this — Reconstruction, the trial of Davis, the trial of the President — deeply troubled Lee and put Mary into such a state of brood-
ing that he feared it might worsen her physical condition. Writing to
his twenty-seven-year-old cousin Annette Carter, Lee's tone differed
from the bantering, flirtatious letters of earlier years. Along with many
Democrats and some Republicans, he saw the trial of the President as
an effort to destroy the power of the executive branch and to realign
the traditional balance of power among the executive, the legislative,
and the judiciary. To Annette, he deplored what he saw as "this grand
scheme of centralization of power in the hands of one branch of the
Govt. to the ruin of all others, and the anihilation [sic] of the Constitution, the liberty of the people and of the country . . . I grieve for poster-
ity, for American principles and American liberty. Our boasted self
Govt. is fast becoming the jeer and laughing-stock of the world."

Although Virginians could not vote for President in this election
year because their state was not readmitted to the Union, Lee believed
that every white Southerner who could vote should do so. This was in

contrast to the views of many recent Confederates, who felt that casting a vote in either a state or national election was to indicate approval of Federal Reconstruction policies. In their view, the new racially integrated state legislatures left almost all of the eight million Southern whites out of the political process: the blacks did not represent their interests, and the non-Confederate whites who had been the only whites eligible for election did not represent them either.

Lee agreed that the majority of white Southerners had no effective representation, but he felt that the only way to change this was to act as he had counseled his young officers to act on the way home from Appomattox: vote if you can; get a toehold. Although he said in a conversation, "I am rejoiced that slavery is abolished," Lee was opposed to granting the vote to the blacks. He saw the alliance between blacks and Republicans as a threat to white Southerners. In a letter to Rob, he characterized the blacks as "those who are plotting and working for your injury and all of whose sympathies and aspirations are antagonistic to yours." In the next sentence he softened somewhat: "I wish them no evil in the world — on the contrary, will do them every good in my power, and know that they are misled by those to whom they have given their confidence; but our material, social and political interests are naturally with the whites."

☆   ☆   ☆

News of the impeachment trial's results came from Washington. By three identical votes of thirty-five to nineteen on three separate charges, the Senate had defeated the Republican attempt to throw Andrew Johnson out of the White House. If the Republicans could have mustered just one more vote on any of the three charges to reach the thirty-six needed for a two-thirds majority, Johnson would not have survived. In Virginia, Lee wrote of the trial of Jefferson Davis, "God grant that, like the impeachment of Mr. Johnson, it may be dismissed."

It was not yet to be, for Jefferson Davis. Lee was summoned again to Richmond for the Davis trial, to find that it had again been postponed, from June 3 to November 30. Returning to Lexington, where the students were starting their final examinations, Lee found political talk everywhere. The Republican convention in Chicago had, as expected, nominated Ulysses S. Grant as the party's candidate for President.

Grant was discovering that politicians are treated less politely than conquering generals. The brilliant and snobbish historian Henry Adams, a Bostonian certainly sympathetic to the Union cause, was aghast at the thought of Grant as President; he saw Grant as a man so primitive that he should have been extinct "for ages"; this prehistoric throwback should live in a cave; instead of a uniform, Grant should have "worn skins."

If that was a Northern opinion, there were equally unflattering Southern ones. In a group that included Lee, one member of his faculty unburdened himself of some scathing words about the Republican candidate.

Lee's face flushed. For him there was only the Grant of Appomattox, the man who had sent the officers of the Army of Northern Virginia home with their swords and pistols at their sides, the man who had re-leased captured horses to be taken home to plow Southern fields for a desperately needed crop.

"Sir," Lee said, "if you ever again presume to speak disrespectfully of General Grant in my presence, either you or I will sever his connection with this university."

Though he did not wish it, a public comparison of himself with Grant was about to be made. Soon after the graduation ceremonies in the newly dedicated chapel that meant so much to Lee, the *New York Herald* printed a fascinating editorial.

The last time Lee had been mentioned in Northern newspapers was to be flayed in the aftermath of the Johnston fracas in Lexington. Now the *Herald* began by pointing out that, though the Republicans had chosen General Grant, the Democrats had yet to hold their convention and name their candidate. It seemed to be a year for considering soldiers as candidates, the *Herald* said; the Democratic Party was thinking about various Union generals who were Democrats as a counterpoise to the Republicans' Grant.

Now the surprise. Let the Democratic Party forget the Union generals. "We will recommend a candidate for its favors. Let it nominate General R. E. Lee. Let it boldly take over the best of all its soldiers, making no palaver or apology. He is a better soldier than any of those they have thought upon and a greater man."

Here, thirty-eight months after Appomattox, in the city where they had yelled for his blood, a leading newspaper was putting forward his name for President of the United States. "For this soldier, with a handful of men whom he had moulded into an army, baffled our greater Northern armies for four years; and when opposed by Grant was only worn down by that solid strategy of stupidity that accomplishes its object by mere weight."

This was, of course, appearing in a newspaper heavily committed to the Democratic Party and strongly opposed to Republican Reconstruction policies, but the paper was going far out of its way in recommending Lee to Northern Democrats, among whom were so many Union Army veterans who had risked their lives as surely as had their Republican comrades. The action spoke volumes for the special place that Lee was coming to hold among his former enemies. The *Herald* warmed to its endorsement.

> With one quarter the men Grant had this soldier fought magnificently across the territory of his native state, and fought his army to a stump. There never was such an army or such a campaign, or such a General for illustrating the military genius and possibilities of our people; and this General is the best of all for a Democratic candidate. It is certain that with half as many men as Grant he would have beaten him from the field in Virginia, and he affords the best promise of any soldier for beating him again.

There it was, the highest compliment that they could pay him. Naturally, the proposal was doomed; it was possible that the *Herald* did not understand that Lee had not been restored to citizenship and was not eligible to run. Democratic Party leaders were not even remotely considering Lee, and he would have considered such a move to be the surest way of reopening the wounds of war he was trying to heal, but it was a startling tribute.

Chapter 25

POLITICS would soon seek him again, but for the moment Lee could rest from the labors of his third completed year as head of Washington College. Long visits from relatives and friends were a constant backdrop to his life in Lexington — indeed, this past winter yet another Mildred Lee, the daughter of his brother Carter, had lived with him, and her two brothers were at the college — and he particularly enjoyed it when children were among the guests in the crowded house. Little girls had always been his favorites, and he had come to expect a delighted response to his teasing and compliments. Now, to his real annoyance, it appeared that his charm was to have its first failure. A neighbor chronicled the mounting crisis and its resolution.

He took a great deal of notice of a little girl whose mother was a friend of one of his daughters and was visiting at his house. All his advances, however, were steadily repulsed by the child. Some weeks passed, and he had not succeeded in winning a smile or kiss from her, when one morning she passed his study door and pausing before it, was invited to come in.

She did not do so, but stood and glanced around the room. Suddenly spying a figure of a man in a costume of a century back made of pasteboard and stuffed, and very showily dressed hanging on the wall — it was meant for a pen wiper, and was hung over his table by some of his zealous lady friends — she looked at it, and then at him, and advancing a few steps toward him, asked, "Is that your doll baby?"

"Yes," he said. His possession of a doll baby seemed at once to establish a feeling of fellowship with him and going to him at once she sat on his lap, and was always his devoted friend.

II

By mid-July, the family was ready for the leisurely progression that was to end at the White Sulphur Springs. The start was proving to be so leisurely that, even though there was a large carriage waiting at the door to take the family on the first leg of their journey, the ladies of the family were so far from being ready that Lee had time to write a letter to a great young favorite of his. This was Charlotte Haxall, who had visited her close friend Mildred in Lexington this past spring. Lee was writing now in the hope that Charlotte might come to join them at the White Sulphur as company for Mildred, and his old gallantry was in full flower. "My beautiful Lottie," he began, "if I were to attempt to tell you how sad your departure made us, how much we have missed you, and how depressed Lexington has since been, time and my ability would equally fail."

Lee had correctly discerned that Custis was destined to remain a bachelor, but he missed no opportunity to bring Rob to the attention of Virginia's fairest ladies. Before Charlotte's spring visit, he had playfully written to her about his hardworking farmer son, "May I bring up Robert as your principal escort?" He had added that Rob would have to have his life insured if he did come with her to Lexington, because "he may be murdered by the disappointed" — the Washington College students and V.M.I. cadets who wanted her to themselves.

As Lee wrote Charlotte Haxall now, he had no idea that this time he was really on the right track, and that this was the girl whom Rob would eventually marry, although he would not be alive to see it happen. Lee gave her this picture of the departure from Lexington: Mildred was "flying about this morning with great activity." Agnes, who had been sick, "is following with slower steps." Mrs. Lee was giving last minute "injunctions" to Sam and Eliza, the black yard man and cook. As for Letitia, Mrs. Lee's maid, who was accompanying them to the resorts, she was "looking on with wonder at the preparations, and trying to get a right conception of the place to which she is going, which she seems to think is something between a steel-trap and a spring-gun."

A Lexington widower, Dr. Howard Barton, was an admirer of

Mildred's, and his appearance at this moment produced in Lee the usual negative reaction concerning suitors for his daughters. "To add interest to the scene, Dr. Barton has arrived to bid adieu and to give Mildred an opportunity of looking her best. I believe he is the last rose of summer. The others, with all their fragrance and thorns, have all departed."

III

The cheery confusion of leaving was soon followed by serious illness, not for Lee, not for Mary, but for Mildred. The family had progressed only to the first resort, the Warm Springs forty miles to the northwest, when Mildred was stricken with typhoid fever. This frequently fatal disease had killed Mildred's sister Anne Carter Lee during the war. Lee became Mildred's chief nurse. To Rooney, who quickly sent a get-well letter to his sister, Lee replied, "I am writing in Mildred's room, who is very grateful for your interest in her behalf. She is too weak to speak."

Here was another battle, against disease this time, and Lee was an experienced nurse. As a boy, the youngest child, it had fallen his lot to nurse his mother when she became an invalid, and the pattern had repeated itself as he nursed Mary through years of increasing invalidism.

In her delirium, Mildred insisted that she could not sleep unless her father held her hand. She did not want him to leave the room. Lee had a cot set up in the corner of Mildred's little room upstairs in their cottage at the Warm Springs. Every night, as the music from the dance in the ballroom came across the lawns and through the trees, Lee sat by Mildred's bed, patting her hand and wiping the sweat from her fevered face. Only when she fell into her restless sleep would Lee stretch out on his cot, ready to respond when she woke again.

This went on for a month. Mildred's hair fell out. Finally, she was pronounced convalescent; instantly, Lee's spirits rose. Writing to E. C. Gordon, he said of some mutual friends, "Tell Misses Maria and Nettie, that I am greatly alarmed about their sister E. There is a young Presbyterian clergyman just arrived, has taken his seat by her at table. He may do so at other times too — she would not tell me."

With Mildred able to travel, the family moved on to the Hot Springs. Here Lee left Mildred with her mother and Agnes, going on by himself to the White Sulphur for what was by now a rest from his vacation.

Chapter 26

THE SUMMER BEFORE, Lee had been at the White Sulphur with his family. In the evenings he had been surrounded by his court of adoring Southern belles. This time he was alone, and it was very different. The White Sulphur was the same, but he was tired and stood more to the side. In a letter he wrote, "The place looks beautiful — the belles very handsome, and the beaux very happy. All are gay, and only I solitary. I am all alone." The year before, Traveller had been with him, but Lee's health had slipped to the point where he could not handle the long cross-country rides necessary to bring his horse here. Even in the midst of Mildred's typhoid attack at the Warm Springs, Lee had written Gordon, "How is Traveller? Tell him I miss him dreadfully and have repented of our separation but once, and that is the whole time since we parted."

There was another situation that made Lee feel, and act, even more withdrawn. To a far greater extent than the previous summer, the hotel and cottages were filled with men who had been prominent in the Confederacy. Everywhere he strolled, he encountered his former officers or those who had been high civilian officials. Alexander H. Stephens of Georgia, Vice-President of the Confederate States of America, was there, as was General P. G. T. Beauregard of Louisiana.

While Lee was happy to greet these men, and glad to see that they could once again afford the pleasures of fashionable resorts, he found the beautiful grounds seething with political talk. To oppose Grant, the Democrats had nominated former Governor Horatio Seymour of New York. The vice-presidential candidate was Francis Preston Blair, Jr., son of Lincoln's intermediary who had offered Lee command of the

Union Army at the war's outset. The Blairs — father, son, and a brother who had been postmaster general under Abraham Lincoln — had broken with the Republicans because of their postwar treatment of the South and had come over to the Democratic Party.

The great majority of white Southerners, Lee along with them, hoped for a Democratic victory as their best chance for salvaging what was left of the prewar South; it would reduce the effect of the new black vote and remove much of the Federal control in Southern state government. To this end, the prominent Southerners at the White Sulphur were busy forging every sort of alliance with the Democrats of the North and Midwest. Nearly every conversation in which Lee found himself reverted to this subject; feeling that his views had been made clear by his example and not wishing to be misquoted in this heated atmosphere, Lee excused himself from each gathering after a few minutes.

In the midst of this informal but influential Southern caucus, there appeared a recently resigned United States Army general. This was William Starke Rosecrans, who in 1861 had opposed Lee with considerable success in mountains not far to the north. During the summer preceding this at the White Sulphur, Federal officers were treated with nothing more than cool correctness, but Rosecrans was greeted with enthusiasm. Rosecrans was no vacationer; he was one of the managers of the Democratic national election campaign. He had just come from New York. There, and particularly in the Midwest, the Republicans were hammering on the theme that the South had never accepted the results of the war and was mistreating the blacks; a victory at the polls for the Democrats would negate the victory won at enormous cost on the battlefields.

To see if this Republican theme could be undercut, Rosecrans had come to call on the foremost man of the South. What was needed, he told Lee, was a statement by prominent Southerners to the effect that they realized that this was a new day, that they were fully committed to one national destiny, and that the blacks would receive fair treatment in the South. If Lee would associate himself with such a declaration, his name would have greater influence than any other.

There were men at the White Sulphur who would have leapt through hoops to sign a statement helpful to the Democrats. As usual, Lee was reluctant to have his name brought before the public, but his conception of duty prevailed. He wanted the Democrats to win, but whether they won or lost, he felt that a properly worded statement might improve Northern feelings toward the South. He was barred from voting, but he could influence voters, and now he invited to his cottage thirty-one of the most prominent men at the springs. Among them they represented eight of the Confederate states. They packed into his small living room, and Lee turned the meeting over to Rosecrans.

While Lee remained silent, Rosecrans stated his purpose and went around the room, asking for reactions and suggestions. The nearly unanimous response was that Southerners recognized the Federal government as the valid national authority and intended to be just in their dealings with blacks. Only the last man to speak, F. W. Stockdale, the wartime governor of Texas, said frankly that the South was through fighting but was not a dog that would lick the hand of the man who kicked it.

The result, after a final consultation between Lee and a Virginia lawyer named Alexander H. H. Stuart, who had attended the meeting, was a document that became known as the White Sulphur Letter. The text was written by Stuart, but was expressive of Lee's views and used a number of phrases that occurred in his letters. Promptly published in newspapers throughout the nation, it was regarded as the most important political statement to come out of the South since the war. Lee headed the long list of signers; his name was followed by those of Beauregard and Stephens.

Taking nothing for granted about Northern ideas as to the South's state of mind, the first point made was that the South was finished with slavery and secession. As for the blacks, "we have from childhood been accustomed to look upon them with kindness." Economically, the two races were dependent upon each other: "Self-interest, if there were no higher motive, would therefore prompt the whites of the South to extend to the negroes care and protection."

Then the statement tackled the subject of a vote for the blacks.

It is true that the people of the South, in common with a large majority of the North and West, are, for obvious reasons, inflexibly opposed to any system of laws that would place the political power in the hands of the negro race. But this opposition springs from no feeling of enmity, but from a deep-seated conviction that, at present, the negroes have neither the intelligence nor the other qualifications which are necessary to make them safe depositories of political power.

In claiming for this view "a large majority of the North and West," this position paper was engaging in a combination of conjecture and wishful thinking; it was true, however, that six Northern states still refused blacks the vote, and that the last congressional elections had produced some significant Democratic victories that were in effect a referendum on this issue.

Finally, the declaration spoke of the feelings of white Southerners about the restrictions that the victors still placed upon the vanquished. They wanted an end to Federal regulations controlling which Southerners could and could not vote and hold office. They wanted Northerners to understand that Southern legislatures were filled not only with blacks who did not represent the whites, but also with whites whom they regarded as being Northern carpetbaggers who never could have been elected to office in their own communities, and "scalawags" — white Southern Republicans who were allowed to hold office because they had not served the Confederacy.

> They ask a restoration of their rights under the Constitution. They desire relief from oppressive misrule. Above all, they would appeal to their countrymen for the re-establishment, in the Southern states, of that which has justly been regarded as the birth-right of every American, the right of self-government. Establish these on a firm basis, and we can safely promise, on behalf of the Southern people, that they will faithfully obey the Constitution and the laws of the United States, treat the negro populations with kindness and humanity and fulfil every duty incumbent on peaceful citizens, loyal to the Constitution of their country.

☆ ☆ ☆

When the White Sulphur Letter appeared, those who read it among the twenty-four million Americans living outside the South believed that they were indeed hearing the voice of eight million white Southerners. On balance, they found it a reassuring statement. The Democrats had no doubt it would help them at the polls.

Returning to Lexington in time for the opening of the college's fall session, Lee resisted further efforts to draw him into the closing phases of the campaign. There was dramatic evidence of the impact of the statement and of the fact that growing numbers of Northerners placed Lee in a category of his own. The most striking tribute in the pile of mail awaiting Lee in his new office in the basement of the new chapel was from Isaac Hale, Jr., of Newburyport, Massachusetts. On behalf of the organizing committee, he invited Lee to be a principal speaker at the Salisbury Beach Festival, which thirty thousand people were expected to attend.

"Allow me to state," Hale's letter said, "that no citizen of this country could receive a more cordial reception than would be extended to you on that occasion." Referring to the White Sulphur Letter, he said that it "has been received by the people of the North as the most important document that has been put forth since the close of the Civil War. And will influence to change the minds of thousands of undecided voters to the support of Seymour and the Constitution. We desire to see you and to hear your words of wisdom, and to honor you as one of our greatest warriors and statesmen."

Lee declined, but who, three years before, could have dreamed that Lee would be entreated to address a crowd of thirty thousand in Massachusetts? Democratic politics had much to do with this, but that Democratic Party leaders thought a speech by Lee in this bastion of abolition would aid them was in itself a tribute to his unique position in the postwar scene.

Chapter 27

T HE AUTUMN OF 1868 was a pleasant time for Lee. Politics and unwelcome national notice receded from his life, even though the newspapers were filled with news of the forthcoming election. A parade of family and friends came through Lexington; during their visits Lee gave them a conducted tour of the new President's House, which was under construction next door, a project in which he took the greatest interest. The most important event of the fall was the arrival of Rooney and Tabb at the beginning of November, for a stay of three weeks. Lee's tall, beautiful daughter-in-law was the focus of added attention and excitement because she was expecting a baby in February. Tabb, only twenty, was, pregnant or not, a great attraction to the college students and V.M.I. cadets who called at the house in the evenings.

In the middle of Rooney and Tabb's visit, Lee read the results of the election. Ulysses S. Grant was to be the new President of the United States; he would be inaugurated in March.

Grant was President-elect, but the South could not be expected to welcome as the national leader the man who had commanded the armies that brought it ruin. In this hour of Republican victory, there was another man on the South's mind and in its heart. In Alabama, General John T. Morgan expressed this yearning:

> Eight millions of people turn their eyes to Lexington seeking instruction and paternal advice in the severe trials they have to undergo. They read in the example of their General . . . the lessons of patience, moderation, fortitude, and earnest devotion to the requirements of duty, which are the only safe guides to them in their troubles. His history, his present labors, and his calm confidence in the future kindle the flames of hope in the hearts of millions, that else all would be darkness.

II

On Christmas morning, Lee wheeled Mary into the festive dining room. Rooney and Tabb had gone back to their farm, but all the other Lee children were here. Everyone gathered at the table — Custis, Rob, Daughter, Agnes, Mildred — and Lee said the morning prayers as usual. As they sat down to breakfast, each found a few beautifully wrapped presents, but there was a mountain of gifts in front of Mildred, who was wearing a silk cap to conceal the fact that her hair was only now beginning to grow back after her typhoid-caused baldness. Not long before, Rob explained, Mildred had "enumerated, just in fun, all the presents she wanted — a long list." Lee had overheard; his fabulous memory had needed no written notes of her recital. "To her great surprise," Rob said, "when Christmas morning came she found each article at her place at the breakfast-table — not one omitted."

During the time between breakfast and the hour for church services, Lee mounted Traveller. A large sack was handed up to him, filled with presents for the children of Lexington — mittens for little boys, knitted by Mary Lee and her daughters, and dolls whose dresses they had sewn. Like a Confederate Santa Claus in grey with a trim white beard, Lee rode off to deliver them to his young friends.

☆   ☆   ☆

There was a special present on this Christmas Day of 1868, a farewell gift from outgoing President Andrew Johnson. It was a proclamation of general amnesty for the Confederates who had not been restored to their civil rights by earlier actions. It meant that no Confederate could henceforth be prosecuted for treason. It was the end of the government's long series of postponements in the case of Jefferson Davis; he would never be tried.

It would be seven weeks until the formal dismissal of the indictments still pending against Lee, his sons Custis and Rooney, and thirty-three other prominent Confederates, but it was all over as of Christmas Day.

Lee was free from the threat of arrest, trial, and imprisonment. By following the prescribed procedure in the future when Virginia was readmitted to the Union, he could again become a voter, but by then he would be a very sick and preoccupied man. Even with the amnesty, he was still barred from holding office and would remain so because his application for a special pardon was misplaced, but the long uncertainty, the possibility that the Radicals might still find a way to strike at him, all that vanished on this Christmas Day.

III

In mid-February of 1869, Rooney and Tabb wrote joyously to announce the birth of a healthy son. He was to be named Robert E. Lee III, the same name as that of the earlier grandson and namesake who had died in infancy.

In this hour of domestic happiness, Lee's name was again brought before the public, in a manner he detested. On the initiative of a friendly congressman from Illinois, James May, it had been arranged that Mary Lee should recover a few of George and Martha Washington's possessions that had been at Arlington when it was occupied by Federal troops. These heirlooms had been left to Mary by her father, and included a set of china that Lafayette had given to her great-grandmother Martha Washington. After what the government called their "capture," they had been removed from Arlington and displayed in an obscure corner of the Patent Office; along with the china, there was a punch bowl from Mount Vernon, a mirror, a dresser, some tent poles and tent pegs that George Washington had used in the field with the Continental Army, and a few other items.

The return of these objects to Mary had been arranged quietly, but not secretly. President Johnson thought this was a very small thing to do for a woman who had lost Arlington and its eleven hundred acres by confiscation; about to leave office, it was one of the last kindnesses he could perform, and with the approval of his Cabinet he told the secretary of the interior to hand over Mary's possessions to anyone she designated to receive them. Mary named her cousin who lived in Washington, Mrs. Beverly Kennon. Lee was not a party to the matter.

Just as this transfer was about to occur, the *Washington Evening Express* appeared with the story on February 29. It was laden with inaccuracies and written in an emotional vein. Lee had asked for the objects; they were going to be whisked out of Arlington, now a National Cemetery filled with Union dead, rather than from a corner of the Patent Office; Lee was sending someone to take away from the people of the United States these priceless possessions of George Washington, which belonged to the nation as a whole.

The Radicals leapt on this. In their eyes this was a last disloyal act by the outgoing traitorous President whom they had failed to impeach; it was only to be expected that this Southerner would be in collusion with Lee on the eve of his departure. A resolution was quickly introduced on the floor of the House, asking "by what right the Secretary of the Interior surrenders these objects so cherished as once the property of the Father of his Country to the rebel general-in-chief." On March 3, the day before Grant was to be inaugurated, the Radical-controlled Committee on Public Buildings, of which Arlington was now one, sent to the House a resolution that concluded that the objects belonged to the Federal government, and that "to deliver the same to the Rebel General Robert E. Lee is an insult to the loyal people of the United States." As one of its last acts before adjourning, the Congress voted to keep Mary Lee's china and other possessions in their corner at the Patent Office.

Lee seldom put bitter words on paper, but learning of this decision he wrote, "It may be a question with some whether the retention of these articles is more 'an insult,' in the language of the Committee on Public Buildings, 'to the loyal people of the United States' than their restoration."

☆ ☆ ☆

The morning after the vote to deny Mary Lee her china, a bizarre situation remained unresolved in the hours before the inauguration. The bitterness between President Johnson and President-elect Grant had frozen into glacial hostility. The kindness in Grant that Lee was so ready to acknowledge had for the moment vanished. Just days before the inauguration ceremony that was to take place at noon on March 4,

Grant had informed the Arrangements Committee that he would not ride in the same carriage with Johnson to the Capitol to be sworn in, and would not speak to him even if he arrived separately at the ceremony.

The startled committee frantically discussed ad hoc arrangements. Would President Johnson consent to ride in an identical carriage, moving beside Grant's? Should there be *two* processions up Pennsylvania Avenue, Johnson the focus of one, and Grant of the other?

Inquiries to Johnson produced silence. Finally, the distraught committee decided that its principal responsibility was to get Grant to the Capitol and in front of Chief Justice Chase to take his oath of office. As always, seats for the outgoing President and his Cabinet were reserved within a few feet of the incoming President's chair, and it was left for Johnson and his outgoing secretary of state, secretary of the treasury, and other highest officials to get to those chairs by whatever means they chose.

That was still the preposterous situation, with less than an hour until the inauguration. As they arrived at the White House one by one, dressed for the ceremony at noon, the members of Johnson's Cabinet found him at his desk, signing the bills passed during the final days of the congressional session. Not long before twelve, Attorney General William M. Evarts hurried in. Without taking off his overcoat, he remarked that it was getting late; perhaps they should all be starting for the Capitol?

Johnson raised his eyes from the stack of documents. "I am inclined to think that we will finish our work here."

Secretary of State William H. Seward came in puffing on a cigar as always; there were knife scars on his face, the result of the attempt on his life made at the same moment that Lincoln received his fatal wound. Seward observed that it was almost twelve o'clock. The President said he had more papers to sign. Seward stood there fidgeting and smoking his cigar.

The clock struck noon. Ulysses S. Grant was President, taking the oath of office without his predecessor being present. It was the beginning of an administration that was to be one of the most corrupt in American history, although Grant was innocent of wrongdoing in its many scandals.

Johnson pushed back his chair, shook hands with the men who had served him, and walked out of the White House.

Chapter 28

A T THE END OF MARCH, Lee and the trustees met to review the college's academic development during the three and a half years of his presidency and to chart the future. The moment was a plateau from which all could see how far the school had come under his leadership; combined with new programs that were now announced, the array of accomplishments and proposals attracted attention far beyond Lexington.

The faculty and trustees had been working toward this time, when existing programs would be expanded and more innovations introduced. Only a few of the new ideas adopted during Lee's presidency had originated with him. His special gift was the ability to see the essence of a worthwhile suggestion and to relate it to what was already in existence or planned. Then he would encourage and shape the new project, repeatedly redesigning the curriculum so that a new department or course could have a comfortable place in which to grow and offer its benefits.

During the past forty-two months, Lee had led Washington College through a complete reorganization and a great change in emphasis. In line with his belief in "practical education" to help rebuild the South, the science programs had been greatly expanded. Rather than create new technical schools, the idea was to have such subjects as mining engineering and industrial geology flourish amid the liberal arts; engineering students were required to take courses in French.

In more traditional studies, the law school run by Judge Brockenbrough in Lexington had been increasingly assimilated, and after Lee's death would become the Washington and Lee University School of Law. With the dawn of the modern "social sciences," history, which had been moved away from the study of Greek and Latin but was still coupled with English literature, was now given a new home in a separate department of history and political economy. Fifty years before it was offered in some large universities, there would be a course at the college in international law.

It was in this meeting with the trustees, more than a decade before the Wharton School of Commerce was started at the University of Pennsylvania, that Lee proposed that a full-scale business school come into being. This was an entirely new concept in American education. Through a local secretarial school some of the students were already taking penmanship, bookkeeping, and commercial law, but now the college would offer such courses as "geography applied to production and commerce" and "commercial history and biography." Students could take "commercial technology, or the productions of mechanical and chemical manufactures of trade," and courses in the financial management of "banks, insurance and joint stock companies, railroads, canals, ships, steamers, telegraphs, etc." Modern languages were to be learned so that graduates could do business abroad.

Even more innovative was a proposal for fifty "press scholarships." This was the first mention in the world's history of a school of journalism, and the idea emerged full-blown, aimed at "young men intending to make practical printing and journalism their business in life." In the small-town newspapers of the day, the same man often was editor, reporter, and printer. The typographical unions of the South were invited to nominate candidates to come to Washington College, take the regular college courses leading to a degree, and work one hour a day at the printing plant of Lafferty and Company in Lexington. The object was to attract bright boys, with little prospect of further education, who were already working on newspapers. The college's intention was to "give them as thorough a training as possible in the ways of their profession and to give them as good an education as possible that they may make better and more cultivated *editors*."

In the forerunner of "junior fellows" programs later adopted by some American universities, each year the faculty was to select three graduates of the master of arts programs. These particularly promising young men were invited to remain on campus for an additional two years as "resident masters," paid to teach one hour a day, but with the rest of their time free to pursue independent study.

In addition to plans for a school of agriculture and "demonstration farm," of which Virginia had none, the idea was projected for one of the nation's first summer schools, utilizing buildings that customarily were deserted from June to September. There was also a proposal for free tuition "for candidates for the Christian Ministry" — not a new idea, but one close to Lee's heart.

Lee's stamp was heavily and unmistakably on a project known as the Board of Survey. This was a mapmaking enterprise under the direction of Major Jedediah Hotchkiss of Staunton, Virginia, a former Confederate cartographer. Created for the purpose of instructing engineering students, its first product was the most accurate map yet drawn of neighboring Augusta County. In preparing this, Lee had received cooperation from his old corps, the Engineers, as well as the United States Coast Survey and the Smithsonian Institution. The school's results would be shared with local and state governments and with Federal agencies; the next project was to resurvey the boundary line separating Virginia and North Carolina.

This battery of achievements and innovations was reported in the nation's press, with particularly admiring reactions throughout the growing Midwest. The *New York Herald* saw this "practical education" as the wave of the future, and believed that Lee "was likely to make as great an impression upon our old fogy schools and colleges as . . . in military tactics upon our old fogy commanders in the palmy days of the rebellion."

Most of these ideas were to succeed, but two of them were inescapably in advance of their time, and two others never found enough money. The press scholarships were offered for nine years, but older newsmen were skeptical of them, and there is no record of how many young candidates they sent along. More business courses were instituted, but the undergraduate School of Commerce, Economics, and Politics did not evolve until much later. The agriculture courses that Lee believed to be so important to Southern postwar recovery were offered, but a full-scale agriculture program never materialized. Lee's hopes for starting a medical school, an idea that even he thought would have to be deferred, were never realized. With those exceptions or modifications, everything Lee started at Washington College came to fruition.

In contrast to this ambitious planning, an impromptu conversation Lee was to have with a novice instructor was an example of how the

superior educator, like the great general, never loses sight of the importance of the last man in the rear rank. The young man had been
teaching for only a few months when one day he met Lee coming the
other way on the campus. The general stopped and "inquired how I
was getting on with my work. I replied that I hoped I was doing fairly
well. 'May I give you one piece of advice, sir?' Of course, I said I should
be delighted to receive it. 'Well, sir, always observe the stage driver's
rule.' 'What is that, General?' 'Always take care of the *poor* horses.' "

II

Since coming to Lexington, Lee had been troubled about its inaccessi-
bility. When he traveled to the annual meetings of the Episcopal
Church in Virginia, or to those of the Virginia Educational Association, he was faced with the choice between two difficult routes. The
first leg of one route to Richmond required twelve hours on a canal
boat that went fifty-four miles south to Lynchburg for a connection
with an east-west railroad line. The other method, taking between
seven to twelve hours, depending on the weather and the condition of a
rough mountain road, was to ride twenty-three miles on a stagecoach
north to Goshen, where there was another east-west railroad line.
When a visitor to Lexington asked Lee the best way to start back to
Washington, he replied, "It makes but little difference, for whichever
route you select, you will wish you had taken the other."

Now, at the end of April, Lee went to Baltimore with a delegation in
an effort to organize financing for the Valley Railroad, a proposed line
that would connect the other lines serving parts of the Valley of Virginia. This north-south route would open the entire valley to rail service and act as a new corridor connecting such states as Maryland and
Tennessee. Lexington would be on the line.

This was to be the only commercial enterprise that Lee assisted, despite his many job offers and requests that he endorse everything from
pens to pianos. Lee knew a great deal about railroads; in the spring of
1862 he had invented railway ordnance by ordering that a heavy ar-

tillery gun protected by armor be mounted on a flatcar. In the first major war in which railroads were available, Lee mastered the new mode of transportation so well that his movements of men and supplies would be studied in the world's military academies for generations. By his adroit shifting of his limited forces, he had in effect made his army larger.

As Lee and the Valley Railroad's hopeful supporters were to discover, the large crowd that turned out to hear Lee ask the Baltimore City Council to underwrite the new line was less interested in railroads than in seeing him. Lee's careful reading of his long statement urging the purchase of a bond issue to finance much of the construction was by far the longest speech he ever made; in contrast to this thousand-word appeal, he had accepted command of Virginia's forces from the Virginia legislature with seventy-eight words. Lee explained to his Baltimore audience that the proposed railway would open an entirely new market for Baltimore, bringing it "directly within the circle of competition." The railway would "complete the last link in the great chain from the Northern Cities to the South and South-west" and would "afford the shortest line of travel from the large and populous portions of the North to much of the best part of the South."

All this was true, but the City Council felt that there were more pressing uses for Baltimore's funds. There would be a railroad into Lexington, but not yet. Lee's remarks were warmly received as an appearance by him and promptly forgotten as a financial proposal.

☆ ☆ ☆

Lee was about to have a meeting far more important than that with the Baltimore City Council. Ulysses S. Grant, now President for seven weeks, had used go-betweens to pass him a message; as Lee's son Rob put it, "It had been intimated to General Lee that it would be most agreeable to General Grant to receive him."

It was a bold stroke on Grant's part. Many thousands of the Republicans who had recently voted for him would have been aghast at the idea of the President welcoming Lee at the White House, but that was just what Grant intended to do. In inviting Lee, he was inviting the South.

As for Lee, he had no desire to spend time in a city where he could not escape the long vista across the Potomac, at the end of which Mary's beloved Arlington sat on its heights. Because he understood Grant's gesture, he accepted.

On the morning of Saturday, May 1, 1869, Lee boarded an early train from Baltimore to Washington. He was accompanied by his Baltimore hosts, Mr. and Mrs. Samuel H. Tagart, whom he had met at the White Sulphur, and he was wearing a suit that was not of Confederate grey.

It was an interesting moment in American history; the nation was on a pivot between past and future. In nine more days, at Promontory, Utah, two railroad crews, one working west out of the Rockies and another coming east from San Francisco, would meet; a golden spike would be driven, connecting the rails that would make it possible to travel by train from the Atlantic to the Pacific. That was the future: bright, unburdened, seemingly limitless.

In the carriage driving him and the Tagarts from the station to the White House, Lee carried the bloody past. He was as forward-looking as any man, in education, in his efforts for a badly needed railroad, in his efforts to reunite North and South, but people seeing him saw only the past, with all its valor and horror. As he and his friends were driven into the White House grounds at eleven in the morning, it was six years to the hour since the first shots were fired at the opening of his great victory at Chancellorsville. Grant was not opposing him then, but a year later on this date, the two generals were about to clash for the first time in the bloody nightmare of the Wilderness campaign. For the next eleven months Grant had thrown immense forces at Lee, and Lee's men had piled up walls of Union corpses before they went under. The last time Lee and Grant had seen each other was at Appomattox.

A butler opened the door of the White House, and Lee and the Tagarts entered. The President was in his office conferring with John Lothrop Motley, the historian and wartime minister to Austria, whom he was now sending as minister to England. Told that Lee had arrived, Grant rose and asked that he be shown in. Lee entered with the Tagarts. Grant's young secretary, Robert M. Douglas, the son of Lincoln's debating opponent Stephen A. Douglas, was also in the room.

Grant and Lee shook hands; Lee presented the Tagarts, and Motley and Douglas were in turn introduced by Grant. Everyone stood for a few moments as Lee and Grant exchanged small talk. The atmosphere was friendly, but Lee was the more reserved of the two; young Douglas felt that seeing each other stirred memories that saddened both men.

The Tagarts, Motley, and Douglas withdrew; the last thing they saw was Lee and Grant sitting down together. No account of what they discussed was ever recorded. There was some reason to think that Grant hoped to get Lee's ideas of what Federal policy should be in the South under his administration, but that was to remain speculation. Grant's secretary, Douglas, called the visit "merely one of courtesy," and Lee's son Rob said years later that "neither General Lee nor the President spoke a word on political matters."

Grant made only one recorded reference to his conversation with Lee. He later told an aide that when Lee explained that he had been in Baltimore in an effort to start construction of a railroad line, he remarked to Lee, "You and I, General, have had more to do with destroying railroads than with building them." According to Grant, Lee passed over this remark without even acknowledging it and went on to speak of other things.

Lee rose after what he thought was about fifteen minutes, and the two men shook hands and parted courteously. It was the last time they would meet.

Chapter 29

O N MAY 31, the keys to the new President's House were presented by the trustees to Lee in a formal ceremony. The family wasted no time moving into the handsome square brick structure, nearly twice as large as the nearby house they had been living in since December of 1865. The house had the latest inventions, including new systems of running water for every purpose, all of which fascinated Lee. From two five thousand–gallon cisterns, water was pumped to a tank at the top of the house, from which the force of gravity enabled the water to be distributed by pipes throughout the house. A furnace that had poured out smoke when first tested was at last in good working order, ready to supply the warm air that would be circulated through a novel system of air ducts — just in time for summer.

Several features of the house were entirely Lee's idea. A wide roofed-over porch ran around three of its sides; a short ramp from a French window enabled Lee to wheel Mary onto this verandah and walk her around to see three separate views — something impossible to do at the last house, which had only a portico by the front door, and where she had been virtually confined indoors. Mary spent hours on her new porch, even when there was no one to push her back and forth; passersby saw her sitting in her rolling chair, a shawl around her shoulders and her favorite cat, Mrs. Ruffner, asleep in her lap. In an effort to cope with Mildred's ever-growing brood of cats, Lee had designed a special little outbuilding for them. There was a "cow-house" for the Lees' milk cow, and also a small greenhouse and a woodshed.

Firmly connected to the house was a large, warm, sunny stable made of the same brick as the rest of the house. In this equestrian wing were two spacious stalls for Traveller and Lucy Long; hay was stored in the stable's loft and was dropped into the troughs for feeding. Lee wrote a friend that it was gratifying to live under the same roof with Traveller.

Everyone began settling in. Lee quickly found a favorite place to sit, looking out the large bay window of the dining room. In one direction he could see the campus, and in another, Rob said, "his eyes could rest on rolling fields of grass and grain, bounded by the ever-changing mountains."

That was the quiet side, but with a bigger house there was more room for guests; for the impending Commencement Week, Agnes and Mildred had invited six of their friends to come and stay. One of them, Virginia Peyton, found that life at the Lees' was exacting, but with memorable rewards. She was expected to be at the breakfast table at seven o'clock sharp; as the clock struck Lee would step in from the garden and present each lady with a freshly picked rosebud, still wet with dew.

II

In the last week of June, Lee handed their diplomas to the members of the fourth class to graduate during his presidency. There was another departure from Lexington at the end of this 1868–1869 academic year. Lee's invaluable young assistant, Edward Clifford Gordon, had saved enough money so that he could begin his studies at Virginia's Union Theological Seminary, then at Hampden-Sydney.

For three years, Gordon had been Lee's aide on a daily basis during the months the college was in session. They had spent many hundreds of hours together, and Gordon saw Lee as he was. It amused Gordon to read accounts in which people who had known Lee pictured him as being well over six feet tall; "he stood five feet and eleven inches in his cavalry boots," Gordon pointed out, and "among men of the Scotch-Irish race in the Valley of Virginia where I knew him, he was constantly overtopped by men taller and heavier than himself."

No man had a higher opinion of Lee than Gordon did, but there was nothing slavish about his admiration. Listing Lee's virtues, Gordon mentioned among them his modesty, his kindness to animals and love of children, and added, "But these characteristics were combined with what I may call a fierce and violent temper, prone to intense expression." Usually, Gordon said, when some visitor to his office annoyed Lee, he allowed the transgressor to leave in peace. "But the next comer, unless he was unusually wary, was apt to catch the fire."

During pauses in their work, these two Confederate veterans, one sixty-two and the other twenty-six, occasionally spoke of the war; it was something that Lee seldom did. Gordon had no hesitation in writing later, "It was also certain that he was fond of war," and cited Lee's answer when an officer beside Lee had said "Isn't it splendid?" at the sight of Federal troops retreating from the heights of Fredericksburg. "Yes," Lee had replied, "but it is well war is so terrible, or we would become too fond of it."

On his way to study for the ministry, Gordon was of a spiritually analytical turn of mind. He was impressed by Lee's astonishing memory, his ability to manage scores of varied matters, and his intuition about people and events, but what fascinated him was Lee's spirituality. Gordon did not mistake him for St. Francis of Assisi in the woods of Mount Subasio: "He was fond of elegance of every sort; fine houses, furniture, plate, clothing, ornaments, horses, equipage. But he could and did deny himself and his family the enjoyment of such things when he did not have the money to buy them." Gordon saw him as a devout man who "abhorred cant," a man who did not preach but whose every action was a good example, a man who studied the Bible and "was usually found at some other church" if his own had no services on a given Sunday.

What, then, did Gordon conclude? What was the essence of Robert E. Lee?

> Intellectually he was cast in a gigantic mold. Naturally he was possessed of strong passions. He loved excitement, particularly the excitement of war. He loved grandeur. But all these appetites and powers were brought under the control of his judgment and made subservient to his Christian faith. This made him habitually unselfish and ever willing to sacrifice himself on the altar of duty and in

the service of his fellows . . . He is an epistle, written of God and designed by God to teach the people of this country that earthly success
is not the criterion of merit, nor the measure of true greatness.

That summed it up for Gordon; Lee had a simpler explanation of
how he, or anyone, could meet terrible trials and disappointments, and
pray for one's enemies all the while. He believed that all people should
do their best according to their lights, and recognize that what they
wanted might not be what God intended. In odd moments during the
busy days at his desk, Lee jotted down on slips of paper thoughts that
came to him. After his death a stack of these maxims was discovered
in a drawer. The shortest of them read, "God disposes. This ought to
satisfy us."

III

July brought Lee both sorrow and pleasure. On July 22, his brother
Sydney Smith Lee died unexpectedly at his house on the Potomac
south of their boyhood home of Alexandria. Lee had seen little of his
brother Smith in recent years, but felt a deep affection for him.

After attending his brother's funeral, Lee visited Rooney and Tabb
on their farm, and for the first time saw his five-month-old grandson,
Robert E. Lee III. Lee felt that neither Tabb nor the baby looked well,
and suggested that they come with him to the cooler air of the Rockbridge Baths near Lexington, where Mary was staying for the summer.
Safely delivering his daughter-in-law and grandson to Mary, Lee decided to follow the advice of his doctors, who were not at all pleased
with his health and wanted him to drink considerable amounts of the
waters at the White Sulphur.

☆ ☆ ☆

Accompanied by Agnes and Mildred, Lee arrived at the spa at the end
of the first week in August, finding a flamboyant social season under
way. The explosive growth of the nation's railroads was heralding a

new era of great fortunes to be made in cattle, oil, timber, steel, and a score of other industries. A thousand guests, twice the number present the previous summer, packed the White Sulphur. The Southerners were there, eight Confederate generals among them, but now there were vacationers from places as distant as California. Two summers before, the Northern girls sat meekly on the sidelines; now Kate Chase Sprague, daughter of the nation's chief justice and wife of a rich senator from Rhode Island, swept through the halls in stunning Worth gowns from Paris. Her supremacy in fashion was challenged daily by Laura Fair of San Francisco, whose jewelry and wardrobe were financed by the Comstock Lode silver-mining fortune. A flour merchant from Minneapolis wrote home, "One word tells what people do here. Dance." The nightly Treadmill and ball were no longer enough; there were square dances, concerts, and even dances known as "morning germans," which began at eleven and went on until one in the afternoon. The lawns were filled with people playing a new game called croquet; happy the girl who had arrived with a Godey's "croquet suit," with its wide ruffled skirt of Swiss muslin.

Mildred, now twenty-three, and Agnes, twenty-eight, promptly set sail on these interesting social seas. Lee did not have Traveller with him, so there were no long rides, which gave him all the more time to wonder where his daughters were. In his first letter to Mary he said, "The girls are well. I do not know how long they will continue so. They seem to be foot-free." He closed, "The girls would send love if I could find them." Four days later he reported, "The girls are always busy at something, but never ready."

The mineral waters did not improve Lee's health, but his presence at the spa soon benefited Washington College. At his table in the dining room he once again had the company of the art collector and philanthropist W. W. Corcoran of Washington, and through Corcoran's good offices Lee eventually had at his table the greatest philanthropist of his day. This was George Peabody, who, at the age of seventy-four, had less than three months to live. Peabody was from Massachusetts and had spent much of his time as an international money-broker in England, but the largest of his benefactions had been given not to his native North but to the South, which he knew was desperately in need of every kind of help after the war. In 1867 he had created the Fund for

Southern Education, endowing it with what was for that time the stupendous sum of three and a half million dollars.

Peabody was so sick that he spent most of his stay at the White Sulphur in bed, but he had not lost the decisiveness that had characterized his business career; within a few days of meeting Lee he assigned to Washington College a litigation-entangled claim for fifty thousand dollars, which he had against the state of Virginia for state bonds lost when a ship carrying them from England sank in 1854. It was generosity with a touch of Yankee shrewdness: You Southerners go fight it out among yourselves, the genial old man said with his gesture. If General Lee can't get fifty thousand dollars out of the Virginia legislature, nobody can.

Chapter 30

THE COLLEGE OPENED smoothly early in September; in addition to the large group of students from Virginia, there were ten or more from each of the Confederate states and twenty from the North. At home, Lee enjoyed the company of Tabb and his grandson, who had come back to Lexington from the Rockbridge Baths with Mary. But he went right to work with "that quiet zeal and noiseless energy" noted by his faculty colleague Colonel William Preston Johnston, son of his old comrade General Albert Sidney Johnston, who was killed at Shiloh. He did as much as ever in his office, but his doctors were concerned about him, and he had put on weight. Lee still looked magnificent on Traveller, but anyone who saw him making his way on foot had a different picture. An incoming freshman said, "The impression left on me is that of a stout old man who had no too great strength."

II

Near the end of September, a Swiss painter named Frank Buchser arrived in Lexington on horseback. This gifted man was famous in his own country; in Lexington no one knew him or expected him, but they certainly noticed him. The black-haired artist had a thin face from which exploded bushy eyebrows, a goatee, and a waxed mustache

whose tightly rolled tips tapered to their ends in midair six inches on
either side of his nose. He wore a flowing shirt with a Byronic collar
and a bright kerchief. Buchser intended to call on Lee, who did not like
posing for even a photograph, and ask that he spend many hours sitting for a portrait.

Lee's unannounced visitor had packed a lot into his forty-one years.
At the age of eighteen, while he was apprenticed to a piano builder in
Berne, his master discovered him in bed with his daughter and at-
tacked him with a large wooden mallet used for constructing pianos;
Buchser knocked him unconscious with his fists and fled to his destiny.
In Paris he built pianos to pay for his studies at the Beaux-Arts; in
Rome he studied art while earning money serving in the brilliantly
uniformed papal Swiss Guard. With a growing reputation and a fluc-
tuating income, he spent a decade traveling through Europe, North
Africa, and the Middle East, painting, speaking the five languages, including Arabic, that he taught himself, and making love to women of
many nations. By the time he returned to Switzerland in 1866, he was
one of his country's best-known artists, but he re-entered his native
land almost as he left it: in a tavern brawl he sent a government official
to the hospital and faced a jail sentence.

At this time a group of Swiss liberals decided to commission a painting to celebrate the Union victory in the Civil War; it was to be hung in
the Swiss parliament in Berne. A Swiss artist must go to the United
States. Buchser grabbed the chance.

By the time Frank Buchser rode into Lexington, he had parlayed a
trip for one painting into forty months of travel through the North,
South, and Midwest. He loved the United States; born Franz, he
changed his name to Frank and kept it that after his eventual return to
Europe. During his travels he had done many landscapes and studies of
agricultural workers, selling them to European collectors, but he still
had not satisfied the men who sent him over. President Johnson had sat
for him, as had Secretary of State Seward and the South's nemesis,
General William Tecumseh Sherman; but the Swiss liberals wanted
a portrait of Grant, who had repeatedly refused to sit. Buchser's reason for coming to Lexington was that he believed if he could do a
fine painting of Lee and have it shown to Grant, then Grant would
consent.

☆ ☆ ☆

Different as the two men were, when Buchser presented himself Lee liked him. Frank Buchser's father had died when he was a baby; despite his independent career he looked for father figures, and his best portraits were of strong, authoritative men. Perhaps Lee sensed this. He explained to Buchser that his college duties made it impossible for him to sit for the next few days; after that he would give him an hour or two each day until the painting was completed. Lee finished by inviting Buchser to stay at his house.

As a guest, Frank Buchser's performance was a tour de force. His hand-kissing European manners were eminently acceptable to the Lee ladies and their Lexington friends. Along the way this piano builder had learned to play not only that instrument but the guitar, and to sing lively songs in his native German and in Arabic, English, French, Italian, and Spanish. As he accompanied himself on the guitar, he gave off the aura of a man whose diary contained entries such as:

> I despise no colors, even the snow-white ladies. The Caucasian descendants in the Atlas and the blond-haired Berber children are not to be despised, yet dark colors, gypsy girls, love more, love more fervently, know more about the pleasures of love. Then come the next ones on the color scale . . . The Indian woman is a worthy companion-piece to the gypsy girl; darker and darker; the black child in the Sudan has the most delicate skin and the sweetest voice. But as I said, let's not despise our own whites.

Buchser listened as well as sang, and enjoyed the ladies' performances at the piano. He was discreet; in his diary he said only that when a lovely Lexington woman sat down to play, "our two artists' hearts met."

By the time that Lee was ready for their first sitting, Buchser had an entirely new idea about the portrait. Suppose, he asked Lee, that we do the surrender at Appomattox? I could paint you in your uniform standing on one side of a table, and leave the other half of the canvas blank. Then I could go to Washington, and I am sure General Grant would consent to be painted standing on the other side of the table in his uniform.

Lee was by now treating Buchser as if he were an impetuous younger relative. What bothered Lee was the idea of being painted in uniform; if Buchser could get Grant into the other half of the picture, that was his business. "I am a soldier no longer," Lee said. He was a college president, and he would wear the black broadcloth suit he had worn to

Rooney's wedding. In recognition of the past, on the table beside him in the portrait Buchser could arrange the sword, sword belt, sash, and uniform coat he had worn at Appomattox, along with his binoculars and one of his wartime hats. Lee would get them out for him.

Buchser saw that this was the end of his new idea; no one in Switzerland wanted Lee and Grant in civilian clothes standing on opposite sides of a table. It would be a portrait of Lee alone in a dark suit, and on the table beside him would be the sword and the gold-braided sword belt and the silk sash.

For three weeks, Lee sat for Buchser at the hours permitted by his schedule. Soon Buchser fell under Lee's spell. On October 3, he wrote in his diary, "What a gentle noble soul, how kind and charming the old white-haired warrior is!" Two days later he added, "One cannot see and know this great soldier without loving him."

As for Lee, he unburdened himself on several matters in a way that he did with no American. Since the war, he had said not a word against the performance of Jefferson Davis as Confederate President, or about his refusal to surrender even after Appomattox, a decision that had cost additional lives. Now, while warmly praising his character, Lee said that Davis "was, of course, one of the extremest politicians." He would also make his only recorded critical remarks about Grant.

Buchser later explained how their serious conversations developed, and why the sixty-two-year-old Lee looked like a man of fifty in the finished portrait. During the first sittings, Lee was unbending in his posture and chose neutral subjects in his conversation. As Buchser worked and talked, he convinced Lee of his desire to know the truth about the recent past — arriving in the United States soon after the Civil War was like arriving at the scene of an accident and asking the survivors what had happened and what should be done now — and soon Lee was talking earnestly. He spoke about secession, about the war, and as he remembered moment after moment, Lee's face took on even more of the high color that had always been his; the brown eyes became darker and shone with emotion. Years dropped from him; Buchser's brush moved; he painted only what he saw. "I painted his left eye today," he wrote; "it is the living eye of this great man. One can read in it the heavy history, the heavy storm his heart underwent."

☆ ☆ ☆

The conversations they had during the day moved Buchser to put thoughts of his own on paper during the evenings. He had spent a lot of time in Washington and was disillusioned by many of his meetings with the figures in government. "The conviction is growing in me that if the American statesmen of the last fifteen years had been half as intelligent and only half as honest and capable as the soldiers, that is the Generals Grant, Lee, Sherman, etc., then the war would never have been started."

In their conversations, Lee was now talking without reserve:

> Speaking of the war altogether he agreed with me fully that the war was only created by a set of poor politicians, but that it was by no means a necessity and could easily have been avoided, but that the republican party wanted to get control of the country and to obtain this they did not shrink back from anything.
>
> Of Grant he says that he never liked him so well as at the time of the surrender, that he was then really magnanimous, but since then that he allows himself to be guided almost entirely by the party who elected him, but that he believes that if he could follow the dictates of his heart that he would act otherwise. All these things will work around in time.

Buchser did not lack confidence in his work. In his last diary entry in Lexington he said, "The picture of R. E. Lee is going to be remarkable." Then he recorded Lee's views on the hanging of Major Henry Wirz, the Confederate officer who had been commandant at Andersonville prison, and on the subject of exchanging prisoners.

> He told me today that the accusation against Wirz was the world's most unjust calumny, and his subsequent hanging was pure judicial murder; that they, Confederate States, offered everything to arrange an exchange of prisoners of war, but that the North never agreed to it. Grant personally included in this. Lee asserts that ultimately the Confederate States offered to release their prisoners of war unilaterally if the Union would merely provide the means of transportation. Grant is supposed to have refused this also.
>
> When the Confederacy indicated to the North that it did not have enough doctors or medical supplies to treat sick prisoners and requested that the United States government might possibly provide it with doctors and medical supplies, that it, if so desired, would use this aid only for Union prisoners and not for its own Confederate troops, this too was without success.

On the evening of October 18, there was a special party at the Lees' to honor Buchser and to display the completed portrait. The face that looked from the canvas was less handsome than the one the family saw every day; with its quizzical twist of the eyebrows, it could have been the picture of a shrewd, suspicious farmer who was wearing his best suit. But it was an immensely arresting face; a zealot might have possessed those gleaming eyes. On the lips was the trace of a smile; after all, there were those many hours a few feet from a painter whose mustache ends were twelve inches apart. The Lee in this portrait was younger, slimmer; he looked as if he could toil in the fields all day and relish every minute. If he shouted for something you would certainly hear him back at the house.

And so Frank Buchser left Lexington, carrying his canvas aboard a canal boat for Lynchburg. Of the paintings of Lee done from life that survived, this was the third. The first showed a striking, vital young first lieutenant of Engineers, his face all optimism and confidence; the second was a prosaic effort that pictured an able, self-controlled superintendent of West Point; and now there was this far more interesting face. Buchser was on his way back to Washington, but he had lost interest in having this portrait of Lee shown to Grant. He had the painting boxed in Lynchburg and sent on to Norfolk for shipment across the Atlantic. The most original picture of Robert E. Lee would go to Europe and stay there.

Frank Buchser wrote his Swiss patrons that they should accept this picture of Lee instead of the one they wanted of Grant; he told them that "all agree he is the greater character." In terms that would have startled the Republicans, Buchser claimed that Lee "is furthermore the ideal of American democracy. Therefore, of all my American portraits, the one of Lee is the perfect picture to hang in the democratic Swiss parliament."

Buchser's patrons were dumbfounded by this culmination of their effort to commission a painting to celebrate the Union victory. They refused to pay him. Time changed things; a century later this painting of Lee, considered to be Frank Buchser's finest portrait, was on permanent display in the Swiss National Museum.

III

On the day Buchser left with his vibrant portrait, Lee came down with what at first appeared to be only a severe cold. He stayed in the house for a week, chafing to get on with his work for the college. On November 2, he attended a faculty meeting and afterward went for a ride on Traveller in the cold dusk. That put him back in bed.

By now his Lexington physicians, Drs. Howard T. Barton and R. L. Madison, were putting together a more comprehensive picture of their patient's condition. When Lee complained of aches, they thought of rheumatism; a later medical generation would have looked first for a deteriorating heart, which could supply the other symptoms. These doctors were ready to talk about a combination of pericarditis, an inflammation of the membranous sac surrounding the heart, and arthritis, which Lee may have developed independently. In fact, their patient had been suffering from angina pectoris, a symptom of blockage of the coronary arteries, a condition that probably started about the time of his undiagnosed heart attack at Fredericksburg in the spring of 1863.

What these physicians saw was a body that had enjoyed splendid health for most of its life, a superior system still capable of remarkable efforts, and a patient whose normal pace was to push himself hard. The doctors began to understand that what they were encountering — fluid in the lungs, aches in chest, arms, back — was all related to a heart and circulatory system that were badly worn. But there were limits to what they could do, other than to urge their patient to rest.

Lee knew that his body was in trouble, but he dug within himself for strength. After eighteen days in his house, he emerged, returning to duty. To his office there came from New York, at last, the new edition of his father's Revolutionary War memoirs, edited by Lee and with a new introduction by him. As for his projected history of his own campaigns, the idea that had been uppermost in his mind at Derwent in the summer of 1865 until Judge Brockenbrough unexpectedly arrived with the offer that brought him to Lexington, Lee would soon write, "I have not commenced the narrative." He never would.

Even at half-strength, Lee could overlook nothing. Slowly walking

down the path from his house to his office, he saw a high-spirited student, with no malice in mind, pick up a stone and loft it toward the
cupola that rose from the roof of the chapel. The stone knocked a shingle off the upper part of the cupola, and the student went on his way,
still unaware of Lee coming down the path behind him.

The summons to appear in Lee's office was delivered by the janitor,
Lewis. Lee still knew every face, every name, and the family circumstances of all his students. This boy was from Nashville, Tennessee,
where his father was a rich man. The student was informed by Lee that
the shingle he knocked off was going to be replaced at his expense. In
the right spot, replacing one shingle would not have been expensive,
but this scar at the top of the tower of Lee's beloved new chapel was a
different matter. In awe, another student reported what was involved.
"This was done by a number of mechanics, who built scaffolding up to
the necessary height. The expense was said to be thirty-odd dollars." In
1869, that was enough to feed a boy in the dining hall for two months.

☆   ☆   ☆

The world outside Lexington had no idea that Lee's health was slipping so markedly. He never received more business offers, or financially
more attractive ones. General John B. Gordon of Georgia, who had led
the tattered Confederate column that received the Union Army's salute at the Appomattox surrender, had become a successful lawyer and
insurance executive in Atlanta. He wrote asking Lee to become president of his organization, the Southern Life Insurance Company. Lee
answered, "It would be a great pleasure to be associated with you,
Hampton, B. H. Hill and the other good men whose names I see on
your list of directors, but I feel that I ought not to abandon the position
I hold at Washington College at this time or as long as I can be of service to it."

Chapter 31

As long as I can be of service — that was the problem Lee was considering as 1869 closed. The facts were confusing. In the office, he was working most effectively. As 1870 began, he continued his voluminous correspondence for the college, appeared in classrooms during the midyear examinations, and dealt personally with students, as always. A work of particular satisfaction was accomplished when Lee's mapmaking Board of Survey determined that Virginia's southern boundary was not marked accurately, and Lee was able to write Governor Gilbert C. Walker, "In consequence of these errors, the State of Virginia is deprived of several hundred square miles of territory." Lee was also working hard to have Lexington designated the site of a proposed astronomical observatory.

Here, on one hand, were effort and achievement; on the other, he wrote Rooney, "The doctors still have me in hand, but I fear can do me no good." He made his condition graphic when he wrote to Mildred, who was visiting friends, "I cannot walk much farther than to the college" — a distance of one hundred and fifty yards — "though when I get on my horse I can ride with comfort." Yet in this same letter to Mildred, the man who is exhausted by a walk of less than two hundred yards continues cheerfully about the social life at home that she is missing by being in Richmond: "Gaiety continues. Last night there was a cadet hop. Night before, a party at Colonel Johnston's. The night preceding, a college *conversazione* at your mother's . . . You know how agreeable I am on such occasions, but on this, I am told, I surpassed myself."

For a time, Lee continued in this way. On warm winter days he would ride out on Traveller, accompanied now by Agnes on Lucy Long. He continued his keen interest in the affairs of the day, most particularly the welcome news that on January 26, 1870, President Grant had signed the bill readmitting Virginia to the Union. Military District Number One vanished; the state was occupied territory no longer.

II

For the first ten weeks of 1870, Lee tried to carry on as usual, even though Rob believed that his father "was constantly in pain and had begun to look on himself as an invalid." The family was worried.

Lee's business-as-usual attitude changed abruptly in the third week in March. Declining an offer of the managing directorship of an association for the development of trade in the town of Alexandria, he wrote, "My health has been so feeble this winter that I am only waiting to see the effect of the opening spring before relinquishing my present position. I am admonished by my feelings that my years of labor are nearly over."

It was one thing to write a letter turning down a job, but it was far harder to discuss a possible resignation with his associates. His first concession to what he now thought might be inevitable was in a brief conversation with his faculty friend Colonel William Preston Johnston. "General Lee said to me at his office where I had called on some little matter of routine, that if he did not get better, he would be obliged to resign his position as President of Washington College."

Johnston had to leave at that moment for one of his classes, and simply said that he was sure that Lee would feel better if he would slow the pace he had been setting for himself at the college for four and a half years. The next day Johnston returned, and being encouraged to talk more about it, told Lee "that I was confident that his illness was due to over-confinement and want of relaxation and change of air and scene and begged that he would either visit his many friends at Savannah, as

I knew Miss Agnes wished, or that he would visit General Rooney Lee."

Describing his illness, Lee told Johnston that he could not walk up the slope from the chapel to his house, another walk of less than two hundred yards, without stopping to rest. "He alluded to his age" — Lee had turned sixty-three in January — "his wish to rest, and, on some little farm, to enjoy the outdoor life of the country." Lee added, prophetically, that "he could not go to Savannah without meeting more people than he wanted to."

Johnston noticed something else: Lee "was evidently labouring under great depression of spirits."

The two Confederate veterans, now educators, talked for an hour and a quarter. "I tried to point out to him as delicately as I could," the younger man said, "that what we wanted here was his control, and not work; that he had everything in such excellent running order, that in his absence the machine would run for a while by its own momentum, with the inspiration of the headship to which we all looked."

Colonel Johnston pressed Lee to take a vacation before deciding, but he left Lee's office convinced "that if he was not turned from his purpose he would resign."

In succeeding days, Lee brought up the same subject with Captain James J. White and another Confederate officer who was now a professor, Colonel William Allan, who had been Stonewall Jackson's ordnance officer. These two men consulted with Johnston; the three of them sought the opinions of the rest of the faculty, and a meeting was held out of Lee's presence. Then Johnston, White, and Allan were sent as a delegation to Lee. He received them at five in the afternoon; Johnston's first thought was that "the General was not looking well."

His three younger colleagues handed Lee a letter that begged him to take a vacation for two months and to appoint one of the faculty as acting president while he was gone. By implication, the faculty also begged him not to resign, although Johnston assured him that, whatever Lee's decision, they were all deeply in his debt.

Lee began to speak, with tears in his eyes. He again mentioned his age, his illness, his wish to rest. For the first time, he spoke of his desire to make a permanent home for his wife — the new President's House belonged to the college, and Lee never referred to it as being his. If he died, a new president would occupy that house. He wanted to do better than that for Mary, "who is helpless."

Lee made his final point. "He also said that he felt he might at any moment die."

Three silent and pensive professors walked away from this meeting. In the memorandum he wrote that evening, Johnston summed up, "He promised to consider the communication, and now it is my belief that his purpose is fixed and that we shall soon lose General Lee at Washington College."

III

Professor Johnston was wrong. Lee decided to try the long vacation rather than resign immediately. He wrote Mildred, who was still off visiting, "The doctors and others think I had better go to the South." His own view was: "I think I should do better here, and am very reluctant to leave home in my present condition; but they seem so interested in my recovery and so persuasive in their uneasiness that I should appear obdurate, if not perverse, if I resisted longer."

As in war, once his mind was made up, Lee moved swiftly. He appointed the Reverend Dr. John L. Kirkpatrick, professor of moral philosophy, to act as president while he was gone. He had decided, he wrote Mildred, "to take Agnes to Savannah, as she seems anxious to visit that city, or, perhaps, she will take me." Lee's daughter Mary was in Lexington at this point, and would stay to take care of her mother. Custis would also be on hand. "I am sorry not to be able to see you before I go," Lee said to Mildred in closing, "but if I return, I hope to find you here well and happy."

If I return. Lee repeated that thought in a letter to Rooney just before his departure. Speaking of his daughter who had died during the war, he said, "I shall go first to Warrenton Springs, North Carolina, to visit the grave of my dear Annie, where I have always promised myself to go, and I think if I am to accomplish it, I have no time to lose."

☆ ☆ ☆

On the morning of March 24, 1870, six days after the faculty letter begging him to take a vacation was handed to him, Lee said good-bye to his wife, to Daughter and Custis, and set off with Agnes in the carriage taking them the mile and a half to the canal-boat landing on the river. Along the road he saw scores of his students heading in the same direction on foot; they doffed their hats as his carriage passed. At the wharf, Lee understood: his faculty and hundreds of his students had come to see him off. There was no band, there were no speeches, just his young men standing on the bank as he and Agnes went aboard the packet boat. Lee turned on the deck and raised his hat to them. A member of the junior class was "painfully struck with the change in his appearance" in recent months.

The canal boat cast off; a few of the bolder boys called words of farewell; Agnes waved. Lee lifted his hat again.

In retrospect, it was to be a moment of enormous naïveté. Almost overnight, at the request of his faculty and on the urging of his doctors and his family, Lee was going south. He at least had some premonition that this might not be a quiet rest — he had wanted to stay home and had said that "he could not go to Savannah without meeting more people than he wanted to."

That was to be the greatest understatement ever made by a modest man who truly disliked applauding crowds. Someone — one of his faculty, one of his doctors, one of his more worldly Lexington friends — should have realized that it would be impossible for Lee to take a quiet trip through the South for his health. In the five years since Appomattox he had been to parts of Virginia, to Washington, to Baltimore, and to a few hot springs west of Lexington. That was all. This was the first time he would travel south of Virginia into other ardent Confederate states, where millions wanted to see him. He was on his way, launching himself right at them. Lee was thinking like a tourist, carrying train schedules and wondering about the availability of hotel rooms. The South, once it knew, would receive him as an emperor, almost as a god.

Chapter 32

EVEN THIS first part of the journey to Richmond on the canal boat to Lynchburg was hard on Lee. He wrote Mary that "the night aboard the packet was very trying, but I survived it, and the dust of the railroad the following day." Three of Richmond's leading physicians gave him a thorough examination; Lee described himself as "a little feverish. Whether it is produced by the journey, or the toddies that Agnes administers, I do not know."

Lee was deliberately avoiding crowds and undue excitement in Richmond, a city that was used to seeing him, but going from one part of his hotel to another he encountered Colonel John S. Mosby, whose force of mounted irregulars had made spectacular behind-the-lines raids. "The general was pale and haggard," Mosby recalled, "and did not look like the Apollo I had known in the army." Lee invited him to his room, where they talked of current news. "I felt oppressed by the great memories that his presence revived," Mosby wrote, "and while both of us were thinking about the war, neither of us referred to it."

Leaving Lee's room, within a few minutes Mosby ran into Major General George E. Pickett, whose division had been torn to shreds in the final brave and suicidal charge at Gettysburg; of the forty-five hundred men who went with Pickett up Cemetery Ridge, thirty-three hundred and ninety-three fell dead or wounded, and with them went the Confederacy's last hope of winning its independence. The contemporary historian James D. McCabe wrote, "From his position on Seminary Ridge, General Lee had witnessed the charge. As he saw his men driven back from the heights, it is said that he placed his finger for a moment thoughtfully between his lips." Although the blame for failure at Gettysburg could be shared among several generals in addition to Lee, he had taken the entire responsibility; on the battlefield he said to Pickett, who had behaved superbly, "This has been my fight and upon my shoulders rests the blame."

When Mosby said that he had just been with Lee, Pickett impulsively "remarked that if I would go with him, he would call and pay his respects to the general but did not want to be alone with him." They went back into the hotel, two men in business suits on a busy street, Mosby a successful thirty-six-year-old lawyer, and Pickett a struggling insurance agent of forty-five, both overwhelmed by memories. Pickett, a West Pointer, felt that Lee had sacrificed his splendid division at Gettysburg after the chance for winning that battle had clearly passed, but there was more than that to estrange Pickett and Lee. Eight days before the surrender at Appomattox, Pickett had left his own headquarters to attend a shad-bake two miles away at the headquarters of Major General Thomas L. Rosser. While Pickett was eating fish, the Federals launched a powerful surprise attack that began the disaster known as Five Forks. Just how derelict in his duty Pickett was on this occasion was debatable, but Lee sent an order relieving him of command and transferring him away from the collapsing Army of Northern Virginia. Pickett evidently did not receive the order, because he went on riding at the head of his Five Forks survivors. Seeing Pickett pass by on the eve of surrender, Lee, who always referred to an officer by his name and rank if he knew it, turned to Lieutenant Colonel Charles Venable of his staff and said coldly, "Is that man still with this army?" That was the last time Lee had laid eyes on him.

These two famous officers, Mosby and Pickett, came down the hall to Lee's hotel room. Ironically, Mosby, who was in good graces with everyone, including Lee, had become a Republican and would canvass voters for Grant during the next election. Pickett, who was having a hard time supporting his family, was to refuse President Grant's offer of the post of United States marshal for Virginia. It was Grant's tribute to the valor of Pickett and his men, an effort to help a fellow West Pointer, and an attempt to place Federal authority in Virginia into the hands of a man acceptable to Virginians. Pickett would decline because he felt that to accept such a Federal appointment was a step beyond what a Confederate general should do.

As a social call, the next minutes were the equivalent of Gettysburg and Five Forks combined. Lee's words when he saw Pickett were civil, but as the three men sat down together Lee's tone was icy and his face frozen. Whether this was guilt for Gettysburg or anger about Five Forks or some combination of the two would remain an unanswered question. Pickett instantly regretted his impulse to call on his old commander, and sat matching Lee's glacial manner.

Mosby could not stand it and got to his feet. Pickett and Lee both gladly rose and parted with the briefest of farewells. Going back down the hall, Pickett burst out bitterly against Lee, calling him "that old man," and saying, "He had my division slaughtered at Gettysburg."

Mosby wondered how to reply to that. Thousands of ghosts were listening. "Well," he observed, "it made you immortal."

Lee's next caller was infinitely more welcome. This was Colonel James L. Corley, an able executive who had been Lee's chief supply officer. He had learned that Lee and Agnes were under the impression that they could handle their trip by themselves. Knowing that they could not, he dropped everything, came to the hotel, and politely insisted that Lee turn the project over to him. When he left his former commander, it was understood that Corley would join the Lees in Charlotte, North Carolina, after they had visited the grave of Annie Lee. Corley would travel with them from there, handling the arrangements.

II

On the evening of March 28, Lee and Agnes crossed into North Carolina on a train. They were going through little-populated areas, and their presence was known only to a startled few individuals who boarded their coach.

The state that they were entering had been a tower of strength during the war. With less than 10 percent of the Confederacy's population, North Carolina sent forward 20 percent of the South's soldiers; one quarter of the Confederates killed in action were from North Carolina. Lee had seen them storm the slopes at Gettysburg; the Twenty-sixth

North Carolina started the battle with eight hundred and eighty men and ended it with a hundred and seventy-two. Sick, hungry, sleepless, North Carolinians had been among the very last of the immortal scarecrows who marched up to stack their arms at Appomattox.

At ten o'clock that night the Lees stepped down onto the station platform that served the quiet little town of Warrenton. No one knew that they were coming; Lee assumed that they could find a hotel.

A local merchant named Will White, who was a Confederate veteran, was at the station, meeting his sister on the incoming train. He blinked. It seemed impossible, but that was General Robert E. Lee standing at the depot in the middle of the night, accompanied by a very pretty black-haired young woman, both of them apparently lost. Soon the commander of the Army of Northern Virginia and his daughter were asleep under the roof of this veteran's surprised and delighted parents.

The next morning, when the Lees' impromptu hosts discovered that they had come to visit the grave of their daughter and sister, they tactfully sent them off in a carriage by themselves. As Lee picked up the reins, their hostess handed Agnes an armful of white hyacinths.

Lee was silent as he turned the carriage off the main road and headed through a forest of cedars to the rural cemetery. Annie Lee haunted the family's memories; with all that they had endured, with all that Lee and Custis and Rooney and Rob had risked and survived, it seemed unthinkable that of the seven children the only wartime death was that of Annie, stricken by typhoid at a place far from the fighting and dead at twenty-three. Lee called her "the purest and best" of his children. Because of a childhood eye injury that marred her looks, no picture was ever made of Annie. In a letter he wrote her from San Antonio, Texas, in 1860, Lee spoke openly of family friction in a way that he did with none of his other six children. Back on the frontier after nearly two years spent principally on leave at home at Arlington in his effort to save the family farms, Lee said to Annie, "It is better too I hope for all that I am here. You know I was much in the way of everybody, and my tastes and pursuits did not coincide with the rest of the household. Now I hope everybody is happier." No letter to or from Lee added to this clue that life at Arlington was not always the idyll that the family, including Lee himself, remembered it as being. He was

at that time a worried man — worried about his army career, which
was at the mercy of a system of promotion by seniority; worried about
the outcome of the struggle to put the neglected Custis farms on a paying basis; troubled about the stark vision of God and humanity that
came to a colonel who had to read the burial service under a summer
Texas sun for "as handsome a little boy as I ever saw — the son of one
of the sergeants, about a year old; I was admiring his appearance the
day before he was taken ill. Last Thursday his little waxen form was
committed to the earth." Most of all he had been worried about the
growing rift between North and South. When it came, Annie Lee
wrote a friend in Georgia that she had received a letter from an equally
dear Northern friend: "She asks me if we intend to make Virginia a
graveyard, and I have replied 'not for us, but for you.' "

Arlington was a Northern graveyard now; Lee and Agnes were ap-
proaching the cemetery in a North Carolina cedar forest where Annie
lay. The news of Annie's death had come in a letter delivered to Lee at
his headquarters near Winchester. He read it and with astonishing
self-control went over some military correspondence brought to his
desk just then by his gallant young aide Walter H. Taylor, who had no
idea that anything was wrong. Taylor left the tent with this sheaf of
papers; when he returned unexpectedly a few minutes later he found
Lee with the letter in his hand, weeping.

Here was the cemetery in the woods. Lee and Agnes got out of the
carriage in the silence, Agnes with the white flowers in her arms. They
had no trouble locating the grave. These far from rich country people
had taken up a collection among themselves to erect a granite column
twelve feet high for the daughter of Robert E. Lee.

III

That evening, the Lees boarded the train that was to take them all the
way to Augusta, Georgia. It was the first night that either had spent in
that recent invention, the Pullman sleeping car.

As Lee and Agnes retired for the night in their curtained berths along the aisle, they were unaware that the nature of their trip was about to change dramatically. At midnight the train would stop to take on passengers at Raleigh, the capital of North Carolina. The telegraph operator at the Warren Plains station had wired ahead four words: GENERAL LEE IS ABOARD. Even at this hour, the news went through Raleigh like a flame; people poured down streets to the station. Long before the train pulled in, the crowd was waiting.

A startled Agnes awoke to hear a roar of "Lee! Lee!" coming from the platform outside the curtained window next to where she was lying in her Pullman berth. She did not raise the curtain, and her father, also blasted from sleep by this cheering, did not look out his window either. "We were locked up and 'mum,' " Agnes wrote her mother of this first mass encounter with her father's admirers.

By sunrise, the telegraph lines of the South were humming. At little depots where the train did not even slow down Lee's veterans were out, many holding on their shoulders children born since the war, hundreds of them named after him. The Lees had their curtains up now; for them, shortly after dawn, the South was passing by as a succession of babies being held up to the train at red-clay crossroads, women waving handkerchiefs from buckboard wagons, and dignified-looking men suddenly thrusting their hats into the air and howling the Rebel Yell.

It was before the day of dining cars; at meal times, the train stopped and the passengers went into a nearby restaurant, sometimes located in the station itself. Lee saw that even in a small place he would be mobbed, and he and Agnes decided to stay on the train and forgo breakfast. In a few minutes a procession crossed the platform and entered the car; it was the proprietor of the restaurant and his staff, carrying an enormous breakfast on trays. After the train pulled out, the porter appeared with a basket of fruit. There were some Federal soldiers on the train, enlisted men of the Regular Army, and they had chipped in and bought this fruit for General Lee while the train was stopped.

Now came the larger towns. Salisbury, North Carolina, had its entire population there, and a band thundering out the Confederate battle songs. Lee still stayed inside the train. On to Charlotte, North Carolina, and a larger crowd and a bigger band. Out of the throng came

Colonel James L. Corley, Lee's self-appointed guide through what lay ahead, reporting for duty just as he had promised back in Richmond, shouldering his way through just the sort of tumult he had expected.

The train soon crossed into South Carolina. Here was the state that had been wildest for secession; a colonel who watched a South Carolina brigade withstand three hours of Federal assaults at Second Manassas wryly called it "the consummation of the grand debate between Massachusetts and South Carolina." In those terms, there had been much more to come; after his "march to the sea" reached Savannah, Georgia, Sherman turned and marched north through South Carolina, leaving an avenue of wreckage forty miles wide. The correspondent for the *New York Herald* who was with Sherman for the entire campaign wrote, "As for wholesale burnings, pillage and devastation committed in South Carolina, magnify all I have said of Georgia some fifty-fold." Half the state's property values were lost during the war. South Carolina's Reconstruction government was one of the South's worst: two hundred trial judges were said to be unable to read, and an historian wrote of the notorious general assembly that "legislation was by bribery."

It was pouring rain when the train reached Columbia, the state's capital. Two thirds of the city was burned at the war's end. For Lee's arrival a holiday had been declared. Stores and offices were closed. There was a parade to the station; to the sounds of trumpets and drums, a long grey column of Confederate veterans marched in step through the rain, followed by more bands and many civic groups. The organizer of the welcome was Colonel Alexander Haskell, commander of the Seventh South Carolina Cavalry and a man who repeatedly had been invaluable to Lee's army in crucial combat situations. His was a fighting spirit that enabled him to say that when he and his men withdrew from Richmond a week before Appomattox, "the idea of subjugation never dawned upon us."

Columbia, too, was only a fifteen-minute stop on the train's route south, but when Lee looked out the window he knew that this time he would have to emerge. On the platform in the rain stood a long rank of his former officers. The first to catch his eye was Brigadier General E. Porter Alexander, who had been the young commander of Longstreet's artillery. It was Alexander who suggested on the last morning of fighting at Appomattox that Lee turn his army into small guerrilla bands that should slip through the Federal lines and organize further fighting throughout the South. Had Lee acted on the suggestion instead of quickly rejecting it, the cost to the South in additional lost lives and property and prolonged suffering might have been incalculable. So many had died as it was, but at least these men on the platform were alive; Alexander was standing with his little daughter beside him, her hand in his.

Lee put on his hat and coat and stepped into the cold rain, his eyes looking from under the dripping brim at men who had saluted him in a hundred rainstorms, on battlefields and on the march. The band struck up; little girls came forward and handed him bouquets as the crowd cheered itself hoarse. Everyone wanted a speech, but Lee simply lifted his hat in the rain and bowed. The band thundered on again. General Alexander came forward with his little daughter; Lee swept the child up in his arms and smiled at her reassuringly amidst the drums beating, the trumpets, and the sound of his veterans giving voice to the Rebel Yell.

☆　☆　☆

After traveling for twenty-four hours on the train, they reached Augusta; there they were, as Agnes put it, "whirled" off to the Planter's Hotel to spend the night. Lee had hoped for a day and a night of complete rest before going on to Savannah, but even Colonel Corley was unable to save him from a morning-long reception at the hotel. "Crowds came," Agnes wrote home to Lexington, describing a line that passed through for hours — veterans on crutches, farmers and laborers and their wives, and "the sweetest little children — dressed to their eyes." Those who were too young to introduce themselves had "tiny cards in their fat little hands — with their names." In the case of the boys, often the first part of the name was Robert E. Lee.

A boy of thirteen came to the hotel that morning on his own. He wiggled his way through the crowd until he got right next to Lee and then stood silently and unabashedly admiring him. The boy's name was Woodrow Wilson.

IV

Leaving Augusta the next morning, the Lees were no longer ordinary tourists who bought their own tickets. At the station they and Colonel Corley were escorted through a cheering crowd of veterans to a luxurious private railroad car attached to the rear of the train.

By evening they would be in Savannah, a hundred and sixty miles away. For Lee, their destination was a city filled with particularly fond memories. As a bachelor second lieutenant just out of West Point, his first assignment had been to assist in the construction of a fort at Cockspur Island, twelve miles below Savannah. The site for the fort was a miserable marshy place, but in Savannah he was warmly received at the home of his West Point classmate and close friend Jack Mackay. In addition to Jack's two brothers, there were four daughters in the family, the oldest two being Margaret, aged twenty, and Eliza, eighteen. Lee promptly displayed great interest in Margaret, and when she soon married a local doctor, he transferred his affections to Eliza, who was petite, had deep brown eyes, and was gifted at drawing and painting. Going home to Virginia on leave, he became engaged to Mary, whom he had known from childhood; returning to Savannah, he remained a constant caller at the Mackays', enjoying the company of a large and charming family who were devoted to him, and he kept up his gallant attentions to both the married Margaret and to Eliza.

In the case of Eliza, his heart was to some degree involved. While he was truly fond of Mary, it was a day when marriages were based on many things besides love, and he was making a most advantageous match. Less than three months before his wedding, from his post down the river from Savannah he was writing Eliza about his impending transfer to Fort Monroe at Old Point Comfort, Virginia, where he would be living with Mary. Complaining that he had received no letters from Eliza during these last days at Cockspur Island, he said to her, "It did grieve me so to see the Boats coming down one after another, without any of those *little comforts* which are now so *necessary* to me. Oh me! I do not know what I shall do for them at Old Point. But you will send some sometimes, Will you not Sweet — ? How I will besiege the P. Office."

Lee proved to be a faithful husband, and over the years his feeling for Eliza turned into a warm and lasting friendship, shared in by Mary. The Lees kept up with all the Mackays; many years later, Eliza, married to a diplomat, brought her daughter to visit at Arlington, and on another occasion the Lees entertained two of Eliza's nephews. Over the years, Eliza had died, Jack Mackay had died, even the daughter Eliza brought to Arlington had died, but several of the Mackays whom Lee had known still lived in Savannah, and he was looking forward to seeing them. Eliza's house in Broughton Street was one of the places where he had been happiest in his life; visiting there on a coastal-defense inspection trip soon after the Mexican War, Lieutenant Colonel Lee sat down to dinner with the family as gaily as in those earlier days. Hugh Mercer, a West Point friend who had resigned from the service, saw him during that visit: referring to him as "Bob Lee," Mercer wrote, "I do not find him at all changed — he runs on just as he used to — He made me laugh very heartily and laughed himself until the tears ran down his face."

That Savannah never faded for Lee. Early in the war he spent time there organizing its seaward defenses, preparations for which he found had "lagged terribly." It was a critical moment, but even then he spent his evenings at Broughton Street with his friends of happier days. Eliza, then in good health but with only six years left to live, mended his shirts and made him three new ones. Through all the years, Savannah was for Lee what he had said in an early letter to Jack Mackay: "That spot of spots! That place of places!! That city of cities!!!"

V

In contrast to the places through which Lee had passed on the first part of his trip, Savannah had received ample time to prepare its reception for him. Before Lee's train got there, it stopped to take aboard a delegation of his former officers, who rode with him the rest of the way.

Shortly after six in the evening, these men escorted Lee and Agnes and Colonel Corley off the train. Waiting for Lee was the largest crowd that had ever assembled in Savannah. The dignitaries greeting him had to push back the cheering throng in the station to make a path to the open carriage waiting on the street. Outside the station, the crowd packed so thick around the carriage that the horses could not move after Lee was seated in it. Finally, he rose and bowed, and the crowd began to fall back.

That evening the fine hand of Colonel Corley showed itself. Lee was at Brigadier General Alexander Lawton's house, which had crowds in the street in front of it. He was spirited out the back way and taken to the house of Andrew Low, a rich cotton merchant who had been married to Eliza's daughter. While two brass bands in front of General Lawton's house were playing "Dixie," "The Bonnie Blue Flag," and other wartime songs, Lee was peacefully asleep in another house.

Chapter 33

WHILE LEE was in Savannah, at Lexington the trustees and faculty began arrangements that would force him into a somewhat more comfortable pace if he resumed his college work. Captain White was assigned to be his secretary and aide. Because the faculty knew that Lee would insist on continuing to see students in his office, they compromised in advance by limiting the hours for such meetings to run only from eight-forty-five to ten-thirty each morning.

Now fully aware that Lee thought he might die at any time and was worried about what would become of Mary, the trustees worked out a proposal to convey the new President's House to her for her lifetime, and to give her an annuity of three thousand dollars a year. The trustees had made maximum use of Lee's presence at Washington College; now they intended to take care of him and his family in every way that they could. They stated their purpose in handsome words:

> The Board realizes that the recent additions to the College endowment are due not merely to aid the cause of education, but are largely also evidence of the desire of his countrymen to promote the personal comfort of the President and his family. The Board consider it a right, a duty and a privilege to provide promptly to that end.

As for Mary, she was reading the mail from her traveling husband and daughter. From Savannah, Lee wrote her two classic understatements — "The old soldiers have greeted me very cordially," and "I do not think travelling in this way procures me much quiet and repose." He said of the trip that he had "more than ever regretted that I undertook it," and that "I perceive no change in the stricture in my chest. If I attempt to walk beyond a very slow gait, the pain is always there."

Agnes was more comforting in her report: "Papa has borne the journey and the crowds far better than I thought he would and seems stronger."

Amidst the attention in Savannah, two bright spots for Lee were his reunion with the surviving Mackays and the visits he was having with his West Point classmate, the redoubtable General Joseph E. Johnston. The two men were prevailed on to go to a photographer's studio. A portrait was made of them sitting on opposite sides of a small round table, each in handsome profile, their backs straight, Johnston looking at a piece of paper, Lee with a pen in his hand and a piece of paper before him — two old grey lions, their faces looking as if they were enjoying tales of long-ago cadet days.

Mary Lee was planning to do some traveling of her own. She had often spoken of visiting Rooney, Tabb, and the baby at their farm, but Lee had always assumed that the trip would be too much for an invalid to undertake. Now Mary was not just talking about it; with her husband away and no debate necessary, she was organizing her visit. Less than a month after Lee and Agnes left, Mary arrived in Richmond by the slowest but most comfortable route for her — canal boat all the way from Lexington. Accompanied by her cousin Markie Williams, she was lifted aboard a train in Richmond that went to Rooney's lower country.

II

From Savannah, Lee and Agnes set off for the most interesting, and for Lee the most enjoyable, part of their trip. They were bound for Florida on the steamer *Nick King*; at Palatka on the St. John's River Lee would have the novel experience of picking an orange from a tree.

First, however, they stopped at Cumberland Island on the Georgia coast so that Lee could visit his father's grave. Reporting this to his brother Carter, he wrote, "Agnes strewed it with beautiful fresh flowers. — I presume it is the last tribute of respect that I shall ever be able to pay it." Lee must have had some complicated thoughts as he stood at the grave of Light-Horse Harry, a father who had left his life when he was six, an able soldier, war hero, a governor of Virginia who was buried there when he died on his way back to Virginia after five years of self-exile abroad caused partly by speculations that brought him to bankruptcy. In contrast to his father — probably because of what he had learned about his father — Lee had a horror of debt. His father had been unfaithful to his mother; Lee had been faithful to an invalid of many years. Whatever his thoughts, Lee added to his letter to his brother only some words about his own physical condition: "I feel better, am stronger and my rheumatism pains have diminished, but" — and what a "but" — "the pain in my chest, along the heart bone is ever present when I walk or make any exertion."

Cumberland Island is just north of Florida, and soon the *Nick King* steamed into the mouth of Florida's St. John's River heading for Jacksonville. Later generations would think of Florida as a tropical vacationland different from the rest of the South, but it had been the third state to join the Confederacy and had thrown itself ardently and bloodily into the war. In this era, there were no Atlantic coastal towns south of St. Augustine — no Palm Beach, no Miami — and tourism was virtually nonexistent. It was an agricultural state; the farms of northern Florida had provided much of the Confederacy's food.

From Florida's small population, fifteen thousand soldiers had come forward — more soldiers than there were registered voters. Because of its location, the military manpower of the state had been sent in many directions: men from Florida had died along the Gulf of Mexico; on the banks of the Mississippi; at Chattanooga, Tennessee; at Gettysburg. The contingent that had come north to fight under Lee arrived with the title of the Florida Brigade, but their swift attacks won them an unofficial name: the Whirlwind Brigade.

These men from Florida were exceptionally close comrades. A private who was courting his major's daughter saw that officer wounded at the Battle of Cold Harbor in 1864, and he and two others crawled forward under fire to rescue him. All three would-be rescuers were wounded; more men crawled out and pulled everyone to shelter. The private, shot through the leg but now in supposed safety within his own lines, reported what happened next:

> There were already three bullet holes in my hat when, as I reclined with my head against the raised side of the traverse, another enfilading shot, very much like a blow from a hickory stick, struck me on the head, made a furrow in my scalp, and clipped as with a sharp knife a lock of my hair, which fell in the lap of a near-by comrade, who picked it up and handed it to me. I preserved it as a memento, and sent it . . . to my sweetheart, who six months later, while I was still on crutches, became my wife and has ever since been my loving and helpful wife.

This was the race of people who were waiting at Jacksonville. The steamer was scheduled to stop here for only half an hour before proceeding on to Palatka. A receiving line was formed in the main lounge, and Lee's veterans, with their wives and children, began filing through to shake his hand. So many came aboard that the ship dropped lower in the water, but it soon was clear that most of the large crowd on the pier and waterfront beyond would have no chance to come aboard and see Lee before the ship sailed.

To oblige them, Lee walked out on deck by himself in the late afternoon sunshine, advancing to the rail with his hat in his hand.

Everywhere else in the South, the crowds had roared as he appeared. Here, silence. Starting at the front of the crowd, men took off their hats; like a ripple through the sea of people, hats were removed until all were bareheaded. Lee gazed at them and they at him. The water could be heard lapping against the pilings.

Chapter 34

RETURNING TO SAVANNAH from Florida, Lee spent a few more days there, allowing time for two of the city's doctors to examine him. Then he and Agnes proceeded up the Atlantic coast. At Charleston, where the war had started with the attack on Fort Sumter, the city's fire companies staged a colorful parade, marching behind a brass band to the house where they stayed. Lee avoided reporters on most occasions, but he was so amazed by the contrast between what he saw and what he knew Charleston had endured that he spontaneously told a journalist, "I am astonished to see Charleston so wondrously recuperated after all her disasters."

The nation's press was chronicling Lee's inadvertent triumphal tour, and invitations poured in on him to come to places hundreds of miles from his route. Writing to Colonel Johnston in Lexington, Lee referred to a letter from the proprietor of the Galt House, in Louisville, Kentucky, and said, "Our kind people seem to think that I am running loose or have a roving commission to travel the country."

II

On the morning of April 30, the Lees left Wilmington, North Carolina, on their way to Portsmouth, Virginia, where they would take the ferry across the Elizabeth River to Norfolk. When Lee got off the train at

Portsmouth, he was greeted with shattering blasts from a cannon —
the one form of noise he had not previously experienced on this trip.
Amidst a storm of Rebel Yells, a small, slender man came toward him,
as composed as he had been when cannon were firing to kill. This was
Lieutenant Colonel Walter H. Taylor, even now only thirty-one years
old, who had been Lee's all-purpose aide, controller of headquarters
paperwork, appointments secretary, and official greeter, and had sometimes dashed into battle when he could get ahead of his desk duties.
The last time that Lee had seen his splendid adjutant was in Richmond, when they parted after the trip home from Appomattox.
Escorted by Taylor, the Lees boarded the ferry that would take them
across to Norfolk. Roman candles and rockets filled the sky as the ferry
left its slip, and on the far shore the United Fire Company of Norfolk
began a series of salutes from its cannon.

Lee's first morning in Norfolk was a Sunday. He wanted to go to
church, and invited Miss Caroline Selden, one of his host's daughters,
to accompany him. She wrote that, as they neared the church, "the street
was lined with adoring crowds. For one block before reaching Christ
Church we had almost to force our way through a narrow pathway
that they seemed to have left for him." Because it was a Sunday, the
crowd refrained from cheering, but Miss Selden summed up his
Southern tour in six words: "Every hat was in the air."

☆   ☆   ☆

As suddenly as it began, the public part of Lee's trip was over. By taking a steamer that went up the James River from Norfolk, he and
Agnes left the coastal cities behind and entered upon leisurely days,
visiting relatives who lived quietly on their riverside farms. One young
female cousin who had never met him before remarked on how charming he was, and added, "We regarded him with the greatest veneration.
We had heard of God, but here was General Lee!"

Going by way of Richmond, father and daughter took the opportunity to go to Rooney's farm on the Pamunkey River, where Mary was
visiting. The morning after this reunion, Mary wrote Mildred, who was
back in Lexington after her own extended visits to friends. She spoke of
"your papa, who arrived last evening with Agnes. He looks fatter, but I
do not like his complexion, and he still seems stiff." As for Agnes, she

"looks thin, but I think it was partly owing to the *immense chignon* which seems to weigh her down and absorb everything."

Mary closed with this picture of grandfather and grandson. "The General has just come in. Robbie is riding on his knee, sitting grave as a judge."

Chapter 35

SURPRISED that he was still alive, Lee arrived back in Lexington on the morning of May 28. He had been gone for two months and four days. Mildred was waiting to greet him, but his wife was enjoying her travels so much that she was staying away for another week, visiting more relatives in the company of Markie.

Lee did not reopen with anyone the subject of his resignation. It was clear that he had decided to die in harness. On the day of his return, he found awaiting him the resolution of the Board of Trustees giving Mary the new house and providing her with an annual income in the event of his death or incapacitation. Within hours, Lee rejected the offers with thanks, writing the trustees, "I am unwilling that my family should be a tax to the college, but desire that all of its funds should be devoted to the purposes of education. I know that my wishes on this subject are equally shared by my wife."

Since their first encounter in September of 1865, when Lee had told the trustees that he was not going to be part of an elaborately staged installation as college president, the trustees had followed his wishes in all matters. This time, in the words of Dr. Kirkpatrick, who had acted as president in Lee's absence, they "declined to recede from the position they had taken," and without arguing the matter left on the books their resolution protecting Mary Lee.

Throwing himself back into the work of the college at the time of final examinations, Lee was again seeing and counseling students. One of the freshmen coming to the end of his first year, James R. Winchester, said that "General Lee led us all by cords of love," but thus far his classmate W. H. Tayloe was an exception. A shy, self-described "green country boy" from Uniontown, Alabama, he had found his first interview with Lee "very perfunctory." Tayloe studied hard and successfully, and soon his mathematics professor had begun choosing him to go to the blackboard and solve a problem whenever Lee entered the back of the room. "I could never see that any impression was made upon him. Nor did anything occur to make me have any particular impression of the person. I had no idea but one of fear and distance."

During this 1869–1870 academic year, some of the students had never seen Lee on Traveller, due to his combination of illness during much of the autumn and winter and his two-month trip south during the spring. Now, in June, Tayloe saw Lee on Traveller for the first time.

> He was passing just as I came out of the gate at the Episcopal church. I saw him but a moment; the picture is with me yet. Traveller moved as if proud of the burden he bore. To me the horse was beautiful and majestic. It was the only time I was impressed with the greatness and beauty and power and glory of the man. He sat erect in the saddle. The gloved hand held the bridle, the other hung gracefully at his side. He was every inch a king. It was only a moment, but the impression will last a lifetime. It is one of the joyous moments of life on which my memory loves to dwell.

On a morning during the week before graduation the winners of prizes were announced. Tayloe learned that he had won the coveted scholarships in three subjects: Latin, Greek, and mathematics. In addition to being awarded the badly needed money, he was designated a Distinguished Undergraduate. Having finished his examinations, he had nothing to do, and in the middle of that morning he was standing by himself in front of the main college building that faced the chapel down the slope.

> I saw the General coming up the walk towards the college. I hid behind the last pillar of the portico in front of the main building. I had no idea that he had noticed me. I considered myself safely concealed and there was no one in sight. My back was turned to the door of the main building. I heard a voice, turned and found him with hand extended to me. His soft notes of congratulation fell upon my ears and the hope that I would return the next session. That was all. I hardly knew what had happened. I was so utterly confounded I knew not what to say or do.

II

On Thursday, June 23, 1870, in the chapel he had caused to be built, Lee handed their diplomas to the last students he would see graduate. With his fifth year at the college completed, he was prevailed upon to go to Baltimore to consult Dr. Thomas H. Buckler, an eminent physician of that city who had been living in France since the war and was just in the United States briefly. Lee stayed with his friends the Tagarts, whom he had taken with him on his visit to President Grant at the White House the year before, and then spent time visiting relatives in both the Maryland and Virginia countrysides.

In Alexandria, Lee consulted with his lawyer, Francis L. Smith. Lee had made a will years before, and with Smith's assistance had recovered and conveyed to Rooney and Rob a Custis property known as Smith's Island, so this meeting dealt with Lee's lingering hope of regaining some or all of Arlington's confiscated acres. Smith had been working on this in recent months, but all the news was bad. There were now sixteen thousand Union graves at Arlington, and a bill had been introduced into Congress "to perfect the title of the Government to Arlington and the other National Cemeteries." The end of the story lay twelve years in the future; in 1882 the Supreme Court would rule that Arlington had been taken illegally, and that Custis Lee could at last claim it as his inheritance. At the same time, the government offered to buy it from Custis for one hundred and fifty thousand dollars. Not wanting to move into a cemetery, he accepted.

☆ ☆ ☆

Returning to Lexington exhausted by three weeks of travel in July heat, Lee felt his energy restored overnight. On August 6, he called a special meeting of the trustees to see if a hundred thousand dollars could be raised to ensure an endowment for an astronomical observatory whose final site in Virginia had not yet been designated. Lee was eager to have it firmly associated with the college for the benefit of his scientifically inclined students.

One hundred thousand dollars to maintain a huge telescope. It was five years before, almost to the day, that the trustees had elected Lee to the presidency without his knowledge and had borrowed fifty dollars to send Judge Brockenbrough, wearing a borrowed suit, to persuade him to take on the job.

III

Lee's Lexington doctors had more to say to their inconsistent and perplexing patient. They urged him to try the waters of the Hot Springs resort, northwest of Lexington. Captain White accompanied him. They dutifully started off on the roundabout journey through the mountains by taking the railroad from Goshen, but within a few miles the views of peaks and valleys brought back memories of rides they had taken together around Lexington, and they got off the train at the next stop and continued by stagecoach. They were behind horses instead of on their backs, but they much preferred it to a railroad car.

From the Hot Springs, Lee wrote Mary that he was taking a treatment known as the "Hot Spout, which seems to agree with me very well, but it is too soon yet to look for results. I receive the water on my shoulder, back and chest. The sensation is pleasant." After some days of this he was to have the "Boiler." Nine days after starting the whole program, he wrote Mary, "I do not perceive any benefit yet."

Lee read the newspapers at the Hot Springs with particular care. The Franco-Prussian War had broken out, and he was worried about his nephew Edward Childe and his wife, who lived in Paris. "No," he wrote Markie Williams in the last lines of the last letter she would receive from him, "I am not 'glad that the Prussians are succeeding.' They are prompted by ambition and a thirst for power." Perhaps thinking of his own army's stand in northern Virginia, he continued, "The French are defending their homes and country. May God help the suffering and avert misery from the poor."

In a letter written to another friend he said, "I fear we are destined to kill and slaughter each other for ages to come," but then there arrived a letter that brought out his sense of fun. A spiritualist who conducted séances wrote Lee, asking his opinion of the strategy being used by the Prussian general Helmuth, Count von Moltke. Lee replied courteously that "the question was one about which military critics would differ," and that his own opinion on such matters was deficient. He then pointed out that this medium and his associates were in a position to consult Julius Caesar, Alexander, Napoleon, Wellington, and all of history's great captains, and that he really felt that he should not voice his opinions in such august company.

In contrast to his concerns about this new war, Lee's stay at the Hot Springs brought him a piece of joyous news. Rob was engaged to be married to Charlotte Haxall, Mildred's close friend who had stayed under their roof in Lexington and whom Lee had addressed in playful letters as "My beautiful Lottie." He had done everything in the world to bring Rob to her attention; two days after the high seriousness of completing the White Sulphur Letter he had written her, concerning her sister's impending wedding: "An idea has been revolving in my head . . . What trouble your dear mother, father, sisters indeed your family will be saved if you will only make up your mind to marry my son Robert at the time of Miss Mary's wedding. The feast will be prepared, the minister present, a goodly company assembled, he by your side, and four persons made happy instead of two!"

That had been two years before, and until this moment Lee did not know if anything would ever come of that revolving idea. Now he wrote her of "the happiness you have given us and my gratitude at your consent to enter our family." There was a note of urgency: "I already love you as a daughter. I can do nothing more than beg you quickly to become so, for I have little time to wait, and now want to see you more than ever." To Rob he wrote, "I shall be ready to help you in any way that I can and you must let me know what I can do for you and when."

Lee was spared a look into the future. His death would cause a postponement of Rob and Charlotte's wedding. Then, a year after they were married, Charlotte would die — the second Lee daughter-in-law named Charlotte to die at a young age.

Chapter 36

T HE PROFESSORS were heartened by what they saw of Lee as his sixth autumn at Washington College began. Colonel Johnston emerged from the first faculty meeting presided over by Lee with this reaction: "An unusual elation was felt by those about him at the increased prospect that long years of usefulness and honor would yet be added to his glorious life." Lee was equally impressive in two meetings with the trustees, and at the formal opening of the college session on September 15 he rose after the invocation by the Reverend William Nelson Pendleton to make a vigorous appeal to both students and faculty to attend the daily morning prayers at the chapel. He had even taken on the presidency of the proposed Valley Railroad, for which he had traveled to Baltimore in the spring of 1869, and was involved in new efforts to raise money for its construction.

☆   ☆   ☆

Lee rode out on Traveller in these September afternoons. Starting off on one of these rides, he found that two little girls, daughters of two of his professors, were both on the back of a gentle old horse riding on one of the back streets, afraid to venture far from home. Lee invited them to ride with him to a point beyond the fairgrounds, from which there was a magnificent view of the mountains. The little girls happily accepted, and off they all went. One of the children was recovering from the mumps and had a handkerchief tied around her face. Lee pretended that his horse might catch the disease.

"I hope you won't give Traveller the mumps!" He shook his head, and said again in a concerned tone, "What shall I do if Traveller gets the mumps?"

The afternoon in Lexington ended this way. "An hour later, this party was seen returning, the two little girls in sun-bonnets on the one old, sleepy horse, and General Lee by their side on Traveller, who was stepping very proudly, as if in scorn of his lowly companion." Lee "took the children to their homes, helped them to dismount, took a kiss from each, and, waving a parting salute, rode away."

II

In his office, Lee was once again dealing with matters small and large. His nephew Fitz Lee had a huge dog that he wanted to send to his uncle in Lexington. Lee was fascinated by the prospect of owning what he called this "mammoth dog" and answered his nephew's letter:

> Your letter on the dog question has been unavoidably delayed. I thank you very sincerely for recollecting my wishes on the subject . . . First I must inform you that it is not my purpose to put my dog to towing canal boats or hauling dirt carts, but want him to play the part of friend and protector. His disposition is therefore of vital importance — he ought not to be too old to contract a friendship for me — neither is his size so important as a perfect form.

Lee accepted the dog and gave his nephew directions about sending him by rail to Lynchburg and on by canal boat to Lexington.

An entirely different sort of letter went from Lee to his wartime aide Lieutenant Colonel Charles Marshall, the man who had drafted Lee's famous General Order Number Nine, his farewell to his Army of Northern Virginia. In a sense it was Lee's judgment of himself, and of what he had seen of the world in his sixty-three years. Under it all was Lee's ever-present combination of realism and optimism, and a word of encouragement to others.

> My experience of men has neither disposed me to think worse of them nor indisposed me to serve them; nor, in spite of failures which I lament, of errors which I now see and acknowledge, or of the present aspect of affairs, do I despair of the future.

The truth is this: The march of Providence is so slow and our desires so impatient; the work of progress so immense and our means of aiding it so feeble; the life of humanity is so long, that of the individual so brief, that we often see only the ebb of the advancing wave and are thus discouraged. It is history that teaches us to hope.

III

On September 28, Lee concluded his morning's work in his office by writing to his friend Samuel Tagart in Baltimore. "I am much better," he told him, and added, "my pains are less and my strength greater. In fact, I suppose I am as well as I shall be." Referring to a new student from Baltimore who was known to the Tagarts, Lee said that he was "well and handsome and I hope that he will study, or his sweethearts in Baltimore will not pine for him long."

Lee sealed this letter and rose from his desk to go home for midday dinner. As he stepped from his office, he found a sophomore named Percy Davidson outside. The boy explained that he had with him a small photograph of Lee that a girl had asked him to have Lee sign, but that he would come back another time.

"No," Lee said, "I will go back and do it right now." When he reappeared from his office and handed the signed photograph to his pleased student, neither of them dreamed that Lee was walking out of the basement of the chapel for the last time.

After his customary dinner, Lee sat in his armchair. Agnes rubbed his hands as he fell asleep. In the next room Mildred was playing the piano, practicing one of Mendelssohn's "Songs Without Words." Rain fell against the bay window; the distant hills were wrapped in a cold mist.

As usual, Lee's nap was a short one, and he rose from his armchair with little enthusiasm for what he had to do next. There was a meeting of the vestry of Grace Church, and the principal item on the agenda was a discussion of plans for building a new church. Lee was on the fund-raising committee and always had to inject a note of reality into talk of this long-hoped-for project. To Mary he had written this past summer, "Resolutions will not build the church." It took money, and Lee saw that there was not yet enough. Also on the agenda, and a truer indication of Grace Church's finances, was the question of how to make up the deficit in the Reverend Dr. Pendleton's salary.

Lee put on his grey military cape and, with his broad-brimmed hat in his hand, came into the parlor, where Mildred was now playing Mendelssohn's "Funeral March."

"Life," he said to Mildred, "that is a doleful piece you are playing!" He kissed her and added, "I wish I did not have to go and listen to all that powwow."

The vestrymen who welcomed Lee as he entered the cold, damp church after his walk through the icy rain would never have guessed at his reluctance to come. They noted that he greeted them "with marked cheerfulness of manner," but that he seemed a bit chilly and kept on his cape. Because there was no suitable meeting room, they sat in the pews of the unheated church.

The meeting was a long one. Lee presided and, as at faculty meetings, listened to everyone's opinion on each point before giving his own. As they went through the agenda, his colleagues, his physicians Howard T. Barton and R. L. Madison among them, noticed that he was looking much more tired than when he came in. His face was flushed, although the church had become even colder.

The last item was the deficit in the salary of the Reverend Dr. Pendleton, who was not present. In turn, each of the vestrymen pledged himself to contribute a certain sum, varying with his means. When the clerk of the vestry added up, the total still fell fifty-five dollars short of what it had been agreed that Pendleton must have.

Lee, who had already made a generous pledge, said, "I will give that sum." The meeting was over.

Lee came into the house and went upstairs to hang his coat and hat in his room. As he came down the steps, he heard Mildred laughing in the parlor with two student callers. Lee knew that Mary had been expecting him at the supper table for half an hour and hurried into the dining room. Just as he expected, she greeted him with "You have kept us waiting a long time. Where have you been?"

Lee did not answer, but stood at the head of the table as usual to say grace. Mary and Agnes bowed their heads. He opened his mouth but no words came. His face blank, Lee sat down in his chair.

"Let me pour you out a cup of tea," Mary said softly, her impatience vanishing. "You look so tired."

Lee tried to say something and again no words came. He straightened up in his chair; Mary and Agnes were staring at him. Lee was sitting as straight as he had as a cadet at West Point, but on his face was a look of resignation that they had never seen.

Mary called out to Custis, who appeared quickly and asked his father if he could do something for him. When Lee continued to sit there without answering, Custis threw on a coat and ran into the heavy rain to get the doctors.

Mildred was called in from her chat with her callers in the parlor; she found her father "bowed down, and looking very strange and speaking incoherently."

Drs. Barton and Madison were still walking home together from the vestry meeting when Custis caught up to them, and they rushed to the house. Within minutes, Lee's "small low single bed" had been brought downstairs and was placed with its head to the dining room's bay window, where he always sat. Lee could speak a little, and helped the doctors take off his clothes as they prepared to examine him. There was no paralysis, and the doctors diagnosed his condition as a "venous congestion of the brain," which a later generation would have termed a cerebral thrombosis, a blood clot lodging in the brain. He also had a throat infection. These new afflictions, combined with his heart condition and hardening arteries, were producing what his doctors called "cerebral exhaustion."

☆ ☆ ☆

Lee slept peacefully that night and on through most of the next day and night. The dining table was removed and the dining room became a sick room. The rain came down at a phenomenal rate — fourteen inches fell in thirty-six hours, starting the worst floods in a century in that part of Virginia. A fire was kept going constantly in the fireplace opposite the window near where Lee lay.

Lee rallied slightly; he wakened easily, understood what was being done, knew everyone. He could turn over in bed and could be propped up to eat soup and bland foods. He could say a few words with clarity, but for the most part communicated by nodding or shaking his head.

IV

The vigil took form. Duties settled on those who gravitated toward them. Agnes administered the medicines and sat with him many hours of the night. Mildred fixed her father's meals and sat with him during the day, often joined by Agnes. Custis and Colonel Johnston alternated being in his room from midnight to dawn so that he was never alone.

"Mother would be rolled in," Mildred wrote, "in her chair, and sit by his side — having the hardest part to act, that of being passive — when she would have given her life to do something." Mary wrote a cousin that "Robert . . . Welcomes me always with a pressure of the hand." One of Mary's friends who called daily found her at one moment speaking of "when Robert gets well again," and at another fearing that he would emerge from this crisis paralyzed or in a condition such as hers. Mary had the idea that he would be confined permanently to his upstairs bedroom and that in her wheelchair she would not be able to "get to him." Even in her apprehension she was still able to write this crisp note to General Francis H. Smith, the superintendent of V.M.I.:

> My dear Gen'l:
>
> The Drs. think it would be well for Gen'l Lee to have some beef tea at once and as I cannot get it at market before night I send to beg a small piece, if it can be found at the Institute, lean & juicy if possible; a pound would answer for the present, as I can get some more to-night.
>
> In great haste Yrs.
>
> M. C. Lee

"A week passed in this way," Mildred wrote. The rain kept falling; as a result of the first great downpour, bridges, boats, and docks were all swept down the river, and the locks of the canal were broken up. The roads were nearly impassable; for several days the mail was stopped. In the dining room where Lee had stepped in from the garden to present each lady with a rose at breakfast, Mildred said that now "his lips never uttered a sound! The silence was awful! He would lay straight and motionless, gazing with that solemn unalterable look, into the flames that played on the hearth."

Outside, the weather broke for three days; Mildred remembered "how scarlet the berries were in the hedge — and how soft and magical was the October sunshine!" Indoors, "hour after hour Agnes and I would sit by him — rubbing his dear hands in the old way he used to like — never saying a word. Now I wonder I did not read comforting passages from the Bible — did not repeat his favorite hymns — but words seemed frozen in all our mouths; he was speechless — so were we!" Mildred spoke of the house as being filled with "a sort of calmness of despair." The roads were partly open again, but it occurred to no one to send for Rooney and Rob and Daugher.

☆ ☆ ☆

During the break in the storm, word had gone to the outside world that Lee was in grave condition. His illness was news everywhere; the *London Standard* prepared an obituary with a lengthy review of his career.

At the college, the students walked quietly across the campus, their eyes going to the big brick house at an angle up the slope. The town talked only of Lee's condition, and of the storm and its damage. When Northern Lights were seen in the sky on the nights of October 7, 8, and 9 as the weather broke, some took it as an omen; in this Scots-descended town, one woman quoted a Scottish poem that said of the aurora borealis:

> Fearful lights, that never beckon
> Save when kings or heroes die.

Mildred was there each morning when Lee awoke; "his beautiful sad eyes always gave me a look of love and recognition." One day as she sat stroking his hand, he pressed her hand to his mouth and kissed it; another time he looked at her and said, "Precious baby."

Traveller was neighing in his stall. On a morning call, Dr. Madison asked Lee how he was feeling.

"I — feel — better," Lee managed.

"You must make haste and get well," the doctor said encouragingly. "Traveller has been standing so long in the stable he needs exercise."

Lee shook his head. When at another moment Custis spoke of recovery, Lee shook his head and pointed toward the sky. When Agnes gave him his medicine, several times he put it aside, saying, "It is no use."

V

On Monday, October 10, Lee for the first time seemed to be suffering not only discomfort but constant pain. When he tried to speak he could not, and his eyes kept looking at his family with an unsaid "Something must be done."

"Ever and ever those glorious dark eyes," Mildred remembered, "speaking with imploring, heart rending tones! Oh, the horror of being helpless when he needed help!"

Mary was in the room now almost all the day. Mildred spoke of "Mama so patient, but being able only to pray."

In the depths of the night, Colonel Johnston quietly entered the room and went over to where Custis was sitting beside his sleeping father. A few whispered words, and Johnston took up the vigil. This is how he remembered those hours.

"As the old hero lay in the darkened room, or with the lamp and the hearth-fire casting shadows upon his calm, noble front, all the massive grandeur of his form, and face, and brow remained; and death seemed to lose its terrors, and to borrow a grace and dignity in sublime keeping with the life that was ebbing away."

Coming downstairs on Tuesday morning, Mildred saw her father struggling to turn onto his right side, "an agonized expression" on his face. He refused nourishment and would take medicine only from Dr. Madison or Dr. Barton. In the last day his pulse had become feeble and rapid. It had rained again the day before; now there were occasional showers, grey skies, cold winds.

During the afternoon Lee sank into a coma. Mary sat beside him in her wheelchair. In her words, "He wandered to those dreadful battle-fields" — at one moment he cried out, "Tell Hill he *must* come up!" The last distinct words that anyone heard him say were "Strike the tent!"

☆ ☆ ☆

Mildred fell into bed that night, exhausted. The doctors were in the house, but they offered no hope. Near midnight, Agnes came in and gently woke her sister. She said nothing, but took Mildred's hand and led her downstairs.

The Reverend Dr. Pendleton was at Lee's bedside, saying the prayers for the dying. Mary was there in her wheelchair, and Custis was kneeling beside the bed. Agnes and Mildred knelt beside Custis. Through the words of prayer Mildred heard her father "breathing hard and painfully."

The minister and the doctors withdrew. Through the early morning hours Mary sat there. Agnes was "kneeling by his side — moistening his lips — fanning him — he lying on his right side — drawing long, hard breaths."

With dawn the storm was gone and the sky was clear. The family remained silent beside Lee. Through the bay window a bright sun rose; Mildred could see that the weather promised "a lovely October day."

At nine in the morning Mildred saw that her father "seemed to be struggling. I rushed out for the doctor . . . he came, looked at him, and without saying a word walked quietly away. In a moment he was dead — "

Notes
Bibliography
Index

Notes

SHORT CITATIONS OF SELECTED SOURCES

Agnes Lee Letter — Letter from Agnes Lee to Mary Lee, April 13, 1870, in the deButts-Ely Collection.

deButts-Ely — The deButts-Ely Collection of Robert E. Lee Family Papers, Library of Congress.

Lee Papers, W. and L. — The Lee Papers, Washington and Lee University.

Letters to Annette Carter — Collection of unpublished letters from Robert E. Lee to Annette Carter, later Mrs. Henry Hall Brogden, in the possession of her granddaughter, Mrs. Charles K. Lennig, Jr., of Philadelphia.

Trustees' Records — Records of the Board of Trustees, Washington and Lee University.

U.S. Congress, House, Report — United States Congress, House of Representatives, *Report of the Joint Committee on Reconstruction*, Thirty-ninth Congress, First Session, House Report 30 (Washington, D.C.: Government Printing Office, 1866).

CHAPTER 1

page
3
"Keep your command": A. L. Long, *Memoirs of Robert E. Lee* (New York, 1887), p. 415.

"If victorious": Lee to W. H. F. Lee, April 24, 1864; J. William Jones, *Personal Reminiscences . . . of Gen. Robert E. Lee* (New York, 1875), p. 401.

page

3   "You are the country": Brigadier General Henry A. Wise to Lee; John Sergeant Wise, *The End of an Era* (New York, 1899; reprint, New York: Thomas Yoseloff, 1965), p. 434.

3–4   "The sight of him": Account of John Esten Cooke, in Stanley F. Horn, ed., *The Robert E. Lee Reader* (New York: Grosset & Dunlap, 1949), p. 433.

4   "I have fought my corps": A. L. Long, p. 421.
"Then there is nothing left": Ibid.
"How easily": Douglas Southall Freeman, *R. E. Lee,* 4 vols. (New York: Scribner's, 1934–1935), vol. 4, p. 121.
The full conversation with Alexander is in Ibid., pp. 122–123.

5–6   New Hampshire soldier: Bruce Catton, *A Stillness at Appomattox* (New York: Doubleday, 1953), p. 425.

6   Lawrence Williams: From the account of Charles Marshall in Horn, p. 441.
Orton Williams: Facts concerning him are in the Honorable Henry T. Wickham, *Address,* Virginia Senate Document No. 10 (Richmond, 1940), pp. 6–7; Margaret Sanborn, *Robert E. Lee,* 2 vols. (Philadelphia: Lippincott, 1966–1967), pp. 95–96; and Freeman, *R. E. Lee,* vol. 3, pp. 211–213. A reason for assuming that it was the war that changed Orton is that Lee wrote an enthusiastic and seemingly knowledgeable recommendation on his behalf prior to the war, in 1860, when he applied for a commission in the United States Army; deButts-Ely, Letter Book No. 2.
Many historians of the surrender refer to Babcock as being a colonel at this time. He had been appointed a brevet brigadier general on March 13, and Grant subsequently referred to him as "General Babcock." See Frank P. Cauble, *The Proceedings Connected with the Surrender of the Army of Northern Virginia* (Appomattox Court House National Historical Park, 1962; revised, 1975), p. 51. This valuable work is the most comprehensive study of the surrender.

7   "I could take no part": Lee to Reverdy Johnson, February 25, 1868; deButts-Ely, Letter Book No. 4.
Grant wept: Gene Smith, *High Crimes and Misdemeanors* (New York: Morrow, 1977), p. 213.
"Bonfires": Horace Porter, "Grant's Last Campaign," *Century Illustrated Monthly Magazine,* 15 (November 1887), p. 138.

8   "I never saw a man": Freeman, *R. E. Lee,* vol. 3, p. 298n. The quotation is from the eyewitness Charles Francis Adams (1835–1915). Grant's aide Horace Porter, *Campaigning with Grant* (New York, 1907; reprint, New York: Bonanza Books, 1961), p. 53, pictures Grant as calm after this day's fighting, but, by his own account, Porter was not with Grant during all of these hours. Some details of Grant's appearance and dress on this occasion are in Cauble, pp. 103–104.
A detailed study of the communications between Lee and Grant that led to the surrender is in Cauble, pp. 41–50. Freeman, *R. E.*

page

        Lee, vol. 4, pp. 129–130, has texts of Lee's three letters to Grant on the morning of April 9.

8   Cheers turn into tears: Cauble, p. 50.

        "the most excruciating": Porter, p. 464.

        "sick-headache": Ulysses S. Grant, *Personal Memoirs of Ulysses S. Grant,* 2 vols. (New York, 1886), vol. 2, p. 485.

        "very much as people": Sanborn, vol. 2, p. 229.

        "much embarrassed": Freeman, *R. E. Lee,* vol. 4, p. 135n.

8–9   Lee and Grant's discussion: Ibid., pp. 136–140.

9–10   In Roy Meredith, *The Face of Robert E. Lee* (New York: Scribner's, 1947), p. 89, the Swiss painter Frank Buchser, writing in English a few hours after talking with Lee on October 5, 1869, said that Lee had told him that he had "asked Grant what terms he would give if Lee should surrender his army and Grant then made the well-known overtures which Lee thought generous in the extreme."

11   "Plenty . . . An abundance": Sanborn, vol. 2, p. 229.

        "And it will be a great": Porter, p. 483.

12   George Forsyth: Sanborn, vol. 2, pp. 230–231.

        "Orderly!": Ibid., p. 231.

        "thrice smote": Porter, p. 485.

        "swung himself": Sanborn, vol. 2, p. 231.

13   "This will live": This remark by Adam Badeau is from William C. Davis, "The Campaign to Appomattox," *Civil War Times,* April 1975, p. 41.

CHAPTER 2

14–15   Lee's headquarters: Jones, p. 172.

15   "The enemy never sees": Freeman, *R. E. Lee,* vol. 2, p. 420.

        ". . . the dirtiest men": Sanborn, vol. 2, p. 77.

        "that array": The quotation from William Swinton is here taken from Robert E. Lee, Jr., *Recollections and Letters of General Robert E. Lee* (New York: Doubleday, 1909), p. 150. This lively biography by Lee's son is of particular value for the postwar period of his life, and is the most comprehensive view of Lee to be recorded by a member of his immediate family.

16   "Any man who will not": Sanborn, vol. 2, p. 101.

        "The effect was": Bruce Catton, *Never Call Retreat,* the Centennial History of the Civil War, 3 vols. (Garden City, New York: Doubleday, 1961–1965), vol. 3, p. 315.

        "General, are we surrendered?": Freeman, *R. E. Lee,* vol. 4, pp. 144–145.

17   Rejoicing within Union lines: Cauble, pp. 174–175.

        Eleven thousand men: Freeman, *R. E. Lee,* vol.4, pp. 118–119, gives Lee an effective strength of approximately twelve thousand when this day began, but this was lowered somewhat by break-outs made by the cavalry.

17   "As soon as he entered": Ibid., pp. 146–147.

18   "shared our food": Cauble, p. 111.

"We are all": Ibid., p. 190.

"There is a rancor": Ibid., p. 189.

19   "Every officer": Douglas Southall Freeman, *Lee's Lieutenants,* 3 vols. (New York: Scribner's, 1945), vol. 2, p. 108.

"I had not gone 100 yards": Ibid., p. 51.

19–20   Lee and A. P. Hill: Ibid., vol. 3, pp. 331.

20   Lee to Jefferson Davis, April 20, 1865: deButts-Ely, Letter Book No. 3.

"Yes . . . and the hell of a git": Freeman, *Lieutenants,* vol. 3, p. 718.

"that enemy": Grant's tribute is in the last sentence of his final report to Secretary of War Stanton on the wartime operations of the United States Army from the time of his appointment as its commander to the close of hostilities. Dated July 22, 1865, a text is in Grant, vol. 2, p. 632.

CHAPTER 3

21–22   Grant's April 10 talk with Lee: Grant, vol. 2, p. 497. It should be noted that Grant and Lee fenced with each other, both in the presurrender correspondence and on this occasion, concerning the scope of their authority to extend the Appomattox surrender to the national scene. A study of this subject is in Cauble, pp. 21–22, 28, 33, 133–135.

22–23   Lee, Meade, and Meade's aide: Freeman, *R. E. Lee,* vol. 4, p. 152.

"There were never such men": Sanborn, vol. 2, p. 116.

24   The most readily available text of General Order No. 9 is Freeman, *R. E. Lee,* vol. 4, pp. 154–155.

CHAPTER 4

26–27   Quotations concerning the surrender ceremony are from Joshua L. Chamberlain, *The Passing of the Armies* (New York: Putnam's, 1915), pp. 260–264. It should be noted that Chamberlain wrote several published accounts of the surrender, all different in their wording.

27   ". . . someone in the blue line": Henry Kyd Douglas, *I Rode With Stonewall* (Chapel Hill: University of North Carolina Press, 1940; reprint, Covington, Georgia: Mockingbird Books, 1974), p. 319.

28–29   Union cavalry sergeant: William B. Arnold, *The Fourth Massachusetts Cavalry in the Closing Scenes . . .* (Boston?, 191–), pp. 31–32.

29   "escorted them": April 12, 1865, entry in the diary of Lieutenant Samuel C. Lovell, Fourth Massachusetts Cavalry. Photostatic copy at Appomattox Court House National Park; original in possession of Stuart H. Buck, Takoma Park, Maryland.

"You see I am in my own": Sanborn, vol. 2, pp. 239–240.

". . . he shook my hand": Lovell diary, April 12, 1865.

"Now on the morrow": Chamberlain, pp. 271–272.

CHAPTER 5

30   "bony, weary" and "gaunt and pallid": Sanborn, vol. 2, p. 243.

Cooke had been wounded at Sayler's Creek; Giles B. Cooke, "Just Before and After Lee Surrendered to Grant," Houston *Chronicle*, October 8, 1922.

31   Lee's wartime and postwar health and medical history are studied in Freeman, *R. E. Lee,* vol. 4, pp. 521–525. The present author has had the advice of William H. Mitchell, M.D., who has reviewed this in the light of current medical knowledge. Robert Penn Warren, *Jefferson Davis Gets His Citizenship Back* (Lexington, Kentucky: The University Press of Kentucky, 1980), p. 53, points out that Lee's doctors, from the time of his 1863 heart attack until his death, diagnosed his condition as rheumatism. Lee's vulnerability to a stroke was shown by the thrombosis that precipitated his final illness. His arteries were hardening during the postwar period.

Lee was not bankrupt: His postwar financial condition is summarized in Freeman, *R. E. Lee,* vol. 4, pp. 385–394.

33   Lee on the Great Lakes: Lee to Mary Lee, September 2, 1835, in Norma B. Cuthbert, "To Molly — Five Early Letters from Robert E. Lee to His Wife, 1832–1835," *The Huntington Library Quarterly,* 15 (May 1952), p. 275.

"They convert themselves": Freeman, *R. E. Lee,* vol. 1, pp. 149–150.

34   "the very best soldier": Jones, p. 58.

"You have only to blow": Freeman, *R. E. Lee,* vol. 4, p. 374n.

34–35   Lee's advice to Marshall and Taylor: Ibid., vol. 4, p. 159.

"The continued self-denial": Walter H. Taylor, *Four Years With General Lee* (New York, 1877; reprint, New York: Bonanza Books, 1962), p. 154.

A description of Lee's voice and accent, by a woman who frequently spoke with him, is in J. Bryan III, *The Sword Over the Mantel* (New York: McGraw-Hill, 1960), p. 81.

Lee to Taylor: Sanborn, vol. 2, p. 243.

CHAPTER 6

page
36   "Polly, come with me": Freeman, *R. E. Lee,* vol. 4, p. 161.
     Description of W. H. F. (Rooney) Lee: J. S. Wise, p. 334.
36–37   Various characterizations of Henry Lee, known as "Light-Horse Harry," and a description of his activities, are in Freeman, *R. E. Lee,* vol. 1, pp. 1–17. Sanborn, vol. 1, p. 13, gives several references to his marital infidelity.
37   "It is time": Sanborn, vol. 1, p. 250.
     "In the lone hours": Jones, pp. 398–399.
37–38   A Baptist minister: Freeman, *R. E. Lee,* vol. 4, p. 161.
38   "the grinning ruins": J. S. Wise, p. 458.
     "It is enough": Gamaliel Bradford, *Lee the American* (Boston: Houghton Mifflin, 1929), p. 96.
38–39   "I have been up to see": George Taylor Lee, "Reminiscences of General Robert E. Lee, 1865–1868," *The South Atlantic Quarterly,* 26 (1927), p. 236.
39   "a most splendid": Freeman, *R. E. Lee,* vol. 4, p. 164.
39–40   Lee's final approach to 707 Franklin Street and arrival there are based on Sanborn, vol. 2, pp. 242–243, and Freeman, *R. E. Lee,* vol. 4, pp. 162–164.

CHAPTER 7

41   "He is growing": Jones, p. 307.
42   "That you may know": Sanborn, vol. 2, p. 158.
     Fire threatens 707 Franklin Street: R. A. Brock, ed., *Gen. Robert E. Lee* . . . (Richmond, 1897), p. 340, and Sanborn, vol. 2, p. 247.
     "she sat in her chair": Sanborn, vol. 2, p. 247.
     "The end is not yet" and "General Lee is not": Rose Mortimer Ellzey MacDonald, *Mrs. Robert E. Lee* (Boston: Ginn and Co., 1939; reprint, Pikesville, Maryland: Robert B. Poisal, 1973), pp. 194–195.
     "For my part": Mary Lee to Mary Meade, April 23, 1865; Ibid., p. 197.
43   "It is impossible": Sanborn, vol. 2, p. 248.
     "uncalled for": Ibid.
     "Let 'em up easy": Carl Sandburg, *Abraham Lincoln* (New York: Harcourt, Brace & World, 1954), p. 685.
44   "It is a crime": Lee to Count Joannes, September 4, 1865; Jones, p. 204.
     Mathew Brady: Meredith, p. 64, and James D. Horan, *Mathew Brady: Historian with a Camera* (New York: Bonanza Books, 1955), p. 59.
45   "A partisan war": Lee to Jefferson Davis, April 20, 1865; deButts-Ely, Letter Book No. 3.
     "Tell the little creatures": R. E. Lee, Jr., p. 429.
46   "I think of you": A. L. Long, p. 389.
     Encounter in hall: Channing M. Smith, "The Last Time I Saw General Lee," *Confederate Veteran,* 35 (1927), p. 327.

page
46–47   Rob's closing days of the war: R. E. Lee, Jr., pp. 155–157.
47   "Virginia comes first": Mary Boykin Chesnut, *A Diary from Dixie*
        (Cambridge, Massachusetts: Harvard University Press, 1980),
        p. 315.
47–48   Rob and his father at Sharpsburg: R. E. Lee, Jr., pp. 77–78.
        Slightly differing accounts of Lee's injury are in Freeman, *R. E.
        Lee,* vol. 2, p. 340; A. L. Long, p. 206; and Sanborn, vol. 2,
        pp. 75–76.
49   "All sorts and conditions": R. E. Lee, Jr., p. 158.
49–51   Lee interview: *New York Herald,* April 29, 1865.
50   One hundred and ninety-six slaves: Joseph C. Robert, "Lee the
        Farmer" (Baton Rouge, Louisiana: The Franklin Press, 1937; re-
        print from *The Journal of Southern History*), p. 11. This is the
        most comprehensive study of Lee's prewar management of the
        three Custis farms.
        Liberia: This sole reference to Lee's sending freed slaves to Africa
        occurs in John Leyburn, "An Interview with General Robert E.
        Lee," in *Century Illustrated Monthly Magazine,* 30 (May 1885),
        pp. 166–167. In recounting a conversation that took place in
        April 1869, Leyburn says of Lee: "He declared that, for himself,
        he had never been an advocate of slavery; that he had emanci-
        pated most of his slaves years before the war, and had sent to
        Liberia those who were willing to go; that the latter were writing
        back affectionate letters to him, some of which he received
        through the lines during the war."
        Lee's low opinion of black abilities: See R. E. Lee, Jr., p. 168, in
        which Rob quotes him as saying, in June 1865, "I have always
        observed that wherever you find the negro, everything is going
        down around him, and wherever you find the white man, every-
        thing around him is improving."
        Lee thought that Virginia would be better off if its free black pop-
        ulation migrated south: Lee's testimony in U.S. Congress,
        House, *Report.*
        "Slavery as an institution": Lee to Mary Lee, December 27, 1856;
        Freeman, *R. E. Lee,* vol. 1, p. 372.
        "I am rejoiced": Leyburn, p. 167.

CHAPTER 8

52–54   Lee's conversation with Meade, May 5, 1865: Freeman, *R. E. Lee,*
        vol. 4, pp. 195–196.
53   "You would not have your General": Ibid., p. 192.
54–56   Lee's meeting with Texan: Clement Sullivane, "Last Meeting with
        Gen. R. E. Lee," *Confederate Veteran,* 28 (1920), p. 459.
54–55   Lee and Texas soldiers: J. G. Wheeler, "Lee to the Rear," *Confeder-
        ate Veteran,* 11 (1903), p. 116; Freeman, *R. E. Lee,* vol. 3,
        pp. 287–288; Freeman, *Lieutenants,* vol. 3, pp. 357–359.
56   "Tho' it has not": Mary Lee to Mary Meade, April 23, 1865;
        R. M. E. MacDonald, p. 197.

page
56   "I know you sorrow": Lee to Martha Williams, May 2, 1865, in Avery Craven, ed., *"To Markie": The Letters of Robert E. Lee to Martha Custis Williams* (Cambridge, Massachusetts: Harvard University Press, 1934), p. 60.

"Why *will* you": Brock, p. 342.

"I'm thinking of the men": Bryan, pp. 81–82. This conversation with Belle Stewart took place in Lexington, Virginia, probably in 1868.

"The sad truth": Mary Lee to her nephew Edward Lee Childe, May 5, 1865; Lee Papers, W. and L. This letter exists in the form of an unidentified European newspaper clipping printed in English, but its authenticity seems assured by the accompanying original of a letter from Edward Lee Childe to his uncle Robert E. Lee, dated July 16, 1865. It explains the circumstances under which his aunt's letter to him was released to the press and apologizes for its publication. Childe refers to a letter of June 19 from Lee, and to "my Aunt Mary's of the 20th," both of which apparently reproved him for this indiscretion.

CHAPTER 9

57   "armed resistance": The text of this proclamation is from E. B. Long, *The Civil War Day By Day: An Almanac, 1861–1865* (Garden City, New York: Doubleday, 1971), p. 687.

Details of the treatment of Davis are in John J. Craven, *Prison Life of Jefferson Davis* (New York, 1866), pp. 33–39. See also Warren, pp. 71–81.

58   George W. Julian: Claude Bowers, *The Tragic Era* (New York: Blue Ribbon Books, 1929), pp. 16–17.

"Hang Lee!": Myrta Lockett Avary, *Dixie After the War* (New York: Doubleday, Page, 1906), p. 89.

Grant to his wife: Ibid., p. 114.

58–59   Colonel taxi driver, officers as laborers: J. S. Wise, pp. 457–459.
60   "I am looking": Lee to A. L. Long, n.d.; A. L. Long, p. 439.

"There were three children": R. E. Lee, Jr., p. 167.

Presidential proclamation: Kenneth M. Stampp, *The Era of Reconstruction* (New York: Alfred A. Knopf, 1965), pp. 62–64. See also Freeman, *R. E. Lee,* vol. 4, pp. 200–201.

61   "absurd": Avary, p. 70.

"It was but right": Freeman, *R. E. Lee,* vol. 4, p. 203n.

61–62   Veteran from the hills: Franklin L. Riley, ed., *General Robert E. Lee After Appomattox* (New York: Macmillan, 1930), pp. 52–53.

62   "I am old": Jones, pp. 195–196.
62–63   Lee's approach to Grant: Freeman, *R. E. Lee,* vol. 4, p. 203.
63   Lee's letter to Grant, June 13, 1865, and his application to President Johnson of the same date, are found in sequence in deButts-Ely, Letter Book No. 3.

page
64   "will be guided": Bradford, p. 265.
64–65   George Wise and the oath: Avary, pp. 70–71.
65   Henry Ward Beecher: Freeman, *R. E. Lee*, vol. 4, p. 205 and p. 205n.
65–66   Lee and black man at St. Paul's: T. L. Broun, "Negro Communed at St. Paul's Church," *Confederate Veteran*, 13 (1905), p. 360.

CHAPTER 10

68   Canal boat departs; "catch in her voice": Brock, p. 344.
Lee declines bed: R. E. Lee, Jr., p. 171.
"house and bed in the field": Sanborn, vol. 2, p. 260.
68–69   Details of the trip: Gottfried Wälchh, ed., *Frank Buchser, Mein Leben und Streben in Amerika* ... (Zürich: Orell Füssli Verlag, 1942), diary entry of November 7, 1869, translated and kindly made available to the author by Professor Gérard Maurice Doyon of Washington and Lee University. Buchser's trip was four years later, but he vividly described this mode of travel.

CHAPTER 11

70   "You would suppose": Mary Lee to Caroline Peters, July 18, 1865; Lee Papers, W. and L.
Lee to Robert E. Lee, Jr., n.d.: Robert E. Lee, Jr., p. 174.
71   The Palmores: Avary, p. 159; and Freeman, *R. E. Lee*, vol. 4, p. 211 and p. 211n.
"Ah, Mister Palmore": Sanborn, vol. 2, p. 261.
71–72   Exchange with Hunter, n.d.: Jones, pp. 240–241.
72   "Our future will be": Mary Lee to Caroline Peters, July 18, 1865; Lee Papers, W. and L.
"a quiet so profound": R. M. E. MacDonald, p. 200.
"My dear Bertus": Lee to Robert E. Lee, Jr., August 21, 1865; R. E. Lee, Jr., pp. 176–177.
"I am sometimes lonely": Mildred Lee to Lucy Blaine, August 14, 1865; Lee Papers, W. and L.
"Read history": Carl Coke Rister, *Robert E. Lee in Texas* (Norman: University of Oklahoma Press, 1946), p. 59.
"Let him never touch": Sanborn, vol. 1, p. 249.
73   "a pair of ladies' riding gauntlets": Wickham, p. 7. Lee's recommendation for Orton Williams is in deButts-Ely, Letter Book No. 2.
"I know it will": Lee to Eliza Mackay Stiles, August 14, 1856; Sanborn, vol. 1, p. 251.
73–74   "I remember about the horses": Wickham, p. 7.
74   "He was apt": Mildred Lee, "My Recollections of My Father's Death," dated August 21, 1888, in deButts-Ely.

page
74   "We could not understand": Wickham, p. 7.
      Orton proposes to a married woman: Sanborn, vol. 2, pp. 95–96.
74–75 Orton's final mission, final letters, hanging, and Lee's reaction:
      Ibid., pp. 138–140.
75   Agnes' reaction to Orton's death: Wickham, p. 10.
      "haughtiness and reserve": R. M. E. MacDonald, p. 215.
      "to vindicate myself": Jones, p. 180.
76–77 Richardson to Lee, July 28, 1865: Lee Papers, W. and L. A study
      of Lee's efforts to write this book is: Allen W. Moger, "General
      Lee's Unwritten History of the Army of Northern Virginia,"
      Virginia Magazine of History and Biography, 71 (1963), p. 341.
77   "I shall endeavour": Lee to W. H. F. Lee, July 19, 1865; R. E. Lee,
      Jr., p. 178.

CHAPTER 12

78   "chiefly as a Preparatory School": Report of the faculty to the
      Board of Trustees, July 21, 1865; Trustees' Records, W. and L.
78–79 College's postwar financial condition: Report of the Committee on
      Finance for the fiscal year ended July 1, 1865; Trustees' Records,
      W. and L.
79   "Resolved, that a committee": Ibid. This undated memorandum
      appears among the 1865 papers of the trustees. The August 4
      meeting would have been the most likely time to initiate this re-
      quest, in preparing to open the college for the autumn session.
79–80 "Then various members": This and subsequent details and quota-
      tions from this meeting are from Riley, pp. 1–4. It should be
      noted that in Jones, p. 82, Professor John L. Kirkpatrick of the
      Washington College faculty states that an unofficial overture to
      Lee, in the form of a letter written by a friend of one of the trus-
      tees, had preceded the meeting. This is the sole reference to this
      possibility.
81   Lee's effort to avoid 1852 West Point assignment: Freeman, *R. E.
      Lee*, vol. 1, p. 317.
      Lee at Chancellorsville: Ibid., vol. 3, p. 90.
82   Conversation with Wilmer: R. E. Lee, Jr., pp. 182–183.
      Brockenbrough to Lee, August 10, 1865: Lee Papers, W. and L.
83   Letcher to Lee, August 5, 1865: Ibid. This letter's date and some
      remarks at its close indicate that it may have been carried by
      Brockenbrough when he called on Lee.
      Pendleton to Lee, August 5, 1865: Ibid. This letter may also have
      been carried by Brockenbrough.
84   Private assurances: Ollinger Crenshaw, *General Lee's College* (New
      York: Random House, 1969), p. 196, says, "Dr. Pendleton had
      conveyed to him the trustees' assurances that 'the institution
      would in the future be undenominational.' "
      Lee to trustees: August 24, 1865; Lee Papers, W. and L.

page
85   "The decision" and "the healing": Lee to Letcher, August 28, 1865; Jones, p. 203.

85–86   "proper practical relation": Michael Les Benedict, *A Compromise of Principle* (New York: W. W. Norton, 1974), p. 98.

87   "I believe it to be": Lee to Josiah Tattnall, September 7, 1865; Jones, pp. 205–206.

    "They should remain": Lee to Letcher, August 28, 1865; Ibid., p. 203.

88   "I look forward": Lee to Matthew Fontaine Maury, September 8, 1865; Ibid., p. 206.

    "As president": *New York Independent,* September 14, 1865.

    "Aren't you ashamed": M____ LeB____ to President Johnson, October 1, 1865; Walter L. Fleming, ed., *Documentary History of Reconstruction,* vols. 1, 2 (Gloucester, Massachusetts: Peter Smith, 1960), vol. 1, p. 34.

    "He starts tomorrow": Mary Lee to Emily V. Mason, September 14, 1865; R. M. E. MacDonald, p. 204.

CHAPTER 13

89–90   The encounter at Rockfish Gap: J. L. Minor, "How I Met General Robert E. Lee," *Virginia Magazine of History and Biography,* 42 (1934), pp. 241–243. Lee's young friend became Dr. J. L. Minor, of Cordova, Tennessee.

91   "Their impress": J. S. Wise, p. 240.

92   Names of cannon: Susan P. Lee, *Memoirs of William Nelson Pendleton* (Philadelphia, 1893), p. 142.

92–93   New Market details: J. S. Wise, pp. 290–305.

92   "Probably the last": David Macrae, *The Americans at Home* (New York: Dutton, 1952), p. 197.

93   "Well, go on": Freeman, *R. E. Lee,* vol. 2, pp. 523–524. For an analysis of the contributions of Lee and Jackson to this movement, see Freeman, Ibid., pp. 584–589. William Allan's unpublished memoranda of conversations with Lee, in Lee Papers, W. and L., has Lee saying, on February 15, 1868, that he had reached a conclusion that "we must get round on his (Yankee) right," and that Jackson said he had already been "enquiring about roads" that might accomplish this.

94   The University of Alabama: Marshall Fishwick, *Lee After the War* (New York: Dodd, Mead, 1963), p. 85.

    Status and condition of V.M.I.: Henry A. Wise, *Drawing Out the Man* (Charlottesville: University Press of Virginia, 1978), pp. 45–50.

94–95   Lee's arrival: Freeman, *R. E. Lee,* vol. 4, p. 227; Fitzhugh Lee, *General Lee* (New York, 1899), p. 5; Hunter McDonald, "General Robert E. Lee After Appomattox," reprint from *The Tennessee Historical Magazine,* 9 (1925), pp. 87–101.

Chapter 14

96   Lee to Mary Lee, September 19, 1865: R. E. Lee, Jr., pp. 184–185.

"I feel very": Lee to Mary Lee, September 25, 1865; Ibid., p. 186.

"beautifully located": Lee to Mary Lee, September 19, 1865; Ibid., p. 184.

97   Pendleton and occupation authorities: Susan Lee, pp. 421–424.

98   "Damn Yankee bitch": Freeman, *R. E. Lee,* vol. 4, p. 354, has the letter of Miss J. A. Shearman in the *New York Independent,* April 16, 1868, in which she says she was habitually addressed in this manner.

98–99   Quotations and details concerning Lee's installation: Riley, pp. 12–15.

98   Lexington citizens cheer Lee: Ibid., pp. 67–68.

99–100   Lee's signing the oath of allegiance, and that document's fate: Elmer Parker, "Why Was Lee Not Pardoned?" in the National Archives' publication *Prologue,* 2 (Winter 1970). The discovery of this document opened the way for Senator Harry Flood Byrd, Jr., of Virginia to introduce into the Second Session of the Ninety-third Congress the Senate Joint Resolution 189, "To Restore Posthumously Full Rights of Citizenship to General R. E. Lee." This was signed into law by President Gerald R. Ford on August 5, 1975.

Chapter 15

101   Lee's correspondence: Allen W. Moger, "Letters to General Lee After the War," *The Virginia Magazine of History and Biography,* 64 (1956), pp. 30–69, is a comprehensive study of the nature and volume of letters received by Lee from mid-1865 to his death in October 1870. Funded by grants-in-aid from the Carnegie Corporation, it is of particular value in establishing Lee's place in the estimation of both the South and the rest of the nation while he was still alive. One recent study of Lee's place in American history, Thomas L. Connelly, *The Marble Man* (New York: Alfred A. Knopf, 1977), holds that at the time of Appomattox Lee was only one of several prominent Confederate generals who had nearly equal shares of Southern admiration and that, even at his death, "Robert E. Lee was not yet the primary hero symbol of the South" (Connelly, p. 26). The Moger study points to the opposite conclusion, as does the present author's own extensive study of the subject.

102   Beauregard's letter has been lost, but its thrust is clear from Lee's answer, dated October 3, 1865, in deButts-Ely, Letter Book No. 3, which includes the phrase "As you ask my purpose . . ." A correct text is in Jones, pp. 207–208.

103   All places not filled: *Lexington Gazette,* October 11, 1865.

page
103 Givens B. Strickler: Crenshaw, pp. 128, 130-131; Wickham, pp. 13-14; R. E. Lee, Jr., p. 300.
"At times we were": Turner A. Ashby, "Gen. R. E. Lee As a College President," *Confederate Veteran,* 13 (1905), pp. 358-360.
"I am so impatient": Riley, p. 39. The student was Milton W. Humphreys.
104 "My heart cut": Ibid., p. 138.
"He was so gentle": Ibid., pp. 66-67. These incidents are presented here as representative; not all occurred in the autumn of 1865.
"If he met": Ibid., p. 140.
104-105 "It was a general belief": Ibid., p. 132.
106 "He audited every": Thomas Nelson Page, *Robert E. Lee, Man and Soldier* (New York: Scribner's, 1911), p. 661.
Lee and the little boy: R. E. Lee, Jr., p. 167.
106-107 Chewing tobacco: Freeman, *R. E. Lee,* vol. 4, p. 288.
107 "You'll have to do": Freeman, *Lieutenants,* vol. 3, p. 331.
Fox hunting: Riley, pp. 135-136.
"You shall have justice": Sanborn, vol. 1, p. 263.
107-108 Lee, bookseller, and insurance company's offer: Ibid., vol. 2, p. 280.
108 John H. Finley to Lee, November 5, 1865: Lee Papers, W. and L. This letter has not been published previously.
109 Lee's riding clothes: Riley, pp. 49-50.
109-110 Lee and Traveller at the review: R. E. Lee, Jr., pp. 106-107.
110 " 'Traveller' was a mighty": H. McDonald, p. 12.
"dextrous and coquettish": Sanborn, vol. 2, p. 234.
111-112 The first plan for reorganization and expansion of the curriculum is in Trustees' Records, W. and L., meeting of October 24, 1865. Comment on this is to be found in Walter Creigh Preston, *Lee, West Point and Lexington* (Yellow Springs, Ohio: Antioch Press, 1934), pp. 60-70, and in Freeman, *R. E. Lee,* vol. 4, pp. 231-233.
113 Lee to McCormick, November 28, 1865: deButts-Ely, Letter Book No. 3.
Brockenbrough to McCormick, n.d.: Crenshaw, pp. 169-170.

CHAPTER 16

114 Mary Lee, Mildred, and Rob arrive: R. E. Lee, Jr., pp. 195-196, 203-204; R. M. E. MacDonald, pp. 208-209; Freeman, *R. E. Lee,* vol. 4, p. 242; Sanborn, vol. 2, pp. 294-295, 320.
115 The Reverend George Junkin: Crenshaw, pp. 111-125.
116 "to inquire into the condition": This portion of the text of the resolution introduced by Thaddeus Stevens is from Eric L. McKitrick, *Andrew Johnson and Reconstruction* (Chicago: University of Chicago Press, 1960), pp. 258-259.
117-118 Howard's views: Ibid., p. 56; Fishwick, pp. 111-112.

page
118   Lee and Arlington's legal status: Lee to William H. Hope, April 5,
       1866; deButts-Ely, Letter Book No. 3; and Lee to his friend and
       attorney, Francis L. Smith of Alexandria, same date, next in the
       Letter Book.
       "a House that": Sanborn, vol. 1, p. 104.
118-119 Lee and Macomb: A. L. Long, p. 37.
119   "War is": Sanborn, vol. 1, p. 309.
       Letter to Amanda Parks, March 9, 1866: deButts-Ely, Letter Book
       No. 3.
       "I am now considered": A. Craven, p. 68.
120-124 Text of questions and answers is from U.S. Congress, House, *Re-
       port*. The groups of questions and answers are not in every in-
       stance in the sequence in which they were asked and an-
       swered.
121   For an expansion of Lee's views on prisoner exchange, and Lee's
       mention of Union refusal to accept Judge Robert Ould's unilat-
       eral offer to return 15,000 sick Union prisoners, see Jones, pp.
       192-195, and R. E. Lee, Jr., pp. 230-231. For a broader view, in
       which Lee mentioned Andersonville's commandant and person-
       ally criticized Grant, see Meredith, pp. 90-91.
122   Lee to Reverdy Johnson, January 27, 1866: Jones, p. 211.

CHAPTER 17

125-127 Among the many accounts of the Lees' home life are R. E. Lee, Jr.,
       p. 203 et seq., including Lee and closing shutters, p. 245;
       R. M. E. MacDonald, p. 236 et seq.; Sanborn, vol. 2, pp.
       297-298; S. H. Chester, "At College Under General Lee — in
       '69-'70," typescript of reminiscence in Lee Papers, W. and L.
126   "It often seems": R. M. E. MacDonald, p. 240.
       "but I am unable": Ibid., pp. 239-240.
127   "There are so many": Ibid., p. 267.
       "with the exception": Ibid., p. 245.
       "Secession is nothing but": Jones, p. 137.
       "I would lay down my life": Mary Lee to Eliza Mackay Stiles
       (Mrs. William Henry Stiles), February 9, 1861; Robert E. Lee
       Papers, the duPont Library, Stratford Hall Plantation, Strat-
       ford, Virginia.
       "greater than": Mary Lee to Helen _____ (probably Helen
       Bratt), February 1, 1861; Lee Papers, W. and L.
128   "I think the last": Mary Lee to Caroline Peters, May 4, 1866;
       Ibid.
       "I believe it was you": Mildred Lee to Lucy Blaine, February 7,
       1866; Ibid.
129   "the provincial society": Mildred Lee, "Recollections."
       "Saints": Mildred Lee to Emily Hay, dated only March 1; Lee
       Papers, W. and L.

page

129   "I have recently": R. M. E. MacDonald, p. 215.

"We rarely hear": Mary Lee to unidentified cousin, February 12, 1866; Brock, p. 347.

"wholly devoid": Henry Boley, *Lexington in Old Virginia* (Richmond: Garrett & Massie, 1936), p. 123.

"very masterful type"; Chester, p. 5.

"We are all": Lee to W. H. F. Lee, December 2, 1869; R. E. Lee, Jr., pp. 373–374.

"No lady skates": R. M. E. MacDonald, p. 217.

Skiff: Sanborn, vol. 2, p. 347.

129–130   Reading Club: Lee to Mildred Lee, December 21, 1866; R. E. Lee, Jr., p. 254; R. M. E. MacDonald, pp. 215–219.

130   "not beautiful" and "Miss Mildred was": The friend was S. H. Chester, and the quotations are from pp. 5–6 of his reminiscences.

"Experience will teach": Lee to Mildred Lee, December 21, 1866; R. E. Lee, Jr., p. 247.

"I miss you": Lee to Agnes Lee, January 3, 1866; Ibid., p. 207.

"Where is my little": Freeman, *R. E. Lee,* vol. 4, p. 411.

130–131   "To me he seems": Mildred Lee, "Recollections."

131   "After his early": R. E. Lee, Jr., p. 357.

"As to the girls": R. M. E. MacDonald, p. 258.

"Most women": Mildred Lee, "Recollections."

131–132   Lee stops lynching: Account of Charles A. Graves in Riley, pp. 28–30.

133–134   Improved financial condition of the college, fund-raising activities, and expansion of the curriculum: Meetings of April 26–28, June 27–28, and July 18, 1866; Trustees' Records, W. and L. A short description is in Freeman, *R. E. Lee,* vol. 4, pp. 262–267, a somewhat longer account is in Crenshaw, pp. 161–174, and a full study is in Preston, pp. 48–174, with particular attention to the chronological list of accomplishments, pp. 69–70.

134   "to a level": This document, intended for the consideration of the trustees, is dated April 26, 1866, and is signed by Professor C. J. Harris as clerk of faculty and endorsed by Lee; Lee Papers, W. and L.

Lee's room and swords: Christiana Bond, *Memories of General Robert E. Lee* (Baltimore: The Norman, Remington Co., 1926), pp. 47–49.

Also Freeman, *R. E. Lee,* vol. 4, pp. 499–500.

135   "This is a good day": Ashby, p. 359.

Miss Long: G. T. Lee, p. 249.

Jackson monument: Lee to William Beyers, June 2, 1866; deButts-Ely, Letter Book No. 3.

135–136   "I wish these military": Jones, pp. 169–170.

136   "Cut it down": Sanborn, vol. 2, p. 308.

CHAPTER 18

page

137   "as if he had been": Freeman, *R. E. Lee,* vol. 1, p. 106.
       "Do you remember": Ibid., vol. 4, p. 457.

138   "My sweet little Boy": Cuthbert, p. 269.
       Latin dictionary: R. M. E. MacDonald, p. 46.
       "rather stupid" and "intolerably": Ibid., pp. 49, 133.

138–139 In St. Louis: Ibid., p. 73.

139   Lee and Custis slaves: Leyburn, p. 167.
       American Colonization Society: R. M. E. MacDonald, p. 88.
       "my black class": Ibid., p. 54.
       "Let no motive": Mary Lee to Washington Lewis, circa September 1864; Ibid., p. 100.

139–140 Lee to his cousin Annette Carter, November 8, 1859: Letters to Annette Carter. This letter is previously unpublished.

140   "While a beautiful": Brock, p. 328.
       "a desert of dullness": Lee to Mary Lee, circa April 1859; Rister, p. 83.
       "I was invited": Sanborn, vol. 1, pp. 265–266.
       "No one enjoyed": R. M. E. MacDonald, p. 261.

CHAPTER 19

141   Baseball: Wickham, p. 12; Crenshaw, p. 215.

141–142 Gordon's account: Riley, pp. 75–105.

143   "An invitation": Page, p. 661.
       Boy whose mother died: Riley, pp. 50–51.
       Acton to Lee, November 4, 1866: Lee Papers, W. and L. A text is in Freeman, vol. 4, pp. 515–517.

143–144 Lee to Acton, December 15, 1866: John Neville Figgis and Robert Vere Laurence, eds., *Selections from the Correspondence of the First Lord Acton* (London: Longmans, Green, 1917–), vol. 1, pp. 302–305. Excerpts from this letter are in Freeman, *R. E. Lee,* vol. 4, pp. 304–305.

144   Lee to Mrs. Jefferson Davis, February 23, 1866: deButts-Ely, Letter Book No. 3.
       Early to Lee, January 25, 1866: Lee Papers, W. and L.
       Lee to Early, March 15, 1866: deButts-Ely, Letter Book No. 3.

144–145 Harris to Lee, June 6, 1866: Lee Papers, W. and L.

145   "The writer has": Moger, "Letters," pp. 46–47.

145–146 Firewood explosion: Riley, pp. 70–72.

146–147 "Christmas confrontation": Page, p. 663; Riley, pp. 36–39.

CHAPTER 20

148   "Whereas": Avary, p. 248.

149   "It is bad enough" and "They still desire": Mary Lee to Mrs. R. H.

page

Chilton, March 10, 1867, and May 6, 1867; Freeman, *R. E. Lee,* vol. 4, p. 313.

150   "I look upon the Southern": Lee to Maury, May 23, 1867; deButts-Ely, Letter Book No. 4.

"I think all persons": Lee to Ould, March 29, 1867; Ibid.

150–151   Altercation at blacks' schoolhouse: Freeman, *R. E. Lee,* vol. 4, pp. 316–317; Crenshaw, p. 151. See Wickham, pp. 13–14, for Strickler's role.

151–152   "Lee Association": Lee wrote to it on June 18, 1867; Jones, p. 259. Evansville *Daily Sentinel*: Crenshaw, p. 154.

152   "Your release": Lee to Davis, June 1, 1867; Jones, pp. 258–259.

Lee to Robert E. Lee, Jr., October 18, 1866: R. E. Lee, Jr., p. 243.

Lee's sleeplessness over sufferings: H. McDonald, p. 6.

"Madam, do not": Sanborn, vol. 2, p. 308.

153–154   This scene is described by Samuel Zenas Ammen in William Kavanaugh Doty, *Samuel Zenas Ammen and the Kappa Alpha Order* (Charlottesville, Virginia: The Surber-Arundale Co., 1922), pp. 29–30. Background on Stern is from Riley, p. 120, and James Lewis Howe, typescript, "Annals of Washington and Lee University during the Administration of General George Washington Custis Lee (1871–1896)," 1, p. G. 10a, in Lee Papers, W. and L. Background on Ammen is from Richard R. Fletcher, "Lexington Civil War Babies: Three National Fraternities," *Proceedings of the Rockbridge Historical Society* (Lexington, Virginia), 8 (1970–1974), p. 123. Ammen as "most interesting collegian," James Lewis Howe, "The Ugly Club," *The Alumni Magazine,* Washington and Lee University, 16 (November 1940), p. 9.

154   "We likened him": Ammen in Riley, p. 143.

"the chivalrous" and "Something might": Ammen in Doty, p. 31.

155   Statistics, accomplishments, needs, and plans are from Lee to Board of Trustees, June 20, 1867; deButts-Ely, Letter Book No. 4. The existence of a gymnasium at the time has been questioned, but it is mentioned both in this letter and in Royster Lyle, Jr., and Pamela Hemenway Simpson, *The Architecture of Historic Lexington* (Charlottesville: The University Press of Virginia, 1977), p. 165.

"east of the mountains": Lee to W. H. F. Lee, June 8, 1867; R. E. Lee, Jr., p. 260.

"determined to devote": Ibid., p. 376.

"Make no needless": Edward S. Joynes, "Lee, the College President," in *Robert E. Lee: Centennial Celebration . . . of the University of South Carolina* (Columbia, South Carolina: The State Co., 1907), p. 33.

155–156   "The discipline has": Ibid., p. 30.

156   "The great mistake": Riley, p. 38.

Carter Jones: R. E. Lee, Jr., p. 267.

282   ☆

CHAPTER 21

page
157–159 Mildred Lee's account is in R. E. Lee, Jr., pp. 269–273.
160   "one black silk": William Alexander MacCorkle, *The White Sulphur Springs* (New York: Neale Publishing Co., 1916), p. 339.
        "practically the clearing house": Ibid., p. 397.
161   ". . . we were aware": Bond, pp. 19–20.
162   Everyone rises: Freeman, *R. E. Lee,* vol. 4, p. 326.
162–163 West Virginia belle: A. R. H. Ranson, "New Stories of Lee and Jackson," *The South Atlantic Quarterly,* 12 (1913), p. 295.
163–164 Lee and Englishmen: Ibid., p. 294.
164   Corcoran's gifts to the college: Crenshaw, p. 167.
        "Do I behold": Freeman, *R. E. Lee,* vol. 4, p. 330.
165   Lee, Christiana, and Governor Curtin's party: Bond, pp. 31–34. That it was Governor Curtin is stated by Percival Reniers, *The Springs of Virginia* (Chapel Hill: University of North Carolina Press, 1941), p. 213.
166   "I saw the lady": Lee to R. E. Lee, Jr., August 5, 1867; R. E. Lee, Jr., pp. 277–278.
167   Brazil Emigration Agency: *White Sulphur Echo* (West Virginia), August 10, 1867.
        "Well, General Lee": Bond, pp. 39–40.
        "we saw, moreover": Ibid., p. 23.

CHAPTER 22

169   Rooney convinces his father: R. E. Lee, Jr., pp. 284–286.
        Measurements for suit: Sanborn, vol. 2, p. 329.
        Description of Mahone: J. S. Wise, p. 325.
        Lee and Mahone at Sayler's Creek: Freeman, *R. E. Lee,* vol. 4, pp. 84–85.
170   "astonishingly well": Lee to Mary Lee, November 26, 1867; R. E. Lee, Jr., p. 287.
170–171 The positions of Davis, Chase, and Federal prosecutors are in Warren, pp. 80–88.
171   "I am responsible": Riley, p. 97. This is from E. C. Gordon's account of his relationship with Lee, and is presumably based on a conversation with him. Since no minutes of Lee's testimony have been found (see Freeman, *R. E. Lee,* vol. 4, p. 337n.), this appears to be the sole quotation from the proceedings.
172   Lee's trip to Petersburg: Sanborn, vol. 2, pp. 330–331.
172–173 Lee at Mahone's house: R. H. Fitzhugh, *R. E. Lee* (Lexington, Kentucky: J. L. Richardson & Co., 1910), pp. 12–14.
173   "I was so happy": Sanborn, vol. 2, p. 331.
        Lee to Mary Lee, November 29, 1867: R. E. Lee, Jr., pp. 287–288.
        Crowd gathered three hours before: Freeman, *R. E. Lee,* vol. 4, p. 339.

CHAPTER 23

174   "The mountains": Lee to Martha Williams, January 1, 1868; A. Craven, p. 78.

Lee's editing: Richardson to Lee, February 7, 1868; Moger, "Unwritten," p. 348. The letter indicates that Lee had finished the project and was preparing to send it to Richardson in New York. If this was the case, other accounts are mistaken in placing Lee's completion of the task a year later.

175   The status of buildings, library, planetarium, and enrollment are from Lee to the trustees, June 16, 1868; Lee Papers, W. and L.

Lee to Ewell, March 3, 1868: Jones, pp. 117–118.

Offer to Lee and his reply: R. E. Lee, Jr., p. 376. This is undated. Various authors have placed it in different years. It is placed here as being germane to this consideration of Lee's postwar attitudes.

"He looked twenty years": James B. Craighill, "Personal Recollections of the John Brown Raid and the Civil War," unpublished memoir dated March 11, 1912, p. 72. See Manuscript Sources in Bibliography for further identification.

176   Lee to Martha Williams, January 1, 1868: A. Craven, p. 78.

New York fund-raising: Freeman, *R. E. Lee,* vol. 4, pp. 360–361.

179   "I suppose you will go": The subject of Lee's resignation is treated in Freeman, *R. E. Lee,* vol. 1, p. 437 and n., pp. 438, 633–636. According to William Allan's memoranda of conversations with Lee, in the Lee Papers, W. and L., Lee spoke at some length on this subject on March 10, 1868. Lee told Allan that on the occasion of his first conference with Scott on this subject, in March 1861, Scott had showed Lee letters from Lincoln and Secretary of State Seward that made both Scott and Lee feel that "a peaceful solution would be attained." After the situation worsened and Lee had his final conversation with Scott, Lee told Allan, it had been a hard thing, "thinking that secession was foolish and the war wrong, to break loose and come south." Previous biographers seem to have been unaware of this conversation.

180   Lee to Reverdy Johnson, February 25, 1868: deButts-Ely, Letter Book No. 4. Texts are in R. E. Lee, Jr., pp. 27–28, and Freeman, *R. E. Lee,* vol. 4, pp. 361–362.

CHAPTER 24

181   Fund-raising meeting: Freeman, *R. E. Lee,* vol. 4, pp. 348–351.

New York Independent, March 12, 1868, as quoted in Ibid., pp. 351–353.

182   "Residing in Lexington": *New York Independent,* April 2, 1868. W. L. Garrison: Ibid.

182–183 Unfavorable publicity: Fishwick, pp. 164–165; *Chicago Daily Tri-*

bune, April 6, 1868, in Preston, p. 75; *Boston Evening Traveller* in Crenshaw, p. 154.

183   "implements for another": Crenshaw, p. 153, citing *New York Independent,* April 16, 1868.

A Northern woman: This was Miss J. A. Shearman; Freeman, *R. E. Lee,* vol. 4, pp. 354–355, cites this as *New York Independent,* April 16, 1868.

184   "refused to give" and "and said that": Hugh A. Moran to his father, May 10, 1868; Moran Papers, Washington and Lee University. Other accounts of Brockenbrough shooting are Riley, pp. 129–130; Crenshaw, p. 151; Fishwick, pp. 165–166; Freeman, *R. E. Lee,* vol. 4, p. 358.

184–185   Lee to Strickler, May 11, 1868: R. E. Lee, Jr., p. 300.

Impeachment Blue: Gene Smith, p. 266.

186   Lee to Annette Carter, March 28, 1868: Letters to Annette Carter. This letter is previously unpublished.

187   "I am rejoiced": Leyburn, p. 167.

Lee opposed to granting vote to blacks: His fullest statement on this subject is in U.S. Congress, House, *Report,* p. 134: "My own opinion is that, at this time, they cannot vote intelligently, and that giving them the right of suffrage would open the door to a great deal of demagogism, and lead to embarrassments in many ways. What the future may prove, how intelligent they may become, with what eyes they may look upon the interests of the State in which they may reside, I cannot say more than you can."

"those who are plotting": Lee to R. E. Lee, Jr., March 19, 1868; deButts-Ely, General Correspondence folder for 1868. Lee's remarks about the blacks came in connection with his suggestion that his son attempt to replace the black workers on his farm with white laborers. The full text of the first sentence quoted reads: "You will never prosper with the blacks, and it is abhorrent to a reflecting mind to be supporting and cherishing those who are plotting and working for your injury and all of whose sympathies and aspirations are antagonistic to yours." Text in R. E. Lee, Jr., pp. 305–307.

"God grant that": Lee to Mrs. W. H. F. Lee, May 29, 1868; R. E. Lee, Jr., p. 313.

188   Henry Adams: Gene Smith, p. 213.

"if you ever again presume": Bradford, p. 226.

New York Herald: Freeman, *R. E. Lee,* vol. 4, p. 371.

CHAPTER 25

190   Lee and little girl: H. McDonald, pp. 6–7.

191   Lee to Charlotte Haxall, July 14, 1868: deButts-Ely, General Correspondence folder for 1868.

page

192   "I am writing": Lee to W. H. F. Lee, August 14, 1868; R. E. Lee, Jr., pp. 322–323.

192–193   Lee to Gordon, August 18, 1868: Lee Papers, W. and L.

CHAPTER 26

194   "The place looks beautiful": R. E. Lee, Jr., p. 324.
       "How is Traveller": Riley, p. 93.

196–197   White Sulphur Letter, sometimes known as White Sulphur Manifesto: This was in the form of a letter to Rosecrans, with Lee leading the signers, August 26, 1868; deButts-Ely, Letter Book No. 4. A text, omitting only the last two redundant paragraphs, is in Freeman, *R. E. Lee,* vol. 4, pp. 375–377. The *White Sulphur Echo* of August 28, 1868, carries both the full text and a lengthy editorial that conveys some of the feeling that surrounded the election campaign and the evolution of this document at the White Sulphur.

198   Isaac Hale, Jr., to Lee, September 7, 1868: Lee Papers, W. and L.

CHAPTER 27

199   "Eight millions": Crenshaw, pp. 149–150.

200   Christmas morning: R. E. Lee, Jr., p. 324; R. M. E. MacDonald, p. 248.

200–201   Johnson's amnesty: Freeman, *R. E. Lee,* vol. 4, p. 381.

201–202   Arlington relics: Ibid., pp. 382–385.

202–203   Johnson absent from Grant's inauguration: Gene Smith, pp. 300–301; Lately Thomas, *The First President Johnson* (New York: Morrow, 1968), pp. 617–618.

CHAPTER 28

204–206   Studies of Lee's administration used here include Preston, pp. 60–70, 95–103, and Freeman, *R. E. Lee,* vol. 4, pp. 231–233, and, for particular emphasis at this juncture, pp. 420–433. See also Crenshaw, pp. 160–166. The account of J. L. Kirkpatrick in Jones, pp. 88–92, includes the sole firsthand statement by a member of the faculty that Lee kept in his office a fully detailed plan for a medical school, which he hoped to institute if funds became available.
       Lee's own best exposition of what he hoped to accomplish in 1869 and thereafter is in his letter to the finance committee of the Board of Trustees, January 8, 1869, which is accompanied by the more detailed letter of a faculty committee, of the same

date. This is most easily found in Preston, pp. 95–103. Other records of accomplishments and plans at this time are the minutes of the meetings of March 30 and June 22–23, 1869, in Trustees' Records, W. and L. Also see Lee to trustees, June 22, 1869, in Lee Papers, W. and L., for his report on the academic year 1868–1869. This letter goes into particular detail concerning the Board of Survey, proposes free tuition "for candidates for the Christian Ministry," and suggests the idea for a summer school.

205   "give them as thorough": These are the words of Professor William Preston Johnston, in an interview with the *New York Sun*, as given in Freeman, *R. E. Lee*, vol. 4, p. 425.

206   *New York Herald*: Freeman, *R. E. Lee*, vol. 4, p. 428.

207   "inquired how I was": Riley, pp. 27–28.
     "It makes but little": R. E. Lee, Jr., p. 346.

208   A full text of Lee's speech is in Freeman, *R. E. Lee*, vol. 4, pp. 517–520.
     "It had been intimated": R. E. Lee, Jr., p. 349.

209–210 Meeting with Grant: "merely one of courtesy" in Freeman, *R. E. Lee*, vol. 4, p. 521; "neither General Lee" in R. E. Lee, Jr., p. 349. The meeting is described in Freeman, *R. E. Lee*, vol. 4, pp. 401–402, and an appendix, pp. 520–521, gives different contemporary versions and interpretations of this interview. A much later account appeared in the *Brooklyn Eagle* of January 13, 1912. In a story entitled "A Secret of Grant and Lee," the *Eagle*'s editor, St. Clair McKelway, claimed to have been an intermediary in arranging this meeting, at which he said Confederate General Jubal Early was also present, as well as R. M. T. Hunter, a Virginian who had been a prewar United States senator and subsequently the Confederate secretary of state, 1861–1862, and then a Confederate senator. In this account, the three Virginians asked for and received assurances that Federal troops would in no way hinder the forthcoming elections for governor in Virginia. There is no independent substantiation for any of this.

CHAPTER 29

211–212 New house: Freeman, *R. E. Lee*, vol. 4, pp. 408–409; Sanborn, vol. 2, p. 346; R. E. Lee, Jr., pp. 357–358; Lyle, pp. 162–165 et seq.; *Lexington Gazette*, May 29, 1869; Fishwick, pp. 174–175.

212   Lee happy to have Traveller under his roof: Freeman, *R. E. Lee*, vol. 4, p. 408.
     "his eyes could rest": R. E. Lee, Jr., p. 357.
     Virginia Peyton: Sanborn, vol. 2, p. 345.
     E. C. Gordon: Riley, pp. 75–105.

214   "God disposes": A. L. Long, p. 485.

page

214–215 Brilliant season at the White Sulphur: Reniers, pp. 219–229; *White Sulphur Echo,* August 12, 1869; *Lee Week Herald,* White Sulphur Springs, West Virginia, August 25, 1932.

215 "The girls are well": Lee to Mary Lee, August 10, 1869; R. E. Lee, Jr., pp. 365–366.
"The girls are always busy": Lee to Mary Lee, August 14, 1869; Ibid., pp. 366–367.

215–216 George Peabody: It was first announced that Peabody had given $60,000 to endow a professorship. Oddly, in the same August 12, 1869, issue of the *White Sulphur Echo* in which this was announced, there appeared a correction, stating that Peabody had assigned to Washington College a claim against the state of Virginia, said in that item to be worth "about $50,000." Crenshaw, p. 171, states that the matter was settled in 1881, with Washington and Lee University receiving $145,000 for the bonds and another $105,000 in interest after costs of litigation.

CHAPTER 30

217 "that quiet zeal": Jones, p. 447.
"The impression": Riley, p. 125.

217–222 Frank Buchser and his time in Lexington: For details of this visit, unmentioned in previous biographies of Lee, the author has relied principally on Gérard Maurice Doyon, "Frank Buchser, Painter of the Last Life Portrait of Robert E. Lee," a lecture given to the combined audience of the Rockbridge (County, Virginia) Chapter of the Virginia Museum of Fine Arts and the Rockbridge Historical Society, on May 10, 1977, at Washington and Lee University, where Professor Doyon is chairman of the art department and director of the duPont Gallery. Although some of these texts and observations are available in Meredith, the present author has relied largely on Professor Doyon's translation of Wälchh, graciously made available by Professor Doyon, and on his translations from H. Lüdecke, *Frank Buchsers amerikanische Sendung, 1866–1871: die Chronik seiner Reisen* (Basel: Holbein-Verlag, 1941).

220 Lee on Davis: An additional view is set forth in William Allan's memoranda of his conversations with Lee, in Lee Papers, W. and L. Professor Allan's account of a conversation of March 10, 1868, has Lee saying that he "told Mr. Davis often and early in the war that the slaves should be emancipated, that it was the only way to remove a weakness at home and to get sympathy abroad, and to divide our enemies, but Davis would not hear of it. Thinks highly of Davis, but blames him for not conciliating his opponents and trying to unite all in the Cause. Mr. Davis' enemies became so many as to destroy his power and to paralyze the country . . ."

page
223   "I have not commenced": Lee to his cousin Cassius F. Lee, Jr.,
       June 6, 1870; Page, pp. 668–669.
224   Student and chapel cupola: Riley, p. 32.
       Lee to Gordon, December 14, 1869: R. E. Lee, Jr., pp. 376–377.

CHAPTER 31

225   Lee to Walker, February 24, 1870: Printed two-page document,
       "Communication from Gen'l R. E. Lee Relative to Southern
       Boundary Line of Virginia," identified only by printed "Doc.
       No. IX" at top of p. 1; Lee Papers, W. and L.
       "The doctors": Lee to W. H. F. Lee, December 2, 1869; R. E. Lee,
       Jr., p. 373.
       Lee to Mildred Lee, February 2, 1870: Ibid., pp. 381–383.
226   "was constantly in pain": Ibid., p. 380.
       "My health has been": Lee to General Corse and others, March 18,
       1870; Jones, pp. 175–176.
226–228 Meeting between Johnston and Lee, and subsequent meeting with
       Allan and White also present: G. W. Bean, ed., "Memoranda of
       Conversations Between General Robert E. Lee and William
       Preston Johnston, May 7, 1868, and March 18, 1870," *Virginia
       Magazine of History and Biography*, 73 (1965), pp. 474–484. The
       memoranda on which the article is based are in Lee Papers, W.
       and L.
228   "The doctors and others": Lee to Mildred Lee, March 21, 1870;
       R. E. Lee, Jr., pp. 384–385.
       "to take Agnes": Ibid.
       "I shall go first": Lee to W. H. F. Lee, March 22, 1870; Ibid., pp.
       385–386.
229   Lee's departure: *Southern Collegian*, 2 (March 26, 1870).
       "painfully struck": Riley, p. 130.
       "he could not go to Savannah": Bean, p. 481.

CHAPTER 32

230   "the night" and "a little feverish": Lee to Mary Lee, March 19,
       1870; R. E. Lee, Jr., pp. 388–389.
230–232 Lee, Pickett, and Mosby: John S. Mosby, "Personal Recollections
       of General Lee," *Munsey's Magazine,* 45 (April to September
       1911), pp. 65–69.
230   "From his position": James D. McCabe, *Life and Campaigns of General
       Robert E. Lee* (New York, 1867), p. 403.
231   "This has been my fight": Freeman, *R. E. Lee,* p. 129.
       "Is that man": Mosby, p. 69, quoting a postwar conversation with
       Charles Venable.

page

232 James L. Corley: R. E. Lee, Jr., pp. 390–391.

233–234 Visit to Anne Lee's grave: Sanborn, vol. 2, p. 354. Facts concerning the monument are in J. Randolph Smith, "Miss Annie Carter Lee," *Confederate Veteran,* 14 (1906), pp. 325–327.

233 "purest and best": Lee to his brother Charles Carter Lee, October 26, 1862; Freeman, *R. E. Lee,* vol. 2, p. 421.

"It is better too": Lee to Anne Lee, August 27, 1860; Lee Papers, Virginia Historical Society.

234 "as handsome": Lee to an unnamed correspondent, June 22, 1857; Jones, p. 375.

"She asks me": Brock, p. 324.

News of Annie's death: Taylor, p. 76.

235 "We were locked up": Agnes Lee Letter. A text is in R. E. Lee, Jr., pp. 391–394.

235–237 From Raleigh to departure from Augusta: Agnes Lee Letter; Freeman, *R. E. Lee,* vol. 4, pp. 447–449; Sanborn, vol. 2, pp. 355–357.

236 "the consummation": Freeman, *R. E. Lee,* vol. 2, p. 326.

"As for wholesale burnings": Fishwick, p. 190.

"legislation was by bribery": David Duncan Wallace, "South Carolina," *Encyclopaedia Britannica,* fourteenth edition (1929).

"the idea of subjugation": Freeman, *Lieutenants,* vol. 3, p. 686.

237 "Crowds came": Agnes Lee Letter.

238 "It did grieve me": Sanborn, vol. 1, p. 81.

239 Mercer on Lee: Ibid., pp. 201–202.

"lagged terribly": Freeman, *R. E. Lee,* vol. 1, p. 624.

Eliza mends shirts: Sanborn, vol. 2, p. 44.

"That spot of spots!": Ibid., vol. 1, p. 82.

239–240 Reception and stay in Savannah: Agnes Lee Letter; Freeman, *R. E. Lee,* vol. 4, pp. 449–451; Sanborn, vol. 2, pp. 357–358; Fishwick, p. 194; Lee to Mary Lee, April 2, 1870, in R. E. Lee, Jr., pp. 390–391.

241 Captain White assigned: Freeman, *R. E. Lee,* vol. 2, p. 468. New hours were not formally adopted until June 27, 1870; Ibid., vol. 4, p. 484.

"The Board realizes": Resolution of April 19, 1870; Trustees' Records, W. and L. A text is in Preston, pp. 90–91.

"The old soldiers": Lee to Mary Lee, April 2, 1870; R. E. Lee, Jr., pp. 390–391.

"I do not think": Lee to Mary Lee, April 17, 1870; Ibid., pp. 394–395.

242 "Papa has borne": Agnes Lee Letter.

242–243 "Agnes strewed it" and "I feel better": Lee to Charles Carter Lee, April 18, 1870; Lee Papers, W. and L.

page

243   Whirlwind Brigade and Cold Harbor incident: "J.F.T.," "Some Florida Heroes." *Confederate Veteran,* 11 (1903), pp. 363–365.
244   Reception at Jacksonville: Freeman, *R. E. Lee,* vol. 4, p. 452.

CHAPTER 34

245   "I am astonished": Ibid., p. 455. Also on Charleston, see Sanborn, vol. 2, pp. 359–360.
      Lee to William Preston Johnston, April 21, 1870: Lee Papers, W. and L. This was written from Savannah.
245–246 Wilmington, Portsmouth, Norfolk: Freeman, *R. E. Lee,* vol. 4, pp. 456–459; R. E. Lee, Jr., pp. 400–401, and pp. 209–210 for earlier relationship with their hosts the Seldens; Sanborn, vol. 2, p. 360; Fishwick, p. 199.
246   "the street was lined": Freeman, *R. E. Lee,* vol. 4, p. 458.
      "We regarded him": R. E. Lee, Jr., p. 405.
246–247 "your papa": Mary Lee to Mildred Lee, letter begun May 9, 1870, and continued May 13; R. E. Lee, Jr., pp. 405–406. The description of Agnes is missing in this text, but it is in R. M. E. MacDonald, pp. 273–274. The description of Lee and his grandson is in the text in R. E. Lee, Jr., p. 406.

CHAPTER 35

248   "I am unwilling": Lee to John W. Brockenbrough, May 28, 1870; Jones, p. 116.
      "declined to recede": Ibid., p. 116.
      James R. Winchester: Riley, p. 115.
248–249 W. H. Tayloe: Ibid., pp. 125–128.
249   Lee's movements during these weeks, greatly condensed here, are described in more detail in Freeman, *R. E. Lee,* vol. 4, pp. 473–477; Sanborn, vol. 2, pp. 366–368; and R. E. Lee, Jr., pp. 412–419. The last citation includes the texts of three letters from Lee to his wife.
250   "to perfect the title": R. E. Lee, Jr., p. 396.
      The end of the story: Sanborn, vol. 2, p. 385. The Supreme Court decision is *United States* v. *G. W. P. C. Lee* 27 U.S. Law Ed. 171; 106 U.S. 196; 1 Sup. Ct.–240. At the time of this decision, Custis was president of Washington and Lee University, having been elected on his father's death.
250–251 Lee and telescope: Freeman, *R. E. Lee,* vol. 4, p. 478. The telescope was subsequently located at the University of Virginia in Charlottesville.
251   "Hot Spout": Lee to Mary Lee, August 14, 1870; R. E. Lee, Jr., p. 423.

"I do not perceive": Lee to Mary Lee, August 19, 1870; Ibid., p. 425.

Lee to Martha Williams, August 27, 1870: A. Craven, pp. 89–91.

"I fear we are destined": Lee to an unnamed correspondent, August 23, 1870; Riley, p. 158.

252 Lee to spiritualist: R. E. Lee, Jr., p. 316.

Lee to Charlotte Haxall, August 28, 1868: deButts-Ely, General Correspondence folder for 1868.

"the happiness": Sanborn, vol. 2, pp. 369–370.

"I shall be ready": Ibid., p. 370.

CHAPTER 36

253 "An unusual elation": Jones, p. 447.

Lee at beginning of college session: Freeman, *R. E. Lee*, vol. 4, p. 481.

Lee and Valley Railroad: Ibid., p. 480.

253–254 Lee, Traveller, and little girls: R. E. Lee, Jr., pp. 372–375. The incident is given without date.

254 "Your letter on the dog": Lee to his nephew Fitzhugh Lee, September 19, 1870; Freeman, *R. E. Lee*, vol. 4, pp. 309–310. Sanborn, vol. 2, p. 320, adds details.

254–255 Lee to Charles Marshall, n.d.: Freeman, *R. E. Lee*, vol. 4, pp. 483–484. As with the ride on Traveller, this undated passage is placed here because it seems appropriate in summation.

255 Lee to Samuel H. Tagart, September 28, 1870: McDonogh School Archives, McDonogh, Maryland. A text is in R. E. Lee, Jr., pp. 432–433.

Percy Davidson: Freeman, *R. E. Lee*, vol. 4, p. 486.

256 "Resolutions will not": Lee to Mary Lee, July 20, 1870; R. E. Lee, Jr., p. 418.

"Life": Mildred Lee, "Recollections."

"with marked cheerfulness": William Preston Johnston in Jones, p. 448.

"I will give that sum": Jones, p. 448.

"You have kept us waiting": Mary Lee to Mrs. A. L. Long, November 20, 1870, in Lee Papers, W. and L., and to Edward Turner, n.d., in R. M. E. MacDonald, pp. 278–280. See also Mary Lee to Mary Meade, October 12, 1870, as quoted in Freeman, *R. E. Lee*, vol. 4, pp. 487, 488, 489, 492.

257–261 Lee's final illness and death: The most vivid and comprehensive eyewitness account is Mildred Lee's "Recollections." Other eyewitness accounts are the letters of Mary Lee, cited immediately above, and her letter to Mrs. R. H. Chilton, n.d., in R. E. Lee, Jr., pp. 439–440. The account of William Preston Johnston, who was frequently at Lee's bedside, is in Jones, pp. 446–452, as well as in Riley, pp. 207–213, and, in shorter form, in R. E. Lee, Jr., pp. 434–439.

page

257 "venous congestion" and "cerebral exhaustion": Freeman, *R. E. Lee,* vol. 4, p. 524.

258 "Mother would be": Mildred Lee, "Recollections."

"Robert . . . Welcomes me": Mary Lee to Edward Turner, n.d.; R. M. E. MacDonald, p. 297.

"when Robert gets well": H. McDonald, p. 7.

Mary Lee to Francis H. Smith, October 10, 1870: R. M. E. Mac-Donald, p. 280.

"A week passed": Mildred Lee, "Recollections."

259 Weather conditions: *Lexington Gazette,* September 30, 1870, and October 7, 1870. From these reports, it is clear that the "Great Storm" took place on September 28–29. However, Mildred Lee, in "Recollections," speaks of a rainy period of eight days, which would place the break in the weather on October 5 or 6. Sanborn, vol. 2, pp. 375–376, has rain again on October 10, and has the rain stopping and the sky clearing before dawn on October 12, the morning of Lee's death.

  The author is indebted to Mary P. Coulling of Lexington, Virginia, for drawing his attention to the foregoing combination of references.

It occurred to no one: Mildred Lee, "Recollections."

London Standard: Freeman, *R. E. Lee,* vol. 4, p. 490.

"Fearful lights": H. McDonald, p. 7. Freeman, *R. E. Lee,* vol. 4, p. 490n., states that these lines are incorrectly attributed in McDonald and that they are from W. E. Aytoun's *Edinburgh After Flodden.*

260 "I — feel — better": William Preston Johnston in Jones, p. 449. The dashes have been added to conform to Johnston's statement that this was said "slowly and distinctly."

"As the old hero": Ibid., p. 451.

261 "He wandered to those": Mary Lee to Mrs. R. H. Chilton, n.d., in R. E. Lee, Jr., p. 440.

"Tell Hill": William Preston Johnston in Jones, p. 451.

"Strike the tent!" Ibid. This appears to be the authority on which various biographers have written deathbed scenes in which Lee expired immediately after saying these words. Although Johnston refers to them as "those last significant words," his phrase can also be taken to mean the last comprehensible words, certainly containing a nearly poetic significance at the close of a famous military campaigner's life. If Lee had, in fact, said those words and then died, it seems impossible that this would have escaped the attention of his daughter Mildred, who was at his side for hours before his death and at the moment he died. In her "Recollections," she mentions only his "drawing long, hard breaths" and finally "struggling," and then, "In a moment he was dead."

Bibliography

MANUSCRIPT SOURCES

Allan, William. Memoranda of conversations with Lee. In Lee Papers, Washington and Lee University, Lexington, Virginia.

Board of Trustees' Records. Washington and Lee University.

Carter, Annette. Unpublished collection of letters from her cousin Robert E. Lee. In the possession of her granddaughter, Mrs. Charles K. Lennig, Jr., of Philadelphia.

Chester, S. H. "At College Under General Lee — in '69-'70." Typescript in Lee Papers, Washington and Lee University.

Coulling, Mary P. "The Lee Girls." Unpublished paper with footnotes, given as lecture on May 11, 1964, in Lexington, Virginia. Lee Papers, Washington and Lee University.

Craighill, James B. "Personal Recollections of the John Brown Raid at Harpers Ferry and of the Civil War." Unpublished memoir, dated March 11, 1912. In the possession of its author's grandson, James B. Craighill of Charlotte, North Carolina.

The deButts-Ely Collection of Robert E. Lee Family Papers, 1794-1916. The Library of Congress, Washington, D.C.

Doyon, Gérard Maurice. "Frank Buchser, Painter of the Last Life Portrait of Robert E. Lee." Paper presented to the Rockbridge (County, Virginia) Chapter of the Virginia Museum of Fine Arts and the Rockbridge Historical Society, May 10, 1977, in Lexington, Virginia. In the possession of Professor Doyon, Washington and Lee University.

Howe, James Lewis. "Annals of Washington and Lee University During the Administration of General George Washington Custis Lee (1871-1896)." Typescript in Lee Papers, Washington and Lee University.

Lee, Mildred. "Recollections of My Father's Death." In the deButts-Ely Collection, Library of Congress.

Robert E. Lee Papers. The duPont Library, Stratford Hall Plantation, Stratford, Virginia.

Lee Papers. Virginia Historical Society, Richmond, Virginia.

Lee Papers. Washington and Lee University, Lexington, Virginia.

Lovell, Samuel C. (Lieutenant, Fourth Massachusetts Cavalry). Diary. Original in the possession of Stuart H. Buck, Takoma Park, Maryland. Photocopy at Appomattox Court House National Historical Park, Appomattox, Virginia.
McDonogh School Archives. McDonogh, Maryland.
Moran Papers. Washington and Lee University.

PRINTED PRIMARY SOURCES

Arnold, William B. *The Fourth Massachusetts Cavalry in the Closing Scenes of the War for the Maintenance of the Union.* Boston?, 191–.
Ashby, Turner A. "Gen. R. E. Lee as a College President." *Confederate Veteran,* 13 (1905).
Bean, G. W., ed. "Memoranda of Conversations Between General Robert E. Lee and William Preston Johnston, May 7, 1868, and March 18, 1870." *The Virginia Magazine of History and Biography,* 73 (1965).
Bond, Christiana. *Memoirs of General Robert E. Lee.* Baltimore: The Norman, Remington Co., 1926.
Broun, T. L. "Negro Communed at St. Paul's Church." *Confederate Veteran,* 13 (1905).
Chamberlain, Joshua L. *The Passing of the Armies.* New York: Putnam's, 1915.
Chesnut, Mary Boykin. *A Diary from Dixie.* Cambridge, Massachusetts: Harvard University Press, 1980.
Cooke, Giles B. "Just Before and After Lee Surrendered to Grant." *Houston Chronicle,* October 8, 1922.
Craven, Avery, ed. *"To Markie": The Letters of Robert E. Lee to Martha Custis Williams.* Cambridge, Massachusetts: Harvard University Press, 1934.
Craven, John J. *Prison Life of Jefferson Davis.* New York, 1866.
Cuthbert, Norma B. "To Molly — Five Early Letters from Robert E. Lee to His Wife, 1832–1835." *The Huntington Library Quarterly,* 15 (May 1952).
Douglas, Henry Kyd. *I Rode with Stonewall.* Chapel Hill: University of North Carolina Press, 1940. Reprint, Covington, Georgia: Mockingbird Books, 1974.
Figgis, John Neville, and Reginald Vere Laurence, eds. *Selections from the Correspondence of the First Lord Acton.* London: Longmans, Green, 1917–.
Fitzhugh, R. H. *R. E. Lee.* Lexington, Kentucky: J. L. Richardson & Co., 1910.
Fleming, Walter L. *Documentary History of Reconstruction.* vols. 1, 2. Gloucester, Massachusetts: Peter Smith, 1960.
Grant, Ulysses S. *Personal Memoirs of Ulysses S. Grant.* 2 vols. New York, 1886.
"J.F.T." "Some Florida Heroes." *Confederate Veteran,* 11 (1903).
Jones, J. William. *Personal Reminiscences, Anecdotes, and Letters of Gen. Robert E. Lee.* New York, 1875.
Joynes, Edward S. "Lee, the College President," in *Robert E. Lee: Centennial Celebration of His Birth, Held Under the Auspices of the University of South Carolina . . .* Columbia, South Carolina: The State Co., 1907.
Lee, Fitzhugh. *General Lee.* New York, 1899.

Lee, George Taylor. "Reminiscences of General Robert E. Lee, 1865–1868." *The South Atlantic Quarterly*, 26 (1927).

Lee, Robert E., Jr. *Recollections and Letters of General Robert E. Lee.* New York: Doubleday, 1909.

Lee, Susan P. *Memoirs of William Nelson Pendleton.* Philadelphia, 1893.

Leyburn, John. "An Interview with Gen. Robert E. Lee." *Century Illustrated Monthly Magazine*, 30 (May 1885).

Long, A. L. *Memoirs of Robert E. Lee.* New York, 1887.

McKelway, St. Clair. "A Secret of Grant and Lee." *Brooklyn* (New York) *Eagle*, January 13, 1912.

Macrae, David. *The Americans at Home.* New York: Dutton, 1952.

Minor, J. L. "How I Met General Robert E. Lee." *The Virginia Magazine of History and Biography*, 42 (1934).

Mosby, John S. "Personal Recollections of General Lee." *Munsey's Magazine*, 45 (April to September 1911).

Porter, Horace. *Campaigning with Grant.* New York, 1897. Reprint, New York: Bonanza Books, 1961.

————. "Grant's Last Campaign." *Century Illustrated Monthly Magazine*, 35 (November 1887).

Ranson, A. R. H. "New Stories of Lee and Jackson." *The South Atlantic Quarterly*, 12 (1913).

Riley, Franklin L., ed. *General Robert E. Lee After Appomattox.* New York: Macmillan, 1930.

Smith, Channing M. "The Last Time I Saw General Lee." *Confederate Veteran*, 35 (1927).

Southern Collegian, Lexington, Virginia. Issues cited were published by the literary societies of Washington College, later Washington and Lee University.

Sullivane, Clement. "Last Meeting with Gen. R. E. Lee." *Confederate Veteran*, 28 (1920).

Taylor, Walter H. *Four Years With General Lee.* New York, 1877. Reprint, New York: Bonanza Books, 1962.

United States Congress, House of Representatives. *Report of the Joint Committee on Reconstruction.* Thirty-ninth Congress, First session. House Report 30. Washington, D.C.: Government Printing Office, 1866.

Wheeler, J. G. "Lee to the Rear." *Confederate Veteran*, 11 (1903).

Wickham, Henry R. *Address.* Virginia Senate Document No. 10. Richmond, 1940.

Wise, John Sergeant. *The End of an Era.* New York, 1899. Reprint, New York: Thomas Yoseloff, 1965.

SECONDARY SOURCES

Avary, Myrta Lockett. *Dixie After the War.* New York: Doubleday, Page, 1906.

Benedict, Michael Les. *A Compromise of Principle: Congressional Republicans and Reconstruction, 1863–1869.* New York: W. W. Norton, 1974.

Boley, Henry. *Lexington in Old Virginia.* Richmond: Garrett & Massie, 1936.
Bowers, Claude. *The Tragic Era.* New York: Blue Ribbon Books, 1929.
Bradford, Gamaliel. *Lee the American.* Boston: Houghton Mifflin, 1929.
Brock, R. A., ed. *Gen. Robert Edward Lee, Soldier, Citizen, and Patriot.* Richmond, 1897.
Bryan, J., III. *The Sword Over the Mantel.* New York: McGraw-Hill, 1960.
Catton, Bruce. *Never Call Retreat.* vol. 3, *The Centennial History of the Civil War.* Garden City, New York: Doubleday, 1961–1965.
———. *A Stillness at Appomattox.* New York: Doubleday, 1953.
Cauble, Frank P. *The Proceedings Connected with the Surrender of the Army of Northern Virginia.* Appomattox, Virginia: Appomattox Court House National Historical Park, 1962. Revised, 1975.
Connelly, Thomas L. *The Marble Man.* New York: Alfred A. Knopf, 1977.
Crenshaw, Ollinger. *General Lee's College: The Rise and Growth of Washington and Lee University.* New York: Random House, 1969.
Davis, William C. "The Campaign to Appomattox." *Civil War Times* (Gettysburg, Pennsylvania), April 1975.
Doty, William Kavanaugh. *Samuel Zenas Ammen and the Kappa Alpha Order.* Charlottesville, Virginia: The Surber-Arundale Co., 1922.
Fishwick, Marshall. *Lee After the War.* New York: Dodd, Mead, 1963.
Fletcher, Richard R. "Lexington Civil War Babies: Three National Fraternities." *Proceedings of the Rockbridge County Historical Society,* 8 (1970–1974).
Freeman, Douglas Southall. *Lee's Lieutenants.* 3 vols. New York: Scribner's, 1945.
———. *R. E. Lee.* 4 vols. New York: Scribner's, 1934–1935.
Horan, James D. *Mathew Brady: Historian with a Camera.* New York: Bonanza Books, 1955.
Horn, Stanley F., ed. *The Robert E. Lee Reader.* New York: Grossett & Dunlap, 1949.
Howe, James Lewis. "The Ugly Club." *The Alumni Magazine.* Washington and Lee University, 16 (November 1940).
Long, E. B. with Barbara Long. *The Civil War Day By Day: An Almanac, 1861–1865.* Garden City, New York: Doubleday, 1971.
Lüdecke, H. *Frank Buchsers amerikanische Sendung, 1866–1871: die Chronik seiner Reisen.* Basel: Holbein-Verlag, 1941.
Lyle, Royster, Jr., and Pamela Hemenway Simpson. *The Architecture of Historic Lexington.* Charlottesville: University Press of Virginia, 1977.
McCabe, James D. *Life and Campaigns of General Robert E. Lee.* New York, 1867.
MacCorkle, William Alexander. *The White Sulphur Springs.* New York: Neale Publishing Co., 1916.
McDonald, Hunter. "General Robert E. Lee After Appomattox." *Tennessee Historical Magazine,* 9 (1925).
MacDonald, Rose Mortimer Ellzey. *Mrs. Robert E. Lee.* Boston: Ginn and Co., 1939. Reprint, Pikesville, Maryland: Robert B. Poisal, 1973.
McKitrick, Eric L. *Andrew Johnson and Reconstruction.* Chicago: University of Chicago Press, 1960.
Meredith, Roy. *The Face of Robert E. Lee.* New York: Scribner's, 1947.
Moger, Allen W. "General Lee's Unwritten *History of the Army of Northern Virginia.*" *The Virginia Magazine of History and Biography,* 71 (1963).

————. "Letters to General Lee After the War." *The Virginia Magazine of History and Biography,* 64 (1956).

Page, Thomas Nelson. *Robert E. Lee, Man and Soldier.* New York: Scribner's, 1911.

Parker, Elmer. "Why Was Lee Not Pardoned?" *Prologue,* vol. 2, no. 3, Winter 1970. (Publication of the National Archives.)

Preston, Walter Creigh. *Lee, West Point and Lexington.* Yellow Springs, Ohio: Antioch Press, 1934.

Reniers, Percival. *The Springs of Virginia.* Chapel Hill: The University of North Carolina Press, 1941.

Rister, Carl Coke. *Robert E. Lee in Texas.* Norman: The University of Oklahoma Press, 1946.

Robert, Joseph C. "Lee the Farmer." Baton Rouge, Louisiana: The Franklin Press, 1937. Reprinted from *The Journal of Southern History,* November 1937.

Sanborn, Margaret. *Robert E. Lee.* 2 vols. Philadelphia: Lippincott, 1966–1967.

Sandburg, Carl. *Abraham Lincoln.* New York: Harcourt, Brace & World, 1954.

Smith, Gene. *High Crimes and Misdemeanors.* New York: Morrow, 1977.

Smith, J. Randolph. "Miss Anne Carter Lee." *Confederate Veteran,* 14 (1906).

Stampp, Kenneth M. *The Era of Reconstruction, 1865–1877.* New York: Alfred A. Knopf, 1965.

Thomas, Lately. *The First President Johnson: The Three Lives of the Seventeenth President of the United States.* New York: Morrow, 1968.

Wälchh, Gottfried, ed. *Frank Buchser, Mein Leben und Streben in Amerika . . .* Zürich: Orell Füssli Verlag, 1942.

Wallace, David Duncan. "South Carolina." *Encyclopaedia Britannica,* fourteenth edition, 1929.

Warren, Robert Penn. *Jefferson Davis Gets His Citizenship Back.* Lexington, Kentucky: The University Press of Kentucky, 1980.

Wayland, John W. *Robert E. Lee and His Family.* Staunton, Virginia: McClure Publishing Co., 1951.

Wise, Henry A. *Drawing Out the Man.* Charlottesville: University Press of Virginia, 1978.

Index

Acton, Sir John Dalberg, 143
Adams, Charles Francis, 266n
Adams, Henry, 188
Alexander, Brig. Gen. E. Porter,
  4–5, 235
Allan, Col. William, 227, 283n
American Colonization Society,
  139. *See also* Slavery
Ammen, Samuel Zenas, 153–154
Amnesty
  for Lee, 84
  proclamation of, 200–201
Andersonville prison, issue of, 121,
  221–222
Appomattox court house. *See also*
  Surrender
  fighting near, 1
  Lee's decision at, 4
  terms of surrender at, 9
Antietam Creek, battle near, 48
Arlington, 31, 118
  attempts to recover, 118, 250
  Lee family at, 138, 233–234
  legal status of, 277n
Arlington Cemetery, 250
Army of Northern Virginia. *See
  also* Confederate Army
  Lee as field commander of, 3
  difficulties facing, 14
  Northern view of, 15
  news of surrender reaching,
    15–16
  reaction to surrender, 18–20
  myths and realities, 19
  Union salute to, 26
  surrender of, 26–27
Astronomical observatory, Lee's
  project for, 250
Augusta, Ga., in Lee's southern
  trip, 237

Babcock, Brevet Brig. Gen. Or-
  ville, E., 6, 266n
Badeau, Col. Adam, 63
Banister, Anne, 173
Banister family, 173
Barton, Dr. Howard, 191, 192,
  223, 256, 257, 260
Baseball, at Washington College,
  141
Beauregard, Maj. Gen. Pierre
  Gustave Toutant, 101–102, 194,
  196
Beecher, Henry Ward, 65, 176,
  181
Black codes, 85, 86, 87
Black franchise, 86–87, 117, 120,
  149, 187
  in North vs. South, 117
  in White Sulphur Letter,
    196–197
  Lee on, 284n
Blacks. *See also* Slavery
  postwar treatment of, 117
  testimony before Congress,
    117
  Lee's views on, 271n
Blair, Francis Preston, Sr., 180,
  194
Blow, Sen. Henry T., 121
Board of Survey, Washington Col-
  lege's, 206, 225
Bolling, Mary Tabb (daughter-in-
  law), 166, 172, 199
Bolling family, 173
Bond, Christiana, 160–161, 165,
  167
Boston Evening Traveller, anti-Lee ar-
  ticles in, 183
Brady, Mathew, 44, 49
Brandy Station, battle of, 37

Brazil, Confederates settled in,
102, 167
Brockenbrough, Judge John, invites Lee to Lexington, 80, 82,
223, 251
meets Lee in Lexington, 99
money raised by, 112, 113
school of law run by, 133, 204
son's assault on black man,
183–184
Broun, Col. T. L., 65
Buchser, Frank, 217–218, 267n,
273n, 287n
as Lee's guest, 219
portrait planned by, 220
opinion of Lee, 221
work completed by, 222
Buckler, Dr. Thomas H., 250
Buford, Capt. Pascal, 159
Business school, Lee's proposal for,
205

Cameron, Sen. Simon, 178–180
Canal boat, Lee family's journey
on, 68–69
"Carpetbaggers," 58, 197
Carter, Annette, 139, 186
Carter, Col. Thomas H., 60
Cavalry, Lee's, 15. See also Confed-
erate Army
Chamberlain, Maj. Gen. Joshua,
25, 26, 27, 29
Chancellorsville, battle of, 76, 81,
92–93, 209
Chapel, Lee's special project, 133,
142, 188
Charleston, S.C., in Lee's southern
trip, 245
Charleston Gazette, 145
Charlotte, N.C., in Lee's southern
trip, 235–236
Chase, Chief Justice Salmon P.,
170, 185, 203
Chester, S. H., 279n
Chicago Daily Tribune, anti-Lee arti-
cles in, 183
Childe, Edward Lee (nephew), 55,
251, 272n
Chilton, Gen. R. H., 46

Citizenship, restoration of Lee's,
276n
Civil Rights Act (1866), 127
Cocke, Mrs. Elizabeth Randolph,
67, 70
Cockspur Island, 238
Cold Harbor, battle of, 243
Columbia, S.C., in Lee's southern
trip, 236
Commencement Exercises, Wash-
ington College
Lee's first (1866), 133
Lee's second (1867), 156
Lee's fourth (1869), 212
Lee's fifth (1870), 250
Conciliation, Lee's belief in, 136,
152
Confederate Army. See also Army
of Northern Virginia
Lee as commander of, 3
difficulties facing, 14
Grant's view of, 20
and postwar allegiance, 53
Confederate States of America
military aims of, 14
resistance of, 45, 52
and conditions for reentering
Union, 149
Congress, Thirty-ninth, 115. See
also Reconstruction, Joint Committee on
Conness, Sen. John, 180
Cook, Thomas M. (reporter), 49,
51
Cooke, Maj. Giles B., 30
Corcoran, W. W., donations to
Washington College, 164,
215–216
Corley, Col. James L., 232, 236,
237, 238, 240
Correspondence, Lee's, 276n
with Confederate generals,
101–103, 254–255
with students' parents, 105–106
on Washington College, 108
with wife, 138, 173
with Annette Carter, 139–140
with Sir John Dalberg Acton,
143
with Mrs. Jefferson Davis, 144

with sons, 152, 225
with daughters, 191, 233
Craighill, Lt. James B., 175
Cumberland Island, 242
Curtin, Andrew Gregg, 165
Custis, Anna Randolph, 32, 137.
    See also, Lee, Mary

Davidson, Percy, 255
Davis, Pres. Jefferson, 20, 22, 34,
    82, 144
    last resistance of, 45
    and Lee's surrender, 47
    capture of, 57
    imprisonment of, 57–58
    dwindling popularity of, 93
    released from prison, 152
    amnesty for, 200
    Lee's postwar meeting with, 170
    proposed trial of, 170, 186
    Lee's testimony on behalf of,
    171
    Lee on, 220, 287n
Democratic Party, and Lee's politi-
    cal position, 195–196, 198
Derwent
    Lee family's move to, 70
    Palmore family and, 71
    Mary Lee's view of, 72
    Lee plans memoirs at, 76–77
    daily life at, 77
Douglas, Robert M., 209, 210

Early, Lt. Gen. Jubal, 71–72, 144
Eastman Business College, Lee As-
    sociation at, 152
Emancipation, Lee's attitude to-
    ward, 139. *See also* Slavery
Episcopal Church in Virginia, 207.
    See also Grace Episcopal Church
Estill, Prof. Harry, 184
Evarts, Atty. Gen. William M.,
    203
Ewell, Lt. Gen. Richard S., 175

Faculty, Washington College
    during Civil War, 78
    Lee's working relationship with,
    106
    rising morale of, 134
    growth of, 155

and Lee's proposed resignation,
    227–228
Fair, Laura, 215
Farewell order, Lee's, 24, 254
Five Forks, disaster of, 231
Florida
    in Lee's southern trip, 242
    during war, 243
Forrest, Gen. Nathan Bedford,
    146
Forsyth, Gen. George, 12
Fort Monroe, Lee family at, 138,
    139, 238
Fourteenth Amendment, 128, 144
    South's refusal to ratify, 148
    and admission to Union, 149
Franchise. *See* Black franchise
Franco-Prussian War, 251
Fredericksburg, battle of, 73
Freedmen. *See also* Blacks
    Lee's view of, 50–51
    Northern view of, 52
Freedmen's Bureau, 54, 86
    education efforts of, 58, 98
    indefinite extension of, 128
    in Lexington, 150, 151
Fund for Southern Education,
    215–216

Garfield, Brig. Gen. James A., 74
Garrison, William Lloyd, 182
General Order Number Nine, 24,
    254
Generals, Confederate
    Lee's correspondence with,
    101–103, 254–255
    postwar emigration of, 102
    as representatives to Congress,
    116
Gettysburg, battle of, 230
Gilliam, Polly, 36
Gordon, Edward Clifford, 192,
    282n
    arrival at Washington College,
    141–142
    grounds improved by, 155
    view of Lee, 212–213
Gordon, Major Gen. John B., 1, 4,
    26, 38, 224
Government, Lee's views on, 186

Grace Episcopal Church, 97, 125,
255–256
Graham, Jonathan, 146
Grant, Ulysses S., 1, 93, 218, 226
early career of, 7
at Appomattox Court House,
8–11, 13, 21–22, 286n
and Lee's pardon, 63, 64
and Johnson's impeachment
trial, 185
nomination for president, 187
Lee's feelings about, 188
as President elect, 199
inauguration of, 202–203
invites Lee to White House,
208–209
Lee's last meeting with, 209–210
communication with Lee, 266n,
268n
Graves, Charles, 132
Greeley, Horace, 152
Gregg, Brig. Gen. John, 55
Griffin, Caesar, 184
Guerrilla warfare, Lee's attitude
toward, 5, 45, 51

Hale, Isaac, Jr., 198
Harris, Brig. Gen. Nathaniel H., 145
Haskell, Col. Alexander, 236
Haxall, Charlotte, 191, 252
Hill, Maj. Gen. A. P., 19, 107
Hood, Gen. John Bell, 23
Horses, and terms of surren-
der, 10
Horse thieves, 131–132
Hotchkiss, Maj. Jedediah, 206
Hot springs resorts, 159–160
Lee family at, 193
Lee's last visit to, 251
Howard, Sen. Jacob M., 117–118,
122–123
Hughes, Jonathan, 131–132
Humphreys, Prof. Milton W., 104,
156, 276n
Hunter, Gen. David, 71, 78, 94

Jackson, Eleanor, 115
Jackson, Lt. Gen. Thomas Jonathan (Stonewall), 15, 19, 76,
92, 115, 227

Jacksonville, Fla., in Lee's southern trip, 244
James River, Lee family journey
on, 68–69
Jefferson, Thomas, 38
Johnson, Pres. Andrew, 44, 57,
144, 218
amnesty proclamation of, 60,
200
postwar policy of, 85–86
Lee's endorsement of, 120
impeachment trial of, 148, 174,
185, 187
and controversy with Grant,
186
and family heirlooms, 201–202
and Grant's inauguration,
202–203
Johnson, Sen. Reverdy, 62, 122,
179
Johnston, Gen. Albert Sidney, 47,
217
Johnston, E. C., 176–178, 182
Johnston, Gen. Joseph E., 1, 45,
242
Johnston, Col. William Preston,
217, 226, 253, 291n
at Lee's sickbed, 260
and Lee's last words, 292n
Joint Committee on Reconstruction, 127–128. See also Reconstruction
Joint Resolution 189, 276n
Jones, Carter, 156
Joynes, Edward S., 145
Julian, George W. (congressman),
58
Junior Fellows program, at Washington College, 205
Junkin, Rev. George, 115
Journalism, at Washington Col-
lege, 205

Kanawha Canal, Lee's journey on,
68–69
Kappa Alpha Order, at Washing-
ton College, 153, 154, 281n
Kennon, Mrs. Beverly, 202
Kirkpatrick, Rev. Dr. John L.,
228, 248
Ku Klux Klan, 144

Labor contracts, for Southern
blacks, 85
Lafferty and Company, 205
Lawton, Brig. Gen. Alexander, 240
Lee Association, in Poughkeepsie,
N.Y., 151–152
Lee, Agnes (daughter), 45
and Orton Williams, 6, 73–74,
75
and move from Richmond, 68
at Derwent, 72–73
in Lexington, 125–126, 129
and Lee's possessiveness,
130–131
at White Sulphur resort, 215
at Lee's sickbed, 258–261
Lee, Ann Carter (mother), 76
Lee, Anne Carter (daughter), 37
death of, 192
visit to grave of, 233–234
Lee, Annie Agnes (granddaughter), 37
Lee, Charles Carter (brother),
35
Lee, Charlotte (daughter-in-law),
37, 127
Lee, Maj. Gen. Custis (son), 3, 6,
31, 38, 44
Confederate service of, 47
farm inherited by, 59
appointment to VMI, 109
at Lee's sickbed, 258–261
as president of Washington and
Lee University, 290n
Lee, Maj. Gen. Fitzhugh
(nephew), 3, 254
Lee, "Light Horse Harry" (father),
36–37, 76, 139, 174, 243, 269n
Lee, Mary Custis (wife)
invalidism of, 40, 126–127, 139,
192
Confederate service of, 42
attitude toward North, 43, 56
and move from Richmond,
67–68
at Derwent, 70, 72
in Lexington, 114, 126
as bride, 137
attachment to parents, 138
and postwar politics, 149

and return of family heirlooms,
201–202
visit to son and daughter-in-law,
242
at Lee's sickbed, 258–261
Lee, Mary (daughter)
at Staunton, 72, 79
in Lexington, 125–126, 129
and Lee's possessiveness,
130–131
Lee, Mary Tabb Bolling (daughter-in-law), 199, 214
Lee, Mildred ("Life") (daughter),
45, 46, 61, 62, 211
and move from Richmond, 68
at Derwent, 72
in Lexington, 114, 125–126,
128–129
memories of father, 130
and Lee's possessiveness,
130–131, 192
at brother's wedding, 173
typhoid contracted by, 192–193
at White Sulphur resort, 215
at Lee's sickbed, 258–261
and Lee's death, 291n
Lee, Mildred (niece), 190
Lee, Gen. Robert E.
at Appomattox Court House
terms of surrender, 8–13
second meeting with Grant,
21–22, 286n
farewell order of (General
Order No. 9), 23–24
leave-taking from Confederate
troops, 28–29
and Confederate resistance, 45
communication with Grant,
266n, 268n
character, 104, 107, 135
self denial, 35
possessiveness toward
daughters, 131, 191
views on property, 135
Gordon's view of, 213–214
spirituality, 213–214
early life
prewar career of, 7
education of, 32

Lee, Gen. Robert E. (*cont.*)
  marriage of, 32, 137
  as assistant astronomer, 33
  as educator, 112, 134, 156,
    175, 204–207 (*see also* Wash-
    ington College)
  health
    heart condition, 31, 223
    accident during war, 48
    deterioration of, 77, 93, 224,
      227, 269n
    visits to resorts for, 194,
      214–216
    visit South for, 228–252
    cerebral thrombosis, 257
    last illness, 257–261
    death of, 261, 292n
  military career
    headquarters of, 14–15, 28
    early, 33–34
    Union command rejected by,
      178–179, 180
    resignation from U.S. Army,
      180, 283n
  physical description of, 2
  portrait(s) painted of, 220–222
  private life
    on Traveller, 16, 37–38, 71,
      89, 94–95, 110, 249
    return to Richmond, 29–30,
      35–40
    move to Derwent, 67–69
    religion, 82 (*see also* Grace
  Episcopal Church)
    move to Lexington, 89–95
    daily routine of, 105, 131
    open house, 125
    job offers, 175, 224
  public activities
    indictment of, 61–62
    summons to Washington, 118,
      186
    influence of, 136, 144, 152, 199
    and postwar politics, 150
    as witness in Jefferson Davis's
  prospective trial, 171
    Grant's last meeting with,
      208–210
Lee, Capt. Robert E., Jr. (son,
  Rob)

Confederate service of, 3, 31–32,
  46–47
farm inherited by, 59
in Rockbridge Artillery, 92
arrival in Lexington, 114
and Charlotte Haxall, 191,
  252
biography of, 267n
Lee, Robert E., III (grandson), 37,
  201, 214, 247
Lee, Sydney Smith (brother), 47,
  214
Lee, Maj. Gen. William Henry
  Fitzhugh (son, Rooney), 3, 36,
  39
  capture of, 31
  first wife's death, 40–42
  Confederate service of, 47
  farm inherited by, 59
  engagement of, 168
  wedding of, 172
Letcher, John, 83, 87
Letitia (Mrs. Lee's maid), 191
Letters. *See* Correspondence
Lexington. *See also* Washington
  College
  citizens of, 91
  Lee's arrival at, 91–95
  postwar condition of, 97, 128
  under martial law, 98, 226
  Lee's house in, 114–115
  winter in, 129, 174
Lexington Gazette, 103
Liberia, Lee's ex-slaves in, 50
Liberty Hall Academy, 79
Liberty Hall Volunteers, 92, 95,
  103, 151, 184
"Life." *See* Lee, Mildred
Lincoln, Pres. Abraham
  assassination of, 43, 49
  and offer of Union command to
  Lee, 180
"Lodge, The," 153
London Standard, 259
Longstreet's Artillery, 4, 236–
  237
Low, Andrew, 240
Loyalty, Lee's position on, 122
Lucy Long (horse), 212, 226
Lynching, Lee's prevention of, 132

McCabe, James D., 230
McCormick, Cyrus H., donations
to Washington College, 112–113,
133
Mackay, Eliza, 238, 239
Mackay, Jack, 238, 239
Mackay, Margaret, 238
Macomb, Lt. John, 118
Madison, Dr. R. L., 223, 256, 257,
259, 260
Mahone, Gen. William, 169,
172–173
Manassas
first battle at, 95
second battle at, 19, 48, 236
Marriage, Lee's, 137, 140
Marshall, Lt. Col. Charles, 6, 10,
12, 23, 30, 39, 254
Marshall, Chief Justice John, 11
Maury, Gen. Dabney H., 150
Maury, Matthew Fontaine, 102
May, James (congressman), 201
Mead, Maj. Gen. George Gordon,
22–23, 52–54, 93
Mechanical engineering, taught at
Washington College, 111, 113
Medical school, Lee's plans for,
206, 285n
Memoirs
Lee's planning for, 76–77
Lee's father's Revolutionary
War, 174, 223
Memphis, race riots in, 144
Mercer, Hugh, 239
"Mess, the," 48
Mexican War, 8, 34
Military Occupation, 177, 185, 226
Minnigerode, Dr. Charles, 65, 66
Moltke, Gen. Helmut, Count von,
252
Morgan, Gen. John T., 199
Mosby, Col. John S., 230, 231, 232
Mosby's Rangers, 46, 76
Motley, John Lothrop, 209

Newcomb, Warren, donation to
Washington College, 133
New Market, battle of, 92
New Orleans, race riots in, 144

New York City, Lee's work in, 34
New York Herald, 99
suggests Lee for president,
188–189
on Lee as educator, 206
on Sherman's campaign, 236
New York Independent
on Lee as educator, 88
anti-Lee campaign of, 181–182
New York Times, anti-Lee article in,
183
New York Tribune, anti-Lee articles
in, 183
Nick King (steamer), 242, 243
Norfolk, in Lee's southern trip, 246
North
military advantage of, 14
and black franchise, 86–87, 117
and White Sulphur Letter, 198
North Carolina, during war,
232–233
Novels, Lee's attitude toward, 72

Oakland, Lee family's visit to, 70
Oath of Allegiance, Lee's, 99–100,
276n
Occupation forces
and Johnston incident, 177
and Brockenbrough shooting,
185
Office, Gen. Lee's, 99, 105, 198,
255
Old Sweet Resort, 168
Orton, Lawrence, 73. See also Williams, Orton
Ould, Judge Robert, 44

Palmore family, 71
Pamunkey (Lee farm), 152
Pardon, Lee's application for,
63–64, 99–100, 201
Parker, Lt. Col. Ely S., 11
Parks, Amanda, 119
Patriotism, Lee's view of, 102
Peabody, George, donation to
Washington College, 215–216,
287n
Peaks of Otter, excursion to, 156

Pendleton, Mary, 160
Pendleton, Rev. William Nelson,
    83, 97, 253, 256
Pennsylvania Reserves, 165
Perry, Thomas L., 132
Petersburg
    Lee's evacuation of, 1
    siege of, 46, 121, 137, 166,
        168–169
    Lee attends son's wedding at,
        172–173
Peyton, Virginia, 212
Pickett, Maj. Gen. George E., 230,
    231, 236
Politicians, Lee and, 38–39, 124,
    221
Politics
    postwar, 149–150
    Lee suggested as presidential
        candidate, 188–189
    presidential, 194–195
    national, 197–198
    Lee's view of, 221
Porter, Horace, 266n
Portsmouth, Va., in Lee's southern
    trip, 246
President, U.S., Lee proposed as,
    188–189
President's House, Lee family in,
    211
Press scholarships, at Washington
    College, 205
Printing, at Washington College,
    205
Prisoner exchange, Lee's proposal
    for, 221–222, 278n

Race riots, 144
Railway ordnance, Lee's invention
    of, 207–208
Raleigh, N.C., in Lee's trip south,
    235
Rations, and terms of surrender,
    11, 18
Reading Club, Lexington's, 130
Reconstruction
    Joint Committee on, 116–117,
        119–124
    and Johnson's impeachment
        trial, 185–186

Reconstruction acts, 148, 152
Redmond, Maj. Robert C., 97
Reid, Col. S. McD., 95
Republican Party, 86
    Radical faction of, 87, 94, 116,
        148
    and black vote, 118 (see also
        Black franchise)
Richardson, C. B., 75, 76, 174
Richmond
    Lee's evacuation of, 1
    Lee's return to, 29–30, 37–40
    burning of, 42
    postwar recovery of, 58–59
    Lee's family leaves, 67–69
Rockbridge Artillery, 47, 92
Rockbridge County, 91, 92
Romancoke (Lee farm), 31
Rooney. See Lee, Maj. Gen. W. H.
    Fitzhugh
Rosecrans, Gen. William Starke,
    195–196
Rosser, Maj. Gen. Thomas L., 231

St. Louis, Gen. Lee's family at, 33,
    138–139
Salisbury, N.C., in Lee's trip
    south, 235
Savannah, Ga.
    during Lee's early life, 239
    in Lee's trip south, 239–240
Sayler's Creek, rout at, 2, 3–4,
    169
"Scalawags," 197
Schedule, Lee's daily, 105, 131
Scott, Gen. Winfield, 34, 179
Secession
    Lee's attitude toward, 49–50,
        123–124
    crisis of, 119
    Lee's prewar statements against,
        123, 124
    Mary Lee's view of, 127
Selden, Miss Caroline, 246
Seward, William H. (secretary of
    state), 100, 203, 218
Seymour, Gov. Horatio, 194
Sharpsburg, battle at, 47
Sherman, Gen. William Tecumseh,
    218

Slavery, Lee's views on, 50, 119, 139, 187, 271n
Smith, Channing, 46
Smith, Gen. Francis H., 258
Smith, Francis L., 250
Smith's Island, 250
South
    military disadvantages of, 14
    attitudes toward war, 49
    postwar economy, 85
    readmission to Union, 86
    black franchise in, 117
    loyalty of, 121
    Lee as civilian leader of, 136, 144, 152, 199
    military occupation of, 148, 226
    Lee's postwar trip through, 228–252
South Carolina, and Lee's trip south, 236
Southern Life Insurance Co., position offered by, 224
Spanish courses, Lee's introduction of, 112
Spotsylvania, battle at, 19
Sprague, Kate Chase, 215
Stanton, Edwin M. (secretary of war), 57, 186, 268n
State's rights
    Lee on, 143–144
    in White Sulphur Paper, 197
Stephens, Alexander H., 116, 144, 194, 196
Stern, Jo Lane, 153–154
Stevens, Thaddeus, 87, 116, 117
Stockdale, F. W., 196
Stonewall Brigade, 26, 92
Stowe, Harriet Beecher, 65
Strickler, Givens B.,103, 151, 184–185
Stuart, Alexander H. H., 196
Students, Washington College
    Lee's relationship with, 103–105
    discipline of, 106–107, 155–156
    attitudes toward president, 106–107, 109
    rising morale of, 134
    Lee's valuation of, 142–143

    in racial fracas, 150–151
    and Johnston incident, 177
    composition of, 217
Suffrage, black, 120–121. See also Black franchise
Sullivane, Col. Clement, 55
Summer school, Lee's proposal for, 206
Surrender
    terms of, 9–11, 267n, 268n
    ceremony of, 11–13, 26–27, 268n
    implementation of, 22, 25–27
Swiss National Museum, Lee portrait in, 222
Sword, Lee's, 2, 134

Tagart, Mr. and Mrs. Samuel H., 209, 250, 255
Tayloe, W. H., 248
Taylor, Lt. Col. Walter H., 30, 35, 39, 44, 234, 246
Tennessee, in Union, 148
Tenure of Office Act, 185
Texas, Lee in, 34
Texas Brigade, 54–55
Thayer, Col. Sylvanus, 33
Thirteenth Amendment, 86, 143
Thomas, Philip F., 178
Traveller (Lee's horse), 12, 48, 71, 89, 109, 110, 194, 212, 249, 260
Treason charge, against Lee, 61–63
Troops, Lee's, 3–4, 15
Tucker, Sgt. G. W., 12
Tulane, Sophie Newcomb College at, 133
Twentieth Maine, 25

"Uncle Robert," 3
Uniform, Lee's postwar, 53
Union Army
    at Appomattox Court House, 5–6
    and surrender, 17, 20
    casualties of, 31

Vagrancy laws, 85
Valley Railroad, 207, 208, 253
Valley of Virginia
    Lexington in, 91
    war in, 93
    travel to and from, 207

Venable, Lt. Col. Charles, 1, 4, 55, 231
Virginia, as Military District Number One, 148, 226
Virginia Educational Association, 207
Virginia Military Institute, 84, 97
  action during the war, 92
  immediately after the war, 94
  Custis Lee's appointment, 109
Vote. *See* Black franchise
Walker, Gov. Gilbert C., 225
War, Lee's views of, 251
Warm Springs Resort, Lee family at, 192
Warrenton, N.C., 233
Warrenton Springs, N.C., 228
Washington College, 78. *See also* Faculty; Students
  bankruptcy of, 79
  Lee offered presidency at, 79, 84
  grounds of, 96–97, 134, 142, 155
  Lee's installation as president, 99
  Lee's daily schedule at, 105
  curriculum innovations and re-organization, 111–112, 133, 204–206, 277n
  Cyrus McCormick's contribution to, 113
  commencement exercises, 133, 156, 212, 250
  fund raising activities of, 133, 164, 176, 216, 279n
  student evaluation of, 142–143
  accident at, 145–146
  Christmas holiday at, 146–147
  discipline at, 155–156
  Lee's retirement from, 155, 226–227, 241
Washington College, trustees of
  Lee elected as president by, 78–80
  characteristics of, 91
  relationship with Lee, 98

  retirement arrangements made by, 241, 248
Washington Evening Express, 202
Washington and Lee University, 112
  Honor Code of, 155–156
  School of Law, 204
  Custis Lee as president, 290n
Wedding ceremony, Lee's, 137
West Point, Lee at, 34, 94
Whirlwind Brigade, 243
White, James J., 95, 160, 227, 251
White, Will, 233
White, Squire William, 99, 153
White House (farm), 31
White Sulphur Letter, 196–197, 252, 285n
White Sulphur Springs
  Lee family at, 160–167
  Lee at, 193, 214–215
Wilderness campaign, 209
Williams, Brig. Gen. Lawrence, 6, 8, 10, 73–74
Williams, Markie, 75, 119, 174, 176, 242, 251, 271n
Williams, Orton, 6, 73, 273n
  capture of, 74
  death of, 75, 129
  Lee's recommendation of, 266n
Williams, Brig. Gen. Seth, 10
Wilmer, Rev. Joseph, 82
Wilson, Woodrow, 237
Winchester, James R., 248
Wirz, Maj. Henry, 120, 221
Wise, Capt. George, 64, 65
Wise, Brig. Gen. Henry A., 18, 266n
Wolseley, Garnet, 145–146
Woodbury, Levi (secretary of treasury), 119
Wright, Brig. Gen. Ambrose R., 19, 20

Yellow Tavern, battle of, 153
Y.M.C.A., in Lexington, 185